You
Never
Gave
Me
a
Name

You Never Gave Me a Name

One Mennonite Woman's Story

Katie Funk Wiebe

Foreword by
Wally Kroeker

DreamSeeker Books
TELFORD, PENNSYLVANIA

an imprint of
Cascadia Publishing House

Copublished with
Herald Press
Scottdale, Pennsylvania

Cascadia Publishing House orders, information, reprint permissions:
contact@CascadiaPublishingHouse.com
1-215-723-9125
126 Klingerman Road, Telford PA 18969
www.CascadiaPublishingHouse.com

You Never Gave Me a Name
Copyright © 2009 by Cascadia Publishing House LLC
Telford, PA 18969
All rights reserved
DreamSeeker Books is an imprint of Cascadia Publishing House
Copublished with Herald Press, Scottdale, PA
Library of Congress Catalog Number: 2009011525
ISBN 13: 978-1-931038-56-0; **ISBN 10:** 1-931038-56-2
Book design by Cascadia Publishing House
Cover design by Gwen M. Stamm

All Bible quotations are used by permission, all rights reserved and unless
otherwise noted or taken from *The King James Version* in the case of quotes
from pre-NIV days, are from the Holy Bible, *New International Version®*. Copyright © 1973, 1978, 1984 International Bible Society. All rights reserved throughout
the world. Used by permission of International Bible Society.

Library of Congress Cataloguing-in-Publication Data

Wiebe, Katie Funk.
 You never game me a name : one Mennonite woman's story / Katie Funk
Wiebe ; foreword by Wally Kroeker.
  p. cm.
 Summary: "This memoir records Katie Funk Wiebe's search for identity as a
woman left widowed with young children who becomes a writer and an early
Mennonite and biblical feminist." "[summary]"--Provided by publisher.
 ISBN-13: 978-1-931038-56-0 (trade pbk. : alk. paper)
 ISBN-10: 1-931038-56-2 (trade pbk. : alk. paper)
 1. Wiebe, Katie Funk. 2. Mennonites--Kansas--Hillsboro--Biography. I. Title.
BX8143.W43A3 2009
289.7'78157092--dc22
 [B]
                          2009011525

16 15 14 13 12 11 10 09   10 9 8 7 6 5 4 3 2 1

To the women, and men, waiting in the shadows for opportunity to use all their gifts in service to the church

Contents

PHOTO ALBUM

PART IV

Foreword

I first met Katie Funk Wiebe in 1975, when I moved to Hillsboro, Kansas, to work with *The Christian Leader*, the biweekly magazine of the U.S. Mennonite Brethren Church. By then she was already in brisk stride as a writer, well on her way to becoming a literary powerhouse. It was my great joy to "inherit" her as a regular columnist who could deftly wrap words around thoughts that readers struggled with but perhaps could not (or dared not) articulate themselves.

I felt kinship with Katie on many fronts, including our limited appetite for churchly pomp and pretense. We both treasured the Anabaptist heritage of our Mennonite Brethren world and were saddened by those who would squander this capital (either by neglect or design).

It was a time when full service in the church could be relegated according to biological plumbing, which meant many women's gifts were locked away, suspended in amber. Katie provided tonal clarity to those straining to make music in a choir dominated by tenors and basses.

But the women's issue is not the only defining category of her monumental contribution to the Anabaptist world, as this memoir so vividly shows. This "life review," as she calls it, is a wine of late harvest, a story "told right" which many readers can embrace as their own. It is, in a sense, a social history of the Mennonite movement of the second half of the last century, as refracted through her Mennonite Brethren lens. Her opening depiction of earnest but stifling Bible college life, for example, is not simply personal reflection but a candid analysis of Mennonite piety, a textured rendering of a generation in flux.

With skill and soul she reaches out to anyone who has felt their gifts smothered in the church, anyone who cares about Anabaptists in the wider world, anyone who has been ready to toss in the towel over the dawdling pace of ecclesiastical change.

And, one might add, anyone who is growing older. "I write about aging as an insider," Katie notes in the final section. For those who fear becoming old, this section alone is worth the price of the book.

Thanks to Katie's efforts, my young grandchildren have access to a more spacious and ventilated church, with generous rooms and windows that open wide. I plan to set aside copies of this book for them, so they have a better grasp of how it all happened.

—*Wally Kroeker, Editor*
   The Marketplace

Preface

The name my parents gave me was Katie, a plain German-Mennonite name. I didn't like it growing up because it didn't sound sophisticated enough to suit my ambitions. To me it brought up images of *Schlorre* (simple footwear), drab clothing, and dull living of another country and era. A Russian girl in our little community of Blaine Lake had the same name but called herself Katya and later changed it to Katherine. My name seemed so plain, so unimaginative. I couldn't understand any parents saddling a child with such a burden. I considered my Russian-born parents an uncreative lot. I wanted a name with flair.

"Why didn't you give me a real name?" I complained to my mother.

"But we did," she replied. "We named you after my mother, Katarina Boldt." Mother also had a sister named Katarina, always referred to as Tina.

"Why then isn't Katarina on my birth certificate?"

In her thinking I was Katarina. In my thinking, only what appeared on paper counted.

So I was called Katie or derivatives of the name like Trien or Tina that lent themselves to being shrieked loudly and at a great length when someone wanted me. In step with the custom of their ethnic community, my parents picked names from a small list of traditional names like Henry, Peter, Jacob, John, Susie, Helen, and Annie. I don't think the Mennonites in south Russia had more than two or three dozen names in circulation.

A child was frequently given the same name as a deceased sibling—and many children died in infancy. Second names were not important unless they were a patronymic. My ancestors loved diminutives, nicknames, and terms of endearment in the small villages where everyone knew everyone else. A child didn't need a second name. So I was plain Katie Funk. And I was born in Canada.

I checked the family genealogy in my grandmother's handwritten book. Between 1865 and 1920 there were nine Katharina (Katarina) Funks, three by marriage, but no Katie. Katharina was not Katie. My birth certificate name was Katie, plain as could be. I must have had a birth defect to be forever hampered by Katie. It had no magic, no mystery to it, no association with greats of the past like Catherine the Great. I wanted a name like that of school friends, whose names exuded romance and beauty: June, Blanche, Fern, Shirley, and Mona.

The right to name a child belongs to parents. That name, to a certain extent, thereafter defines the child. Different things are expected of a Matthew or Mary than of a Khrysti or Felicity. But the responsibility to establish an identity with that name belongs to the child. The African-American writer Ralph Ellison, in his essay, "Hidden Names, Complex Fate," writes that our names being the gift of others aren't really ours until we make them our own. Then we become our names. He didn't like being named after the famous Ralph Waldo Emerson because of the expectations it loaded on him, but in time he learned that before this name became his own, he had to fill it with his own hopes, hates, loves, and ambitions, not those of Emerson. When his name represented his own values and traditions, it didn't matter whom he was named after.

That was the lesson I needed to learn. It took me many years.

When I left Blaine Lake for the city in 1942, I called myself Kay, a name that sounded more modern. My sisters gave me a gold bracelet with "Kay" engraved on it, which I still have. My new name matched the new image I had developed for myself—sleek pageboy haircut, camel-hair coat with fox-fur collar, bright red lipstick when Dad wasn't watching, high heels, and boyfriends. I felt I could safely shed my immigrant past.

Over a period of years Kay disappeared and Katie returned. As a young married woman, once the lipstick and high heels became less important than books and friends, my interests turned to the world of ideas, spiritual development, theology, and church life. I returned intentionally to being Katie even when people misspelled it and called me Kathy or Katharine on their own accord because they didn't believe Katie was my complete name. I had an obligation to my parents to fill the name they gave me with worth and integrity. It didn't matter who I was or wasn't named after.

The harder I worked to fulfill my destiny as Katie Wiebe, a silent, submissive Mennonite woman who accepted her destined life as wife and mother, the harder I struggled, especially after my husband, Walter Wiebe, died, and his goals, which had also been my goals, grew dim. In my book *The Storekeeper's Daughter* I wrote of a pilgrimage I made back to Blaine Lake, my childhood home, to the house with the fence and gate, to the store with the wrinkled green shade on the front door.

Dad wasn't there behind the counter, but I saw his image, standing there in his sand-colored smock, adding up the day's receipts. I wanted to say, "Dad, you made me a Mennonite when you gave me the name of one, Katie. You had the chance here in Blaine Lake to pass us off as Russians or Germans, but you didn't take it. You loaded your Mennonite background on us children. You seduced me with your stories of a people enduring pain and suffering for the sake of their beliefs.

"I wanted to believe all of it. I wanted that faith that suffered hardship courageously and endured to the end. But now I find nothing but narrow authoritarianism and ecclesiastical pomposity out there. Dad, you escaped the bonds of the past by living here in Blaine Lake all these years. You could observe the situation from afar. But I married into it. I can't get out. Dad, what do I do with this craving inside me to write—to wrap the experiences of life in words and let others see what my life has been? Didn't you ever feel anything like that? You told me never to forget I was a Funk. What did you mean by that?

"Why didn't you and Mother give me a real name? You called me Katie—a peasant name, not a writer's name, not a name for this land. And I have to use it all the time, exposing my past. You offered me the freedom of living in Blaine Lake, but at the same time wrapped a chain around me forged by your past experiences."

As I wandered the streets of my childhood, I heard a voice whispering above the rattle and roar of cars and trucks looking for a parking spot: "I did give you a name, Katie, child of the prairies, child of the Russian steppes, child of many wanderings. But your name, being the gift of others, must be made your own. You didn't select your parents, your nationality, or your name, but you have to choose what you make of these experiences of your parents and of their parents and of all those who searched for freedom of faith. Sometimes that search ended in failure for them. Sometimes it succeeded. It was a triumph of the spirit when those people accepted the gift of their heritage—the weaknesses, faults, mistakes, and the strengths, conquests, and joys—and gleaned from them what was needed to move ahead with courage."

I recalled one of my father's last letters. He wrote me often, mostly short notes. "Yes, Katie, I made many mistakes in life. You only get experience after you have lived, but you need it before you live. And that is why a person makes mistakes. When I look back, I ask myself, why didn't I do it differently? I can't answer. All I know is that I didn't have the experience to do it differently with the little education I had. Life is a struggle."

At that point I embraced my roots–the Mennonite ones nurtured by the soil of the Ukraine and those grafted in by this variegated community of Blaine Lake where I had lived for eighteen years. My ancestors had not been complacent, accepting blindly what others told them to believe about God, life, and themselves. They had chosen. Mother and Dad had chosen a new way of living in a new country. That was their gift to me. I too could choose. As I lived alone with four children, I had to make wise choices. This writing is a record of the choices I made over the decades that made me the person people know as Katie Funk Wiebe.

But I'm interested not just in my family roots but also in the theological and social factors that formed me and drove me to express my thoughts in writing. Reviewing the past to write this autobiography has been an invigorating and provided new understandings of my roots, early environment, and their contribution to the making of Katie Funk Wiebe, author. Other girls could be Kay, Kae, Katherine, Kathryn, Kathleen, Kaylene, and Kathy. The name *Katie* might have been the name of a peasant in the Ukraine. Now it is my name. I wear it proudly.

In 1989 I made a strange discovery. I traveled to the former USSR to study my roots, and if possible, to find Mother's relatives left behind when other family members immigrated to Canada. In Moscow I met my elderly aunt Aganetha Janzen Block, a mentally alert woman, full of stories. As we talked , she brought out a few surviving pictures of my family my father had sent her when I was a child. I turned one over. On the back my father had written the names of us three older girls: Frieda, Annie, *Katarina*. I had always had a real name. Now I didn't need it. I had made Katie my real name.

I have often told groups that after you have lived your life, why hang onto it? Why not share it with others? This book represents aspects of my life after I left home to attend Bible college that I want to share with readers. I have traced the dominant themes that twisted in and out of my life. The telling is not always linear. As I observe in chapter 20, "The Old Testament writers keep retelling the story of the Israelites, first from one aspect, then another, to keep reminding the Israelites how God has dealt with them. . . . I do the same with my past."

The telling is also not complete. That would have taken several volumes. I hope you find yourself also, however, in the themes I have highlighted.

—*Katie Funk Wiebe*
Wichita, Kansas

Acknowledgments

To attempt to acknowledge all the sources that have contributed to a life story is a monumental task. That would mean pulling apart an intricate tapestry of actions, thoughts, and words. Some appear in one part of the tapestry, only to reappear as a motif in another, maybe not in the same way, but there nevertheless. Where did everything that makes a life come from?

This autobiography, many years in the making, is based on memory, of course, but also my journals, correspondence with friends and family, editors, and church leaders as well as much reading of other people's biographies, books, and articles. I dug into yearbooks, as well as files of boards and committees of which I had been a member. I have tried to give credit and to authenticate facts as much as possible. Where I have failed, I apologize. The opinions and generalizations are mine. I take responsibility for them.

I have borrowed from earlier writings that appeared in *The Christian Leader* columns and various church publications. Add to this gleanings from talks I gave at women's and mixed group meetings, conferences, and retreats.

Chapter 13 ("How I Received Shoes as a Communicator") was adapted from a paper presented at a Canadian Mennonite Annual Meeting.

Some of the material on women's concerns was presented at Women Doing Theology, Women in Ministry, Mennonite Experience in America, and Mennonite Brethren study conferences.

I also turned to my books out of print—*Bless Me Too, My Father; Alone: A Widow's Search for Joy; Good Times with Old Times: How to Write Your Memoirs*—to find out what I had been thinking then.

Chapter 21 "Sticking with what you're stuck with" appeared in *DreamSeeker Magazine* (Autumn 2006) in a slightly different version as "Who? Me? A Fundamentalist?"

Parts of Chapter 18, "What I Learned from the Women's Movement," were presented at the EnGendering Conference at University of Winnipeg, Department of Mennonite Studies: *Journal of Mennonite Studies* in a paper, "Me Tarzan, Son of Menno, You Jane, Mennonite Mama."

In particular I thank Herald Press for allowing me to use material from the last chapter of *The Storekeeper's Daughter* in my Preface.

My special thanks go to Margot Wiebe, no relative, who patiently read and commented on every chapter in between her visits to family in Europe and the United States, Don and Connie Isaac, Del and Gerry Reimer, Wally Kroeker, and Rose Buschman who read portions of the manuscript.

I thank Michael A. King and the Cascadia Publishing House editorial council for their affirmation and encouragement as I wrote.

I thank my children for their support even as they wondered what Mother was coming up with this time.

Writing the book was a journey of joy and hope for greater opportunity for service for another generation of women in the church world. I am grateful to God for giving me health and strength to complete it. God too was a source during the writing of this autobiography.

PART I

CHAPTER 1

A beginning that led to many beginnings

In John Irving's The World According to Garp, *the narrator no-
tices his young son wading in the ocean, intently looking for something on the ocean floor. A few minutes earlier the father had
admonished his son to beware of the undertow. The boy had misun-
derstood him. He was looking for the Undertoad. While we are
looking for the Undertoad, the undertow grabs us.*

I stepped off the train at the Winnipeg Canadian National
Railway station and looked around anxiously—or was it eagerly? Would there be someone to meet me as promised? Night
was falling on this Thursday evening in late August 1945. I had
arrived from Saskatoon, Saskatchewan, where I had been working as a legal secretary for two and a half years.

I soon spotted Rev. John B. Toews, president of the Mennonite Brethren Bible College and well-known preacher, in his
black Derby hat. He greeted me warmly. I had met him earlier
that spring recruiting students in Saskatoon for this new school
of higher learning for pastors, missionaries, church school
teachers, and musicians. I planned to be one of those students.

He had described the new college as "committed to the
training of men and women who shall meet qualifications equal
to the challenge, a school which seeks to combine real scholar-
ship—conservative, evangelical and positive—with genuine
Christian love and enthusiasm." His language tended to be ex-
travagant, as I soon found out.

I had blithely written on the college application that I was
preparing for children's ministries, something far from my

goals. I knew that would be an acceptable answer. I didn't know what else to write.

The highest calling for women aspiring to church work was overseas missionary work, not in my list of "future things to do" either. While I enjoyed "foreign" missions reports, as they were called then, I didn't see myself in a pith helmet, khaki skirt, and heavy boots stumbling around in the jungle. Church musician? Hardly. I played the piano enough to satisfy my own need, but that was all.

I wanted a ministry in the church with adults but couldn't describe what I wanted. How could I admit to a vague longing for something I couldn't identify to myself? It was a call to something holy, I knew. Without a husband, church ministry opportunities were limited. All I could think of that might lead me to my nebulous goal was to become a pastor's wife. From my reading and experience I knew this sometimes entitled her to become a sort of "little pastor," who stood by her man or rather, behind him.

In his acceptance letter Mr. Toews had quoted Mordecai's challenge to Queen Esther when she faced requesting the king for help for her Jewish people: "Who knows but that you are come to the kingdom for such a time as this?" I clung to those words. Surely God would have something for me. Why was I leaving my old life behind? I had to do this even though my grandmother couldn't understand my giving up a good-paying, highly respected job as a legal secretary to attend a school that didn't lead to money-making.

Mr. Toews loaded my suitcases and portable typewriter into his trunk and drove to the dormitory/dining hall, a large white frame building, known as the White House, on Kelvin Street. Jovial Margaret Peters, college cook and women's matron, prepared a quick snack for me. The school itself was housed in a former one-story public school building next to the White House.

Before he left, Mr. Toews asked me when I could start work. I had agreed to work part-time in the college office as his personal secretary to support myself while studying. That is why I had come early. "Any time," I said, thinking that tomorrow, Friday, or maybe even next Monday would be a good time after I had unpacked and toured the tiny two-building campus. After all, I had just arrived and had lots of settling in to do.

"I will meet you at the college office in an hour" was his quick reply. His need of a secretary/stenographer was greater than my need to rest after a day's travel.

That was my swift initiation into a two-year stint as Mr. Toews's secretary and MBBC college student, years always enriching and stimulating, if sometimes unsettling. During those years I breathed the same theological air the highly respected "JB" breathed, and glimpsed the theological glue that held the Mennonite Brethren Canadian Conference together. Many Mennonite Brethren had been in Canada only about twenty-five years, having left behind the difficulties of World War I and the ensuing revolutionary years in the Ukraine for a better life in this new land.

A large wave of Russian-born Mennonites arrived in Canada from the Ukraine during the 1920s before Russia closed the exit gates. The MBs, a large proportion of this group, brought with them a zeal for evangelism and missions and, especially, for Bible study. Intermixed with this was an undefined theology. They claimed as their own the emphases of other evangelical groups, such as eschatology, pietism, and eventually child evangelism. They lacked a clear understanding of their historical background and theological distinctives as Mennonite Brethren. This new school of higher learning intended to correct some of that.

The nearly bare office I walked into about forty-five minutes later had a good-sized desk for Mr. Toews, a table for me on which sat his small, well-worn portable typewriter with some stationery and carbon paper. Behind the table stood an ordinary wooden chair for me. So we began. I had left behind a fully equipped business office in Saskatoon working in a law firm with definite hours and lunch breaks. This new venture was going to be a challenge, sort of like a pioneer breaking virgin soil. But I felt equal to it. JB dictated letters, one after the other, to incoming students, and I took down his convoluted sentences in Gregg shorthand. I was a fast typist and a good steno, and I knew it. Confidence was my trademark.

The year was 1945. The war was unwinding. Men were being released from the military, conscientious objector alternative service, and farm deferrals. They were in a hurry to take up the movement of their lives interrupted by the demands of the government. Canada, a British dominion, had entered the war in 1939, two years earlier than the United States, quickly following England into the struggle against Hitler's assault on Europe.

The men, a majority of the students, arrived with heavy brief cases, massive Thompson Chain Reference Bibles, and a zeal to study. Many were probably reasonable preachers, with experience in speaking in their local churches, before conscription forced them to spend the next four to five years in the military or alternative service. Some had been deprived of female company for months at a time. Finding themselves suddenly amid many young eligible women after years of repressed testosterone became an interesting factor in our coed living situation. The men wanted to get married; some needed to get married to be accepted by mission boards. Marriage was high on their list of priorities, yet the newly formed school rules aimed to keep hormones firmly subdued.

The average student age that year was twenty-eight, with the women at the lower end of the age scale and men into their thirties and even forties. A number of men were married, some with children, so not all were as young, naïve, and impressionable as I and my roommate, Vera Isaak, a tall attractive blonde with a wonderful contralto voice from Ottawa, Ontario. Like myself, she also had not grown up in a traditional Mennonite Brethren community. She was a year younger than I, a wonderful friend for the next two years and decades to come. Other students sometimes asked us if we were sisters, or at least related. I can't thank God enough for my compatible roommate. I can't remember a disagreement with her. We joked that we slept in one small bed "like spoons" to keep warm in the cold Winnipeg winter (lesbianism was not an overt issue then), ate together, prayed together, sometimes falling asleep on our knees praying after a tiring day. Daily devotions were sometimes a joy, sometimes a burden. But they had to be done.

I soon learned that not all students had experienced Vera's and my freedom to interact openly with men without wondering if they were overstepping boundaries. Some had come from an immigrant background, considerably more conservative than those of us with immigrant parents who had grown up in more anglicized churches and had never trembled under fiery sermons about the evils of wearing open-toed shoes, sleeveless blouses, and lipstick.

But now at MBBC, students like Vera and me confronted boundaries. High boundaries. Strange boundaries. The more conservative students had less difficulty with these rules. To them they weren't new. We others had to think twice before we hollered "Joe" or "Bill" to the young man across the room. My name at the time was Kay, and it took a while to answer to Miss Funk. We were expected to call one another Mr. and Miss at all times to keep relationships platonic, an amusing thought. I liked boyfriends who had first names, not men I had to call "Mr." and who called me "Miss."

At registration a few weeks later, I registered for the religious education program, which included Bible book studies, German, psychology, philosophy, and religious education courses. The four faculty members were J. B. Toews, New Testament and Systematic Theology; A. H. Unruh, Old Testament; J. H. Quiring, religious education and philosophy; and Ben Horch, music. Adjunct faculty filled other teaching needs. Chapel attendance was expected each school day, lasting a whole hour, most of it a lengthy sermon. I remember none.

We women were advised out of theology classes, which didn't bother me too much because I didn't know what theology was. And homiletics and Greek, of course, was out of the question. No woman in the MB Church would ever be called upon to preach. After all, we were told, we would probably become housewives, and our ministry would be in Sunday school, women's circles, or child evangelism. I had written the expected answer on my application form as to future ministry.

Only one woman, Mary Toews, about ten years older than I and who later became a good friend, enrolled in theology classes. She had already been accepted for missionary work in the Congo, so the administration reasoned she might need theology for her teaching assignment there. The rest of us women declared ourselves as religious education or sacred music majors. Only decades later would I realize the injustice done to us and the deep rut, theologically, I was falling into by accepting without question the thinking that women had only one role in life—that related to her anatomy, not her mind. Unlike John Irving's little boy in *The World According to Garp*, I wasn't even looking for the Undertoad, but it found me, nevertheless.

Enrollment mushroomed from twenty students, mostly local to Winnipeg the year before, to eighty students that year. The proportion was sixty men to twenty women. The mate possibilities for the men were a little slim, but a windfall for the women. Students trickled in until late October, especially the men slowly being released from their alternative service duties or the military. Government red tape is not cut quickly. Work supervisors apparently had the right to release the men when they saw fit.

Students were housed in one dormitory and in private homes scattered throughout the area. The rooms were sparsely furnished with a bed, table, and some orange crates stacked three or four high to serve as a dresser. Local merchants gladly donated them to us. Later in the year, some male students with basic carpentry skills built a small bookshelf for each room. Every student did several hours of gratis work each week to keep costs down, such as kitchen or maintenance tasks. I can't recall any grumbling. We were going to make this school succeed.

Dormitory living was enjoyable. I had grown up with three sisters, all of us in one bedroom with one small dresser and one family closet. My brother was privileged to have his own bedroom. We students had a curfew of sorts but, without cars, we were limited to places we could access using public transportation or our own two feet.

Each of us had an assigned time to bathe. The line near the bottom of the tub clearly marked the water allowance without incurring the gentle wrath of the next bather. Wet hose on the bathroom clothesline slapped our faces when we entered too suddenly. Nylons were rare and precious in those days. Vera's mother sent us each a pair with instructions to wash them gently in a canning jar with a little soap.

One young woman had been praying for money to buy some new hose, and waking up early, assured God answers prayer, entered the bathroom to find the line heavy with hose. A windfall. God had answered her prayer. She took a pair. The owner was not amused.

The student body soon fell into a routine, developing a pattern where there had been an untrodden path. Classes, chapel, meals, gratis work, music practice, service projects, socials, and for me, office work, slowly fell into place. Student government was organized, and I found myself on the staff of *The Harbinger*, the student publication, with an attractive young man from British Columbia as editor. Life was getting better and better. But each minute was precious, as the daily maelstrom of activities sucked me into them. Once in a while, Vera and I escaped for a visit to her grandmother, who provided us with *Nashwerk* (snacks) for the week.

Women students were instructed not to wear makeup or nail polish, short skirts (mid-knee was acceptable), transparent blouses, deep V-neck dresses, short sleeves, or anything that today would be called "sexy." There was little open talk about sexuality, but everyone knew what great sins were being prevented by such precautions. One student often quipped: "*Das kalte Fleisch reisst.*" (The naked flesh tempts.) Later in the year we women all adopted a uniform navy blue skirt and jacket with a white blouse for daily wear to make life less troublesome for the men.

The college administration was modeling the school somewhat after Prairie Bible Institute of Three Hills, Alberta, a highly successful institution in terms of turning out greatly motivated, deeply spiritual men and women, eager to serve in God's army. It had a nationally recognized reputation for producing people with a committed spirituality.

Their president, L. E. Maxwell, had written *Born Crucified,* popular reading in evangelical circles. Numerous Mennonite Brethren young people attended this school. Today I think MBBC was an attempt to draw them away from influences that might introduce teachings contrary to Mennonite Brethren doctrine, and strengthen the denomination's concern about maintaining inner purity by erecting fences to shut out alien social, moral, and theological influences. Church leaders didn't recognize it was impossible to escape being influenced by the broader cultural stream in a modern world, having come from closed Mennonite enclaves in Russia. If not, why were we students advised against attending the popular Youth for Christ meetings held in Winnipeg in a large evangelical church?

At Three Hills, rules regarding the amount and kind of interaction between men and women were strict, and clothing regulations equally rigid. Stories emerged from that highly regarded institution of a few women wearing ACE bandages around their chests to make their breasts less conspicuous to the men. On the other hand, other women were reported leaving the campus with skirts the regulation fifteen inches from the ground and, promptly, on the train home, rolling up their waistbands to make their skirts a stylish length and applying makeup. Giving up earrings and lipstick was fairly easy for me. I wore my blonde hair braided around my head a great deal because it was less work. I gave up my coat with the huge fox fur collar that made me feel special. I was determined to fit into the college's standards.

The college administration found it almost impossible to keep the men and women from fraternizing. Even the hallowed prayer closet where we were encouraged to unload our burdens became the ideal place for a couple attracted to one another to unload their feelings privately for a few minutes. The second spring I attended MBBC, an older student from Ontario, in high esteem in his congregation, threatened to report to his church that students were breaking the rules openly and finding secret trysting spots in the cemetery across the street behind large gravestones. The spiritual life at the college was dangerously low, he warned. The administration was sitting on their hands. I can still hear his solemn prophet-stance denunciations. I didn't think I had sinned according to his thinking, but the pressure was on to find Achan, that Old Testament character who hid his sin.

For a week after his threat, the school was in turmoil—loss of constituency financial support and future students was not what this fledgling institution's administration wanted to hear. Was it as a result of this that the school announced an upcoming day of fasting and prayer in the chapel? I don't remember. This day's program scheduled long hours of singing, Scripture readings related to renewal, admonishments, and much prayer, weeping, and confession of moral and spiritual lapses. Time was also set aside to make amends where one had failed.

Students took their faith seriously at college, almost too seriously. Being in the will of God was always a grave concern, as was taking glory from Christ's name to oneself after a public performance. Several of us girls who had felt annoyed by the new women's matron, Lisa Schulz, newly arrived from the United States to whip us into shape, determined self-righteously to each ask her forgiveness—which we did.

Today I look back on this experience and wonder what this unsuspecting American older woman, obviously unfamiliar with Canadian MB culture and hyper-spirituality, thought as one student after another came to her room to ask forgiveness for having disliked her. She didn't stay beyond that year. Why didn't we women see what was happening? Group-think, not the moving of the Spirit; "Idiots," I say now. But I was too ignorant at the time of spiritual development to know to do anything better than fall in line with older and (I thought) more spiritual students.

In chapel we sang "Oh, to be nothing, nothing, for my Lord" again and again. I recall some of the men referring to themselves as "Thou worm Jacob" when they prayed publicly. Humility was the virtue to strive for, pride the greatest sin. Some of the mature (here read older) male students often ended prayers with words that all was done in weakness (*Schwachheit*) to prevent God from charging them with pride.

At times I was so afraid I might have been taking God's glory to myself, I couldn't play the piano in public. What if, in some subconscious way I had thrust myself into the limelight? Yet this kind of spirituality was not singular to MBBC, but an aspect of other church institutions at the time.

Each class began with prayer. One was always expected to pray vocally at a moment's notice, so I kept a selection of popular spiritual-sounding phrases uppermost in my mind, not to be embarrassed by not having the spirit of prayer. But this statement should not be seen as judgment upon the many honest, inspired prayers sent to God.

During the many prayer meetings, I heard mention of secret sins or unspoken requests. I never knew what they were, but speculate now one secret sin was sexual self-gratification, a gross sin men were warned against, especially in the conscientious objector camps, where female companionship was limited. I was too naive at the time to know what this practice was. My knowledge of men's anatomy and needs was limited.

My future husband, Walter Wiebe, and I found that working on the publications committee brought us together enough to learn to know something about one another and acknowledge our attraction to one another. Many students used what we called "*die Augensprache*" (language of the eyes) to communicate. It worked well. The prevailing sentiment, as I remember it now, was that you were expected to marry any man, even a clod, if God told you to do so.

I did grasp that the unspoken prayer requests were a deep yearning on the part of some women for some small sign of romantic interest from the man they were attracted to. I heard one young woman cry herself to sleep at night because her boy friend ignored her in public. I stand amazed even today at the way some older male students remained coldly distant all year, without once letting on they were interested in a female student, then, on the last evening of school, when all rules were off, asking her for a date, proposing to her, and even setting the wedding date, maybe two weeks in the future to save the expense of a return trip to her home if they were from a distant province. But they had remained consistent to the rules governing separation of the genders.

But not everyone accepted this speedy method to get married or even the pressure to see this sudden proposal as God's will. Angelina came home from such a date on the last night of school and told the rest of us waiting at the head of the stairs for the "dated" girls to come home that she had refused him, because, God's will or not God's will, he was too skinny. She couldn't marry a skinny man. We cheered her.

I don't remember much about classes, except those in which I had unpleasant experiences. In a study of 1, 2, and 3 John, our instructor, obsessed with outlining to the fifth and sixth subdivisions, had us outline these books in minute detail, and, if possible, come up with alliterative words to describe each subclass. For years thereafter I could not read these books. I had dissected them too much. Their words stared back at me like the eyes of a dismembered frog, wide open but blank.

I had also enrolled in German under Henry Wall, a respected German teacher. But he had not counted on several adult students who could find no reason to study the German language if they were headed for the mission field in India or Africa, where they would have to learn a different language. They rebelled against this language requirement. Though only few in number, they made teaching for this gentle, gray-haired teacher from the old school in Germany a great misery. They complained. They laughed in class. They refused to do their homework. Yes, they were adults in their late twenties.

Yet the MB constituency expected, nay, demanded, German to be taught at the college. Most congregations still conducted services fully in German. MBBC graduates were expected to achieve German literacy to serve in the churches. In a few places, like Saskatchewan, where I had come from, some churches were slowly making the transition to English. The MB constituency as a whole, however, had not yet made the switch. I recall vividly Dr. Ben Horch, highly respected choral director in Mennonite constituencies, walking into the office one day quite downcast. The board had asked him to prepare the college choir to sing Handel's "Messiah" in German. Much as he had tried, he found it too difficult to fit German words to the existing glorious oratorio. In the end, we sang it in English.

Next term, Dr. A. H. Unruh, revered Old Testament expositor and experienced teacher from Winkler Bible Institute, who lacked fluency in English though he had been in Canada for several decades, offered to teach the German classes. He would put these students in their places. He taught in German and expected even those who didn't speak German to understand his instructions—even speak the opening impromptu class prayer in German. I floundered miserably and got the only D I have ever received in academic work.

Dr. Unruh had strong traditional views on the role of women: Men were heads of family and of the church; women should know how to cook, take care of the children and husband, and, if needed, work in the local Sunday school—or if on the mission field, as helpers to their husbands, not as missionaries in their own right. His teaching was widely accepted as the norm for women's roles in church and home.

Mennonite Brethren have always stressed the importance of music of all kinds in worship—congregational, choral, instrumental. A worship service was considered anemic without vigorous singing of *Kernlieder* and other hymns. Because lessons were paid for under some government bill for veterans, even if they had never approached a piano keyboard before, they elected to take piano lessons from Alan Borbridge. One man played his first simple recital piece with his foot on the pedal the whole time. Enough, he said, and quit. Both player and audience were relieved.

The college maintained a strong emphasis on missions and evangelism, the dominant doctrinal concern of the entire conference. Mennonite Brethren had been an offshoot from the mother Mennonite church in Russia in 1860 as result of the fiery preaching of Lutheran evangelist Eduard Wuest. They lost none of that fire when they established churches in Canada. The Russian Mennonites had come to America in waves—in the 1870s, a smaller group in the early 1900s, then about 20,000 mostly to Canada after the Russian Revolution in the 1920s. Another group arrived after World War II in the 1940s and 1950s. With the rest of the evangelical world at the time, revival meetings were important to Mennonite Brethren.

Mennonite Brethren were known for their zealous overseas missions program, sending missionaries as early as the 1890s to India, and for fervent revival meetings. At the college every student had a practical service assignment. Personal evangelism was an important course. Many students who came with a rich background of music in their home congregation immediately formed small excellent musical ensembles to visit nursing homes, churches, and whatever opportunities to witness for Christ showed up. A male octet, King's Four, was outstanding in their use of mature voices. Some of their renditions of songs such as "*Gottes Volk darf nie ermueden*" are unforgettable. Monday morning chapel was always the time to report the number of conversions as a result of the weekend forays into the highways and byways of life.

In spring of 1945 another student and I canvassed the neighborhood and started a small children's Sunday school in the administration building as our assignment with fair success.

On Saturday evenings some students rode the streetcar downtown to witness. I tagged along behind Mary Toews, who was older, more experienced, and hovered around her as she confronted person after person with the question, "Are you saved?" I didn't have the courage to follow her example.

This type of face-to-face witnessing was the norm at the time in the evangelical world. Years later, a friend from another denomination told me how he and his father spent Saturday afternoons driving slowly down the street. They had prepared small tubes covered with red cellophane holding gospel tracts. My friend's job as a young boy was to throw them at the feet of unsuspecting pedestrians from the open car window. The 1940s was the heyday of the gospel tract, once considered one of the most powerful means of spreading the gospel.

A group of male students felt God was leading them to start a radio Gospel Hour, which still exists today as the Family Life Network, with an international TV, radio, and event ministry to speakers of German, Arabic, English, Spanish, Russian, and Ukrainian. These students enlisted a fine men's quartet, a pianist, student preachers, and a business manager. Their daring plan excited the whole student body into much prayer for this faith venture. They needed a specific sum of money each week before they were allowed on the air. We prayed. We entreated. We waited anxiously with them for funds to come in; sometimes just the right amount arrived by mail minutes before the deadline. Who needed more proof that God answered prayer?

More than a few students, sometimes boldly, sometimes timidly, confessed to having received a call to the mission field under the steady pressure to "Send the light" to the unsaved of the world, possibly the highest calling to service then known. A few found out several years later on the field they were totally unsuited for mission work and returned. Others enjoyed decades of successful ministry in overseas fields.

I was still in the religious education program, bored with the education courses, and praying for a minister to marry to follow into some kind of ministry.

CHAPTER 2

My new learning begins

The glory of the gospel is its freedom. The Pharisees, who were slaves, hated Christ because He was free. The battle for spiritual freedom did not end when our Lord had risen from the dead.
—A.W. Tozer in *Of God and Men*

When I was asked to speak at a fund-raising banquet for Mennonite Brethren Bible College in Winnipeg in 1989, at first I resisted. What did I have to say to supporters of this institution? I was ready to refuse until I thought through those early years. Something special happened at MBBC. I had to admit it. This school had a large part in forming my spiritual thought and life direction.

Here I met my future husband, Walter Wiebe, of Yarrow, B.C., a mature man with four years of conscientious objector camp experience behind him, a love for the Word of God, a serious student, idealistic and imaginative, and a lover of language. And more than ready to marry. He attended only the first year I was there, but we kept the relationship going for another year, until our wedding in August 1947.

Despite the ban on formal dating, Walter and I managed a discreet dating in a group setting. When a group of students went to a function, we knew we were going as a couple. Once a student bet another man that he couldn't get a "street car" date with me to a concert. Student 2 took the bet. Because I wanted to go to the concert more than I didn't want to go with Student 1, I accepted. But I never understood the chuckles all the way downtown as the street car clanged to its destination.

35

Yet in this place of many new experiences, I began my love affair with the Mennonites and slowly became aware of their origins in Europe and migration to Russia, later to Canada, and church growth in Canada and worldwide. The word *Anabaptist* was still foreign to my vocabulary as it was at the time to many Mennonite Brethren, more closely linked with the evangelical world than other Mennonite groups.

By working in the college office, I learned to know students from all provinces. Even when I meet some today, I sense an immediate bond. We lived through certain experiences that only those who were there can understand. In that close, intense environment, we had seen one another in our strengths and weaknesses in the classroom, dormitories, dining hall, and other settings. We had laughed and cried together. Across the office counter, I talked to students, took their money, mindful of the cheerful one who wore a suit coat with a lining almost in shreds, or the one who carried a large full billfold opened magnanimously before me.

I was unmindful of my influence on these students. Years later, a middle-aged man came to me and said, "You changed my life." How? In some casual conversation over that counter I had encouraged him to attend MBBC. He was wavering, but my words persuaded him. He came. He found purpose for his life there.

Here I was introduced to the inner workings of the Mennonite Brethren Conference and its ministries. Visitors to Winnipeg from across the provinces always stopped off at the college to see how this fledgling institution was progressing. I could name every missionary and many church leaders. I knew the location of every congregation. I enjoyed the rare experience of getting an overview of the entire MB denomination.

Here I gained a solid knowledge of the Bible and the importance of a regular prayer life and spiritual growth.

Here I also discovered I was a *Russlaender* (Russian Mennonite) as opposed to *Kanadier* (Canadian Mennonite). And that family names meant something to some people. Those awarenesses came slowly, without fanfare. The first time a student jokingly called me a Russlaender I didn't know what he was talking about, but obviously it was a slur. These subtle differentiations had never been mentioned in our home or in the more anglicized Mennonite Brethren churches in Saskatchewan. I knew my parents had come from Russia in the 1920s. I wasn't overly concerned about those who had arrived at an earlier time—the Kanadier—and there were a number in our little congregation across the river from where we lived. But at the college I sensed a restrained tension between these two groups as students aimed thinly veiled barbs at each other.

The Russlaender, I learned, looked down on the Kanadier as being less educated, less refined, less progressive. Some more conservative Kanadier in the Old Colony villages of Manitoba and Saskatchewan still did not believe in education beyond the eighth grade. Russlaender leaders came to Canada well-educated and with a measure of sophistication. The Kanadier saw this Johnnie-come-lately group as snobbish, pushing to get control of church and conference, too eager for more education, lacking in humility. The Russlaender had pushed that conscientious objectors be allowed to enter noncombatant service during the World War II because that had been permitted in Russia. Kanadier argued for a more purist approach.

I will probably never know the depth of resentment between the two groups, yet here I was a Russlaender (my parents had come from Russia), who had grown up in an "English" world planning to marry a Kanadier (Walter's parents had come to Canada in the early 1910s) but who had grown up among Russlaender in Coaldale. People today talk about mixed marriages. How would this union of mismatched backgrounds affect our future?

Here at MBBC I learned about sacrifice and what it meant to abandon oneself wholly to the work of God's kingdom. Faculty, staff, and supporters were letting their love for Christ cost them something. They deposited spiritual capital in the bank for the next generation, so that those coming after them had a resource for inspiration, a pattern to follow. Even today I feel sorry for children and young people who have never witnessed all-out sacrificial caring for someone or something.

During my years at MBBC I watched faculty, staff, and supporters pour time, energy, money, and prayers into building up this new institution. School board treasurer C. A. DeFehr, Winnipeg businessman and longtime supporter of Mennonite Central Committee and similar agencies, worked long hours to keep the school debt-free. It was a privilege to watch his and his wife's gracious, giving spirits.

By working in the office I knew the long hours President Toews toiled for the college, traveling among constituents every weekend to garner financial and spiritual support. He was a powerful orator and much in demand. Often he came home late Sunday evening to teach Monday morning. I knew he was worn out from a full weekend and had had no time to prepare a class lecture. But his heart was with his subject matter. As I walked down the hall past his classroom, I sensed he made up in oratory what he couldn't reconstruct of the lesson. He always awed the students with his eruditeness. I think they caught his spirit to always keep reaching. He was much admired by many constituents for his zeal to bring the church to new heights.

Students caught this spirit of self-giving. Recently I found a receipt in my files for a donation for $50 that I had given to the building fund, Ebenezer Hall, a new dormitory for married students in spring 1946. My income from secretarial work was about $30 to $35 a month, roughly 35 cents an hour, which hardly paid for my expenses. But I had saved a little from my previous position, so I gave $50 to the project. C. A. DeFehr, board treasurer, knew my weekly wage and wanted to return my check to me. Too much, he said. But I insisted I wanted to give it. Today I wonder if I would be willing to donate more than my monthly income to some cause. I have lost something over the years.

I see it now, but not when I left the college: I had pulled together from many sources a strange amalgam of faith elements akin to magic. Not that the faculty didn't try to teach us otherwise. But we students, like children in a large family, brought each other up, rubbing ideas together with vigor and passion in after-supper discussions. We discussed our inner lives openly. On the table we dissected eternal security, pre-tribulation, the Rapture, the will of God, prayer, and much more. We naïve younger students grabbed whatever bit of information flew past us we thought might help us in our Christian walk.

Faith boiled down to a simple algebraic equation. You prayed, and if you had filled all God's requirements, God granted your request. A Christian was a conduit only, with God's words the life-giving water flowing through the pipe. "Channels only," we sang. Nothing more. You were an inert vessel through which God poured his blessings. All you needed was a spirit of submission. When you prayed for guidance, a big powerful hand pushed you from behind into the right way. You never made your own decision. You "let go and let God," a popular slogan at the time.

Here at MBBC for the first time I heard about a popular way to find God's will—to put out a fleece like Gideon did. And in a setting like the college, students were floundering to find new directions after years of being told what to do by government agencies. In essence, you bargained with God that if you received a letter with money in it, or some person spoke directly to you about a certain mission field you were in doubt about, it was God's will. The letter, the money, the words, were affirmation that the fleece was wet. You could take action. No wet fleece, no action. The important thing was to trust and not think things through by yourself, for that was going against God. Human intelligence was devalued. Conscious choice not considered important. Living by blind faith was the key to all.

I have since changed my thinking about knowing the will of God and prayer but then I, too, expected specific objective evidence (a visible sign) in response to my prayers—for example, whom to marry. I was inexperienced and impressionable. I wanted a definite sign, like an illuminated "X" on the man's back that he was God's appointed. I did not recognize that God might guide in various ways, such as Scripture, circumstances, inner voice, and that I had to make the decision. Recently I reread a letter from a former college friend who had moved to Kansas in the 1960s. He and his wife were enjoying their new place of service and wanted to stay there permanently. "However, we shall seek the Lord's guidance in this matter, for we do not want to go our own way." They had to have a direct sign from God that he wanted them there.

I had liked myself up to this point. I had always been an excellent student, gotten along well with others, was soon able to move to leadership positions. I had confidence in myself. Now I was being indoctrinated into a different set of behaviors, all labeled spiritual character—with humility at the top of the list and a pressure to not be too decisive or confident, especially as a woman, close behind. I was not a humble person. I was usually decisive. Now I wavered.

In the office of J. M. Stevenson, barrister and attorney, where I had worked previously, I was trusted a great deal. I more or less ran the office. It felt good to be in charge. Here at MBBC I soon found I was a lowly handmaiden. I saw many tasks I could have handled easily in the office, but I was never given those assignments—because they were men's tasks. I was allowing myself to fall wholeheartedly into a world shaped by men, and it didn't bother me, because it was the spiritual way. Above all, I wanted to follow the Lord.

Here at MBBC I began my interest in and love of theology, or the interpretation of God's Word for today. I did not realize I was being introduced to this queen of sciences in a church that was fuzzy about its own theology and was turning to other theological persuasions for help. In Russia where the Mennonite Brethren began in 1860, this small group of believers, upset by the lack of spirituality and high morals among some members of the mother church, broke away, but with new goals and great zeal. The emphasis was on what the Bible taught, on brotherly love (hence the word *Brethren* in the name), on discipleship, and on spreading the Word of God to others, not on theology.

This becoming group in the Ukraine was experiential in their approach to spiritual life and knew theology only intuitively. Like a young child in a candy store with only a nickel to spend, the early Mennonite Brethren, unclear about their theological identity, were open to outside offerings. A nickel doesn't buy much.

Fundamentalism with its emphasis on defending truth looked attractive, especially with the emphasis on literalism and proof-texts. Hadn't they defended truth by seceding? Eschatology (Darbyism) was equally appealing and took strong hold. Now the preachers could point to actual texts to uphold their teaching and show how the bits and pieces became a whole. The result was predictable: conformity to mainline evangelical piety, change in leadership models, and adoption of contemporary evangelical strategies of evangelism and church growth. But it took years for me to sort through this mixture of ideas.

Decades later, J. B. Toews wrote in *Pilgrimage of Faith: The Mennonite Brethren Church 1860-1990*, "We're floating aimlessly and need to refocus our theology." He saw the Mennonite Brethren Church as weak in three areas: hermeneutics (we feel we need to defend the Bible), ecclesiology (we have accommodated our church life to the dominant culture), and eschatology (last things). He saw MBs as bombarded by American fundamentalism and not resisting it. MBs had joined the witch hunt for modernism and in the process thrown out the baby with the bathwater. They had became "card-carrying citizens of the modern world." They had neglected to provide opportunities for study to keep historical and theological distinctives of the Mennonite Brethren sharp and consequently accepted an evangelical subjective piety. Jesus had become another product being marketed to satisfy consumer need, he observed.

I recognize now the privilege to know this man of God at close range in his strengths, weaknesses, and foibles. Over the two years I worked for him, I learned to take down in shorthand his much loved four- and five-syllable words without error. His inverted syntax was often strange to read. But his influence was unquestionable.

Nowadays communion services are often rushed affairs, tacked onto a service, a necessary duty. In the North End MB Church, a few miles from the college, communion was a separate evening service with a full-length sermon and much hymn-singing chosen for the occasion. One evening Dr. Unruh preached in German, the only language he felt comfortable preaching in, from Ezekiel 47. A man is going eastward, measuring the depth of the life-giving river he has entered. First it is ankle-deep, then knee-deep, then waist high, until it is a river that cannot be crossed. At such times, we must trust God to bear us, said Dr. Unruh.

I was deeply moved by his sermon. I felt the Spirit moving. Faith lessons of all kinds lay ahead. As yet the water was only ankle-deep. But I pledged to keep walking. And walking., even if the water kept getting deeper. At the time I didn't know there would be times when I would have to force my body through the water.

CHAPTER 3

Ein halber Russlaender (Half a Russian Mennonite)

Turning points in life are generally few in number ... yet they are always an encounter with an idea or with a person, before which the subject cannot remain neutral. He [or she] has to take sides, to shoulder responsibility, to commit to it.
— Paul Tournier

Friday night, August 22, 1947, I was lying awake in the lower berth of a Canadian National Railway train headed for the West Coast. Beside me lay my sleeping husband of two days. We had been married in Saskatoon on Thursday evening, spent that night in a hotel, and now were headed west to our new life together. I was excited and scared. I was now Mrs. Walter Wiebe.

As the train rumbled and rocked, I pondered what lay head. I never realized then that in an era before king- and queen-sized beds, my portion of our marriage bed for the next fifteen years would be a small triangular section to allow Walter room to stretch his long legs by lying diagonally on the bed. But here we were, crowded close together in a small lower berth. It was a strange but good feeling. I was married. I had said yes to becoming a wife and homemaker and expected to spend the rest of my life happily ensconced in our home-to-be. I was intent on becoming the best possible Christian homemaker. Abundant happiness beckoned me.

Yet who was this man I had agreed to love, honor, and obey after an eighteen-month mostly long-distance courtship that was on again, off again? We had not had a lot of time together to talk intimately about our family backgrounds, life goals, financial status, even thoughts on family planning. It was enough that the Lord had led us together and we were in love. That was the way it was done. The Lord would provide. All we had to do was trust.

In college, one student had commented to me there was something "big" about Walter—his outlook, his Christian commitment, his spirit. I had sensed that also. But I knew little else about him beyond what I had observed in school and we had discussed in brief encounters when we were more concerned about expressing our love than who we were. Over the next years, little by little, we told each other our stories.

His parents, Peter and Helena Wiebe, had come to northern Saskatchewan from southern Russia in 1908 with one-year-old Helena. A son, Jacob, was born at sea. The first ten years were incredibly difficult. The family always lived in rundown shacks, used earlier by other settlers. With four children they moved to Borden in the Great Deer district, where his father was scammed out of the harvest income by the landowner. They moved to another farm. There, after three years, they found they had no legal contract. Finally, in 1918, the year Walter was born, they bought a quarter section of land near Borden. By now the family totaled nine living children with two infant deaths. Erna, the youngest, had not yet been born.

Walter's father, Peter P. Wiebe, was neither a farmer nor a good manager. His great passion was arranging and directing music and writing poetry, not digging in the soil. Yet the government expected homesteaders to become farmers. He became an outstanding choir director for the Borden MB Church, which gave him his identity as farming did not. When the opportunity came to lease a large farm in Acme, Alberta, he jumped at the chance to move to this piece of land despite its rundown buildings. However, at harvest time, he collapsed emotionally. The doctor advised total rest. The family gave up the farm, rented a small home, and the older children went to work for others, something the elder Wiebe had hoped to prevent by living on a farm.

It was now 1930, the beginning of the Great Depression. The family was more or less penniless but managed to scrounge enough money to move to Coaldale into a ten-by-sixteen foot one-room house which had once served as a chicken coop. Their stay there was only temporary until a larger place was available. The at-home members of the family numbered eight.

Here Walter's father regained enough strength to set up a shoemaker shop and to take on the position of church choir director. He suffered another siege of depression as well as hepatitis, yet prayed that, like Hezekiah, the Lord would give him another fifteen years of life. That prayer was granted.

Walter's academic career, which began with excellent grades, plummeted in 1935, possibly because of the death of his closest friend, Jimmy Thomas, as well as the family situation. He didn't take his Grade 11 exams but remained at home, picking up odd jobs. Walter spoke of those years as the "dark chapters" of his life. His father was ill, the economic depression in the nation was deepening, and he was amid a troubled adolescence. He didn't fit into the conservative community of Coaldale dominated by Russian Mennonites. He always felt like a "*halber Russlaender*" (half a Russian Mennonite). The Wiebe family belonged to neither the *Russlaender* nor the *Kanadier*, the Mennonite group that had come to Canada in the 1870s, having come with a small group in 1908. Culturally they were two different groups with the same origins.

On November 17, 1936 (the same date on which he later died in 1962), Walter and some school drop-out friends attended a revival meeting at the Coaldale Mennonite Brethren Church. In those days everyone attended revival meetings and outdoor baptismal meetings, if only to see who would go forward to poke fun at them later. This group of young men usually sat on the back bench, not really in tune with what was going on at the front. When the evangelist gave the altar call, Walter made that long, lonesome walk to the altar, leaving his amazed friends behind. He spoke of this as a pivotal point in his life, for it meant "a new position and new relationships." For him, that decision was like the Israelites' coming out of slavery in Egypt to new freedom in Christ. It gave his life direction.

The following year he was baptized but still had not reenrolled in school. The family situation hadn't improved. His father lost the position of choir director because of some unproven charges against him. Discouraged, the older man took a three-month visit to Manitoba to refresh himself.

In 1938, at age twenty, Walter yielded to years of dental problems without financial resources to pay for care and had the dentist pull all his upper teeth and make an impression for dentures. Going without teeth for several months as his gums healed was not easy for the young man. From time to time he was bothered with appendix attacks, which the doctor did not think severe enough to warrant surgery.

Yet after receiving his dentures, he started grade 11 in Coaldale nearly six weeks late. He had lots of catching up to do. War was imminent in Europe. Sickness continued to plague him in spring 1939 with flu-like symptoms and tonsillitis. Yet despite these setbacks he completed his school work with honors.

The next fall, again late for the beginning of school because of working to help support the family, he began grade 12 and finished it successfully. Normal school, or teacher training, in Calgary was the next step, followed by the plan to teach in a Hutterite Colony near Lethbridge, where he had completed his practice teaching. But that was not to be.

Canadian mobilization for war began in June 1940. The government had promised a civilian alternative for conscientious objectors. Mennonites had assurance their religious convictions regarding war and military service would be respected, but not all provinces had set up alternative service boards.

Before he could begin teaching, he was notified to report to Banff, Alberta, on October 12, as a conscientious objector to war. He was immediately made foreman of a gang cutting sick trees and burning. The men at camp organized study clubs with each one teaching according to his expertise. Walter was elected president and taught public speaking and the book of Romans. After four months service he returned to teaching but was called again to work at Camp Q-2 at Campbell River. He entered what he later called his crucible, his place of testing. Life had been tough, but it was about to get tougher.

He often quoted to me his father's saying: "It is better to spend fifty years struggling for the truth and making mistakes than to live for a short time according to tradition." His intense search for God's way was beginning. He was often perplexed. He desperately wanted a girl friend. He wanted more beauty in his life. In his diary he wrote: "Today I bought (in my mind) a Currier & Ives picture collection." He designed book covers for his father's poetry and music. He experimented with becoming a vegetarian after suffering kidney problems. He kept a scrapbook and spent hours copying parts of poems and writings by great writers expressing noble thoughts. His handwriting was carefully crafted. He indulged himself in calligraphy.

He took long, long walks in the moonlight by himself and with friends, sometimes quite discouraged. He saw his life as a failure, going nowhere. His inner searching led him to write letters of apology to people he might have hurt in the past.

He longed for a deeper spiritual life with purity of body and mind. Purity of body was a particular trial to young Christian men at the time when touching oneself inappropriately was considered sin. Camp preachers warned against the evils of sexual self-gratification. He started fasting for the evening meal several times a week. The hard experiences of camp life tested his mettle. Should he give up his faith as a friend had done? While I never learned the true depth to which he was taken in his struggle for self-integrity, that period when he was not free to go his own way but had to obey the government made him into the man he later became—self-disciplined, conscientious, consistent in his goals. He knew what he believed. Government law confined him to camp. The law of the Spirit of life in Christ Jesus had set him free within. He had survived this crucible.

Although Camp Q-2 at Campbell River was dismantled, that did not end his CO requirements. Blubber Bay on Vancouver Island was the next work assignment at a lime mine, mucking dirt, loading lime, breaking down an old kiln and firing stack kilns. He and a friend bought out some departing CO couple's household and started batching, giving them new freedoms and more privacy. They could get up half an hour earlier for Bible study and prayer. His monthly income was $26.65, yet his parents' needs were always uppermost in his mind. During 1944 he sent home $150 to $160 from his fifty-cents-a-day salary. Toothpaste was a mixture of salt and soda. Haircuts cost a dime. He honed a razor blade on his palm to ensure several more shaves before discarding it. I saw him do this often. He brought these frugal habits into our married life.

By fall he had a new cause for concern—his father was not well. He himself was becoming weary with his uninspiring work and with relationship problems among the men in camp. He became aware of intolerance, murmuring, and ill-feeling within himself. A call from his brother Jake that his father was very ill brought him home to Yarrow, B.C. He received permission to stay until September 1, an answer to prayer. His father did not improve, so arrangements were made for him to spend the next months at Bethesda Home in Vineland, Ontario, a Mennonite institution.

Walter had heard about the new Mennonite Brethren institution for higher learning being started in Winnipeg. He sent for information, but his district alternative service officer could deny the release of men deemed essential to the project they were engaged in. His release came October 1, 1945, and a few days later he showed up in Winnipeg looking across the counter at me in the office. His father was well taken care of in the hospital and his mother, with the help of other children living in British Columbia, would manage. God had answered his prayers. Finally, life was beginning to move forward again. On October 3 he was twenty-seven, free to pursue his goals: prepare for service for Christ and marriage, but which came first?

CHAPTER 4

Mostly a Canadian

"There, there, in a hundred years,
this won't matter. It hardly matters now."

I had been at MBBC about six weeks when Walter arrived, ready to begin this chapter of his life. His roommate was dark-haired, fun-loving Victor Toews from Coaldale. The two made quite a pair.

Within a few days, Walter was elected chair of the Advertising and Literary Committee. A week after arrival, he accepted a part-time position to teach literature and composition at the Mennonite Brethren High School adjacent to the college. He also agreed to tutor an older minister, Jacob Dueck, in English. His financial needs would be met.

For the first time in about five years he was living close to young women. He chose Vera Isaak and me as well as some men to work with him on *The Harbinger*, student newspaper, published in English and German. We both became members of a new constitution committee in the spring, so we had numerous opportunities to see one another in this regulated environment.

By Christmas his heart was smitten, and in true Russlaender tradition, even though he was only half a one, he gave me a hand mirror before I left for Saskatoon for the holidays. In this tradition the presentation of a dresser set was an important first gift from the man to the woman in a relationship. That overtone escaped me. I was too much in tune with Canadian ways. Engagement rings I understood, not hand mirrors.

During these months Walter and I were both learning to know great and influential men of the Mennonite Brethren

Conference. He appreciated President J. B. Toews' advice: "Never let the crowd do your thinking for you; always do the thinking for the crowd." As ever, JB easily swayed people with his powerful oratory.

Only later was I aware that even during this year of limited income, Walter sent regular money orders of $30 per month for his father's upkeep at Bethesda Home in Ontario and received frank reports from the director about his condition, not always encouraging. In letters to Walter, the elder Wiebe expressed the longing to die at home in Yarrow, British Columbia, where his wife lived, not in an institution.

The college office attracted Walter because I was there much of the time and, of course, he had *Harbinger* business to discuss. Leaning across the counter, he proposed to me—just like that. Our intention was to get engaged and return as an engaged couple to MBBC the following fall. Walter returned to B.C. at the end of the school year and I to Saskatoon after another month's work at MBBC.

My grandmother, once again, was disappointed that I was getting married—too young—and it meant the end of my promising career. My mother thought I wasn't ready. My father wrote Walter a long letter asking if he was sure I could go along with him in his calling. Walter had sent his father a picture of me sitting at my desk looking steadfastly into the camera. He replied: "I want to look her in the eyes, into her heart, and ask her if she can love that many-cornered Wiebe forever."

Back in Saskatoon for the summer months, away from the cocoon-like living of MBBC, I came out of my trance. I was back in a Canadian world without talk about Russlaender and Kanadier. The atmosphere was more joyous and lighter than in the Winnipeg cloister of serious-minded would-be preacher and missionaries carrying their huge Thompson Chain Reference Bibles and uttering pious words during any encounter. Here the varsity group I associated with from different denominations had a vastly freer outlook on life. Young dating couples, like my sister Anne and future husband Wes Kruger, were much less burdened about finding and doing the Lord's will or worrying whether even a small misstep might seriously set back their spiritual life.

Walter and I were both glad for a time to think matters through more carefully. I wanted to look at our relationship through a clearer lens. The courtship had moved ahead too quickly in a strained atmosphere.

Our four-cent mail visits began. The letters we exchanged summer 1946 were mushy with love, openly pious, and showed much concern for doing the Lord's will, pussyfooting around real concerns. Walter broached questions about his future ministry. He knew he wanted to serve the Lord, but where and how? He fasted and prayed. His mother commented, "Your wife will cure you of that habit."

"She'll never succeed," he replied quickly.

Walter voiced concerns about what he saw as competition between the cradle and a career for me. In his experience with five sisters, married women became wives and mothers and forsook thoughts of outside work. He couldn't find room for both in our marriage. The husband's role was to provide for his family. He worried that I loved my office work at the college more than I loved him. On the other hand, he wanted to study. How could he support a family and also study? "Woman is man's complement. As long as the complement is missing, part of the man is missing. How could it be otherwise?"

The letters continued in lofty spiritual language and avowals of love, but I felt uneasy. I was marrying a man without a vocation or fixed income. He had come from a family where a steady income for long periods was the exception. Walter was accustomed to living with scarcity. In my family, though never well-to-do, my father always had a regular salary. That was a given. There was always food on the table. I broke off the engagement for the time being. I needed time to think.

In fall I returned to Winnipeg to continue studying and working in the college office. Walter was not among the returning students. His father's general condition had improved to the extent he could return home to Yarrow from Bethesda, but his mother was not strong enough to take care of him. Walter would have to stay home. He confided to me later he had lain on his bed at night and cried in disappointment that his education would again be halted. Yet how could he leave his frail parents alone? He was the only unmarried sibling in the family, so the responsibility automatically fell on him. His father was not yet sixty years old but had been sickly a good part of his adult life.

He wrote that he struggled with witnessing openly about his Christian commitment. He struggled with what he called the "lusts of the flesh," leaving me to fill in the blanks. Once again his life was at a dead end.

A measure of hope came when he received an offer to teach from the board of the Yarrow Bible School, a Mennonite Brethren school. He had no biblical studies or theological degree, only several years of intensive self-study in camp and a grade school teaching certificate. The board recognized his spiritual maturity not achieved in formal studies and ability to assimilate material. He accepted the offer.

I don't know what prompted me to write him a letter in late fall inviting him to come to Blaine Lake, Saskatchewan, where my parents lived, for Christmas. The letter was short and without explanation. I wanted him to know what Russlaender who weren't really Russlaender like those we had known at the college, were like. In his short visit, he fit in well with my family, and my family welcomed him gladly.

The engagement was on again. Walter was overjoyed that I would willingly forgo working outside the home for his sake, always a sore point with him. He believed the husband should provide for himself, his family, and his schooling. "And if he can't do that? Then, let him attempt only as much as he can do, and be satisfied therewith. And his wife too!" Yet he doubted his own words, for he added a qualifying statement: "Who knows how life will shape itself for us. Maybe we'll be forced into such unpleasant circumstances."

Clearly, he had been thinking through our relationship as husband and wife all winter. In June 1947 he wrote:

There is such a tender tone of submissiveness [in your letters]. Evidently that theme has been emphasized very much recently in college. I wonder just from what angle or what method of approach has been used. Well, this is a topic about which I long to talk to you, too. But will leave it for later and maybe after we're married. *Then* it will need more consideration. My love, my greatest concern is not, will you be a proper wife to me; I am much more concerned with this, what sort of husband will I be? May the Lord help me, by his grace.

If Walter was happy about gaining a wife, J. B. Toews was most unhappy about losing his prize secretary. A promised discussion about the matter with Walter when JB was in Yarrow never materialized, and Walter felt slighted. He was offended that JB discussed figuring out a way for Walter to return to MBBC with Rev. C. C. Peters, Yarrow Bible School principal, so that I could continue as his secretary but not with him.

Our engagement was announced in Walter's home church in Yarrow, B.C., and at the North End Church in Winnipeg, where I attended on January 12, 1946. Walter wrote that an audible murmur traveled through the congregation at the announcement. Some people wondered why this eligible bachelor hadn't picked a local girl. The announcement had disturbed some MBBC students who also wanted to get engaged during the school year. We were breaking the rules. After discussion in the administration and an explanation in chapel, we were told we had handled the matter properly with everything in the open.

But Walter faced another hurdle by himself in British Columbia. I wanted an engagement ring. He bought a ring with a small Zirconia stone. Zirconia? In my immature thinking, I told him I wanted a diamond like my Saskatchewan friends would have received. But his intentions had been good, and he didn't like to admit he didn't have the money. I wasn't gracious enough to say that it didn't matter.

I wrote him from Winnipeg that the new married couples' housing, Ebenezer Hall, was nearly finished with many flaws in design. An "apartment" was basically one good-sized room with a kitchen cupboard and wardrobe, back to back, dividing it into two tiny rooms. Sinks, showers, and toilets were outside in the hall without adequate privacy. The women carried hot water into their apartments to wash dishes and bathe babies and little children. Men in their pajamas and women in robes and curlers washed and brushed teeth side by side at the open sinks. I wrote him, "I hope we will never live in that place."

As he began to get invitations to preach in the B.C. area, a new wrinkle introduced itself. Jake Epp, principal of Bethany Bible school in Hepburn, Saskatchewan, invited Walter to supervise the short-term high school held on campus for about ten weeks in spring with about fifteen students, so that they could write provincial exams for their high school diploma. He also offered him a position to teach at the Bible school in fall. Walter had no high school teaching certificate and had only taught grade school for about a year and a half. But he felt equal to the challenge of this high school assignment.

He came to Winnipeg at Easter by train, our mode of long-distance travel at the time, to visit me before he went to Hepburn to teach short-term high school. While in Winnipeg, he finally had a conversation with JB. "Sometimes I think a few of my words did pierce his skin," he commented. The man he had once much admired now irritated him because he opposed our marriage and my leaving MBBC.

He found the tiny community of Hepburn odd. "It seems everybody is about half-asleep. I was reminded of Tennyson's 'The Lotus Eaters,' a land where it was always afternoon. The people were friendly, but in a mild sort of manner. I do prefer something brisker." Preparing zealous adult students to take provincial high school exams was easier than he had expected. He had time to study for and write the grade 12 German exam.

During the spring months at college, I and the other young women were being indoctrinated into the college faculty's view of marriage. J. B. Toews told us to consider the spiritual, social, and biological aspects of marriage. "There is a tendency to over-spiritualize marriage in our circles," he warned. Dr. A. H. Unruh admonished us that a preacher's wife was there to bear the burdens, to cook and darn for her husband. A missionary's wife did not go to the mission field to be a missionary but to be her husband's caretaker. "Queer idea," I wrote Walter. "If he is right, the women might as well quit school." I wanted something more than being the one who ironed his shirts and pajamas and met his physical needs.

Yet Walter's image of me was in a kitchen, looking trim in an apron with flour smudged on my pretty nose. But also as his companion in the Lord's work "seriously discussing spiritual matters, reading God's Word, praying, fellowship." A career for me was always a touchy matter. I agreed to yield to his wishes. He knew he was marrying a topnotch secretary and had visions of dictating his teaching notes to me.

In Winnipeg that second year of Bible college, my mind was awakening theologically. I attended a children's rally. The evangelist asked the children to raise their hands to an altar call, then stand to sing "Into my heart, come into my heart, Lord Jesus." Thereupon he pronounced the children saved. This seemed too much like shoving the children down a funnel into the kingdom of God. Such steam-roller evangelism always bothered me.

By the middle of May, Walter grasped that the money crunch would hit hard before the wedding. He was planning to go to summer school at the University of Saskatchewan in Saskatoon while I continued working at the college. I was floored by his outright statement that lack of money never bothered him, for he always had enough for immediate needs. How to deal with the matter?

I pointed out to him that we had never learned to play together at such activities as tennis, bowling, swimming, bicycle riding, and picnics. Such activities never interested him when there were books to read and ideas to explore. He recognized that he was like the man who had missed the first train and was hours too early for next one.

We tried to write about sex but never got far. He admitted sexual relations had always been a mystery to him. Without childhood sex instruction, when his sexual nature asserted itself, he was unprepared for such a strong desire. I was fuzzy about natural birth control. Artificial methods were out of the question for him.

I returned to Saskatchewan in early July to my parents' home in Blaine Lake, with great avowals to give up all the things that kept me bound to myself and to yield completely to the Lord and to my future husband. My mother told me how she and Dad had prayed through every trial and difficulty. Dad was certain I would long for a typewriter years after I was married. I never doubted his word. In July Walter began summer school, establishing a pattern for years to come.

Wedding expenses were mounting up—a suit for Walter, medical exams, bride's bouquet, furniture, and first month's rent for our apartment in Yarrow. The wedding was held in the Saskatoon Mennonite Brethren Church on Thursday evening, August 21. Thursday afternoons were my father's day off from the store. We spent the first night in a hotel and fumbled and bumbled our way through what was supposed to be a night of bliss.

The next day we left for Yarrow by train to begin married life in the new duplex, across from church, which housed the Bible school. It had a kitchen/dining area and bathroom on the first floor plus two small rooms upstairs. Rent: $25 per month. Married life had begun for Mr. and Mrs. Walter Wiebe.

CHAPTER FIVE

A mixed marriage begins

The thing to do is to live the age you are in.
—Dr. Marion Hilliard

Walter and I arrived by train in Chilliwack, about ten miles from Yarrow, in late August at the height of the raspberry season. Someone, I don't remember who, picked us up at the station. We spent a few days with Walter's parents in their small cottage before moving to the duplex across from the Yarrow Mennonite Brethren Church where the Yarrow Bible School was also housed. Walter had a contract to teach there for the coming term.

I had half expected a Wiebe family gathering to welcome us, but that didn't happen, so I was introduced to those family members who lived in the area over the next few months, family by family. Back in Saskatchewan, a newcomer to the family would have been an occasion for a celebration. Developing family relationships seemed to be a low-priority] item here. After all, I was the tenth in-law to join the Peter P. Wiebe family. Everyone with a berry acreage was busy picking raspberries, a fragile crop that had to be harvested when the berries were ripe. Wedding receptions moved down the scale of importance.

I have described this year as one of the most difficult in my life. I should have been ecstatically happy in my new home with my new husband; instead I felt abandoned. If Coaldale, where Walter had spent many years, was the concentrated essence of Russlaender conservatism, Yarrow wasn't far behind. The dominant language was German, which I understood but spoke haltingly. At home we children spoke English to our parents and they spoke English or German to us. Walter's parents spoke very little English even though they had been in Canada since 1910, so conversation with them was limited to conventional phrases.

They tried to make me feel welcome. I had memorized the phrase *"Es freut mich mit Ihnen bekannt zu werden"* (I am pleased to meet you) to have something to say to someone who spoke no English. But after that, my side of the conversation stopped. I was encountering a new culture in language, customs, and traditions. I hardly recognized being called *Frau Wieb*. Kay Funk had disappeared. This strange land did not resemble Blaine Lake, Saskatchewan, where I'd grown up.

Walter was soon busy teaching during the day and deep into class preparation every evening. Even if he had had time, there was no place to go and no money to do so. Finances became an immediate concern. To take care of the needs of two people was a much bigger matter than Walter had anticipated. What to do? As a single man he had adjusted his needs to his income, large or small. As a married man he now had fixed expenditures to meet every month and, before long, we would have an addition to the family.

I was shocked I had become pregnant almost immediately. Cause and effect escaped my understanding. I felt nauseated to the point of despair. I had not planned for this start to our married life. I knew nothing about being pregnant. Nor about cooking or operating the drafts on a coal and wood stove. Growing up, I had been the child assigned to dusting and cleaning, not cooking. Another deep-seated concern was that the new baby might be born prematurely, as had the baby of college friends. The husband wrote anguished letters to all their friends, explaining with underlining and capital letters that he and his wife had not had sex before marriage, the Greatest Sin in the church at the time. Their infant son was truly premature. I believed him, but the new father anguished that people might judge him. What if our baby was born prematurely?

It didn't help when early one morning the Slavic woman living in the other half of the duplex knocked on the door to borrow some sugar. She watched Walter carrying a tray with oatmeal to me in bed. Her amused comment, *"In Amerika, Frauen wie Kinder"* (In America, women are like children), stabbed me to the core. She had come from Europe recently and could chop wood, carry big sacks of groceries for miles, and manage a household with energy to spare. Her statement humiliated but also pushed me. I had chosen marriage. I would make it through this time of misery. Even though I couldn't see clearly ahead, I decided I would find a way through.

Time lay heavy on my hands. A library? Nonexistent. A shopping mall? The only stores were at least ten miles away. We had no car—and I didn't drive. Friends? How did one make friends in a strange community where everyone was busy from early morning until late at night bringing in the fruit harvest? Walter had assumed that I would simply slip into the routine of being a wife like his mother, sisters, and sisters-in-law had. There were husbands' roles and wives' roles. At the time, a man chose career goals and then fitted wife and children alongside. A woman may have worked outside the home for a time, but when she married, she left all that behind for her new role. Except during raspberry picking season when everyone pitched in. Working outside the home after marriage was considered inappropriate and a reflection on the husband's manhood and earning ability.

Walter's brother Jake dropped in from time to time when he was in the area, as did Jessie, his wife, a gentle, caring spirit who carried her own burdens with a large family in inadequate housing. Pete and Anne Andres, with whom I had boarded while working in Saskatoon, offered encouragement. Pete was teaching at the new Sharon Mennonite Brethren High School. Anne let me cry on her shoulder and pointed out that this was Yarrow, a core Mennonite community, not Saskatoon. She offered the illustration of a clock ticking. Listen for the silence between ticks. I was caught between the ticks.

I gazed into the small bathroom mirror at the strained face looking back at me, wondering what had happened to the care-free young girl in Blaine Lake, where I had spent my childhood. Where was the blue velvet beanie with the soaring feather I wore so jubilantly? Where was the gleaming blonde pageboy I flaunted easily and the ready spirit with which I once faced life? I saw drawn lines on an unhappy face framed by long braids wound around my head. I saw empty eyes.

Soon after we moved into the duplex, one early morning I woke to hear heavy footsteps on our gravel driveway, accompanied by loud muttering. I nudged Walter. He looked out the window and then explained that the man lived by himself about a mile or so from us. In his childhood during the Russian Revolution of 1917-19, he had witnessed his mother's rape and murder. Later, he had spent two years in hiding before coming to Canada as a five-year-old to be reunited with family members. At times the demons from the past asserted themselves.

In the morning bleakness I watched from our upstairs window as this miserable, emotionally disturbed soul sparred and shouted at an imaginary foe, his voice growing louder and louder. Even when I first saw him in daylight, I drew back. He was a huge man, poorly groomed, with an angry mien. He was fighting his battles; I was fighting mine.

A new wrinkle introduced itself when Bible school enrollment was lower than expected, so the board decided one teacher would have to be released. Walter was the likely candidate because he had been teaching only one year. However, graciously the other four teachers agreed to keep him on staff if all five teachers were willing to divide four salaries among themselves. The other men were all established fruit farmers. Walter's monthly salary was even less than we had planned. We were setting up a household. One day Walter found a dime on the church yard. We said, "Thank you, Lord," and bought a loaf of bread. Things looked grim.

For a brief time I played for the church choir, but the director wanted someone who could play by ear. That wasn't me.

Church evening gatherings became my refuge, not in the sense of comfort but to fill time. One evening Mennonite Central Committee workers Peter and Elfrieda Dyck spoke to a packed Yarrow MB Church, which held about 1200 people. They told the unforgettable story of the escape of 900 Mennonite refugees through the Communist Russian zone of Berlin to the coast of Holland to board the *Volendam* for Paraguay. Their clear message of *"Gott kann"* gave me courage. My problems were small compared to those of the refugees.

I also attended congregational meetings but sometimes came away perplexed, not understanding why this church body made the strange decisions I had just witnessed. One evening the congregation disciplined a father of a large family who refused to pay the levy for the local church-sponsored high school. He said he couldn't pay. His large family required all his income. The solemn men in black suits up front said he had to pay—borrow the money, skimp even more, but pay. This new private high school had become a bigger financial burden on the congregation than planned. Everyone was expected to contribute to keep it solvent. It did eventually fold, but this was in its beginning stages. The legalistic harshness of these Russlaender leaders frightened me, as it would again and again, later on, in other congregations.

By spring we had to have more income to meet increasing expenses, so we moved from the new duplex to a small one-room log cabin on the side of Vedder mountain. This meant even more isolation for me, someone accustomed to being amid the action at college. Yarrow wasn't the romantic beginning to married life I had expected.

When Bible school ended in spring, we called it quits. Walter sold our briefly owned furniture, and we boarded the train for Saskatchewan. He had accepted a position to teach the short-term high school at Bethany Bible Institute in Hepburn again, something he enjoyed. I was about seven months pregnant. I owned two maternity dresses. Housing in Hepburn was in short supply so, for a few weeks, we moved into the home of an older woman absent for the winter. When she heard what her real estate agent had done without her permission, she was irate, so we moved again, this time to a small dilapidated one-room building at the edge of town. The yard was bare except for a few outbuildings. An outhouse stood at the edge of the property.

On June 15, 1948, as the sun streamed its first rays through the window, my labor pains began. I was two weeks late, which meant the baby would be born well within the allotted nine months. With each day over the due date, I felt easier. We had not sinned. I had always known that, but now everyone would know. Walter rushed to a friend to borrow a car to drive me to City Hospital in Saskatoon and returned to Hepburn shortly thereafter for classes.

Childbirth was a woman's job. In those days she was expected to labor by herself. Fathers were an unnecessary nuisance. I knew nothing about the birth process. No one took time to explain the stages of labor. I longed for someone to be with me through those long lonely hours as my tense body was racked by pain after pain. But that was the way childbirth was done in large city hospitals.

Toward midnight our first daughter, Joanna Katherine, a big beautiful baby, was born. She became a ray of hope in our difficult circumstances. She needed me and I needed her. I spent the next week flat on my back, as was expected, in a large ward holding fifteen beds in what had formerly been the sunroom. A wonderful woman in the bed next to mine had just given birth to her seventh child. Her positive, refreshing spirit reached me, soothed me. She was an early mentor.

The next evening, I waited eagerly to show Walter our new daughter. All the mothers were receiving guests. I tried to keep an expectant attitude until the end of visiting hours. He never showed up. He had taken a nap and slept through visiting hours. "Imagine me sleeping through a date with you a year ago. How fast a husband degenerates. Oh well, you'll forgive me." I forgave him, yet why do I remember it?

When I was ready to be discharged, the hospital threatened to keep me there until the bill was paid. When Walter arrived, the hospital personnel were satisfied with an agreement to pay $10 per month until the $100 debt was paid.

Walter had accepted an offer to teach at Hudson Bay School, a one-room grade school six miles north of Hepburn. That meant steady income for at least ten months.

For the summer, baby Joanna amd I lived with my parents in Blaine Lake and Walter attended the University of Saskatchewan in Saskatoon once again, using the money he had earned in spring, a pattern that continued until his death. He boarded with Anne (my sister) and Wes Kruger for $45 for six weeks. Anne laundered his shirts. He had four dollars left after paying his fees. I had no money with me when I left for Blaine Lake. The little house in Hepburn where we still had our few household goods had been sold, so we had to move our stuff once again.

At the end of summer school, Walter and I with Joanna re-united at the teacher's residence at Hudson Bay School, a fairly new building but without electricity or running water, five miles from Hepburn. During the cold months, Walter started fires in five stoves and heaters each morning, three in our little house and two in school, a building one student described as "a little old woman squatting on a hill." Children drove to school on horse and buggy or walked. The salary was $1500 per year, a welcome thought. It looked like a gold mine.

Here our real bonding as a married couple began. I said good-bye to college days, determined to make a life for myself somehow in this isolated place. I dug into homemaking as best I could. I learned to bake excellent bread with flour we bought by the 100-pound bag. My first task every morning was to wash diapers by hand in the washtub, no small task, for all water had to be carried in and heated on the stove. Walter accepted his role as public school teacher, but only for the time being, I soon realized. Teaching grade school at Hudson Bay School was just a detour.

Our conflicts in marriage were the same then as they are now in many families: money and sex. Walter had finally accepted the need for some form of birth control. A large family like his own family's would soon end his pledge to continue his education. Birth control didn't seem right to him, but the other solution was to sleep on the couch. He explained how his good friends had finally resorted to birth control because with every pregnancy the wife developed a severe case of eczema, making it impossible for her to do dishes—or diapers. That then became the husband's job. Attitudes toward birth control were changing. Sin was being reconfigured. With the birth of Joanna, I now received a monthly baby bonus check from the federal government of about $5. My own money once again.

My parents often came on Thursday afternoons from Blaine Lake, my father's day off from the store, to visit and to leave a box of dented cans and "unsalable items." They were lonely too and the weekly visit brightened their week. Walter and my father became close friends. My parents accepted him as a son, not just a son-in-law. Dad enjoyed discussing theological issues he was struggling with, and Walter answered as best he could, with great respect for my father and his homegrown theology. They loved one another.

I phoned my grocery list to the Hepburn grocery store once a week, and the manager sent it out with whoever was passing by our teacherage, the Canadian term for the teacher's housing. Local farmers sold me eggs and milk. One year I never left the school yard from Christmas until Easter, for we had no means of transportation in winter. I watched the farmers in their horse-drawn sleighs buck the heavy snowdrifts on the road. I tasted isolation as well as solitude by turns.

Our now-steady income paid all our debts and bought me a gas-powered washing machine and a hand-turned sewing machine. I borrowed books from the Saskatchewan Traveling Library. Somehow Walter bought a car—a half-breed with a Whippet body and Hupmobile engine—from my brother Jack. Our next car was a 1929 Model A Ford.

Always ready to preach, Walter started church services in the school building with the approval of the board during the winter months when car travel was impossible. He loved to preach. A sizable group of local farmers and families attended, happy to have a nearby place to worship.

The urge to continue his education interrupted by the war grew steadily in Walter. He enrolled in correspondence courses from the University of Saskatchewan. My brother Jack, teaching at a nearby school and also enrolled in a course, often discussed their assignments in the evening on the party line. Listeners soon hung up when the discussion moved to Shakespeare's "King Lear" or something similar.

The glue was beginning to settle into the small corners of our marriage. At Hudson Bay School we learned to talk to one another about our future together. Though we had two distinct backgrounds, we found togetherness in a shared future. He had a dream and I dared to join him in this dream. As a married woman, there was no other way.

The dream focused on a literature ministry for the Mennonite Brethren Church, affirmed by an invitation in 1950 asking Walter to become editor of *The Christian Leader*, the English publication started as a youth publication but on the way to becoming the organ of the church in Canada and the United States. Walter declined, citing his lack of preparation for such a position. We started a daily devotional time, which we maintained until Walter died. It was impossible to pray together when angry with one another.

After two years of steady income and some success as a rural school teacher, Walter pushed ahead with his theological degree at Mennonite Brethren Bible College, interrupted when he had to look after his parents. I had once vowed I'd never live in that monstrosity, Ebenezer Hall, married students housing, but acquiesced. We packed our belongings onto a home-built trailer towed behind our Model A Ford and traveled to Winnipeg.

Our apartment was basically one room with a divider consisting of an open closet on the bedroom side and a small kitchen cupboard on the other. The monthly rent was $12.50. The bedroom area barely had room for a double bed and a crib. The kitchen was crowded with a small electric range, table and chairs. The trunk I had received from my parents when I finished high school, a book shelf, and a chair completed the furnishings.

Washrooms were in the hall, as was the community refrigerator, where each couple could keep milk, butter, and a little meat. I carried water into the apartment to wash dishes and bathe Joanna. Crowded? That wasn't the word. It was overstuffed.

Because our quarters were so full with the stuff of life, Walter spent most of his spare time in the college library. The second year he was elected student body president, another reason to spend time away from the family.

The summer of 1951 Susan was born at Concordia Hospital, so Walter moved another crib into the tiny bedroom. We barely had room to walk between our bed and the children's cribs. This time I was determined to learn about pregnancy and childbirth, particularly from the book *Childbirth Without Fear*. Better prepared than for Joanna's birth, I had a fairly easy birth, although the nurses held my knees together to keep the baby from being born before the doctor arrived. My family allowance, now increased to $10, went for necessities, not just infant needs.

After Susan's birth, I suffered post-partum depression, not considered a clinical illness at the time but spiritual weakness. I wasn't trusting God enough. I lacked faith. I descended into a pit of darkness, even contemplated ending it all one evening as I wandered along the shores of the river close to Ebenezer Hall and sought comfort from the inviting, fast-flowing water.

Child-raising in such crowded conditions was a challenge. Early on, a young three-year-old took his frustrations out on his young playmates by biting them. Joanna picked up the habit from him, followed by a mother biting Joanna in desperation. Dormitory councils were held to solve relationship problems without much success. Leaders attempted to keep everything on a high spiritual plane. More prayer, and more prayer, was recommended to resolve issues. I just wanted more space.

Joanna, an active curious child, liked nothing better than to climb onto her tricycle and pedal madly around the neighborhood with the host of dormitory children. She and two other would-be explorers reported one evening they had gone as far as the Louise Street Bridge, a considerable distance, and dangled their feet over the edge, a terrifying distance to the river below.

Financial resources continued to be limited. An old ledger for summer 1952 shows our income for the two years in Winnipeg was meager. Walter, an excellent finish carpenter, worked for Display Fixtures one summer and on the editorial staff of the *Konferenz-Jugendblatt*, a partly German, partly English publication for young people. One Christmas he sold books at the North End MB Church Bible Conference. With the war over, new books and Bibles were again appearing on the market. Commission on his $200 gross sales added another unexpected bit of income.

I typed papers for students at fifteen cents a page on my old college typewriter to add to our limited income. We ate a lot of Australian canned beef and lamb that winter, both cheap. Groceries totaled about $25 per month. We were back to the budget limitations of our first year of marriage. The $5 reward for finding a budgie was a huge boost one week. A nickel earned or found meant a nickel could be spent.

But even from this meager income, Walter always tithed faithfully. Sometimes he borrowed from the Lord's purse, but always with an IOU in it to remind him to repay the debt when we had more money. He kept track of this money zealously. It did not belong to him. I wasn't nearly as precise in my bookkeeping.

In spring 1952, Walter's father, Peter P. Wiebe, died in Yarrow at age sixty-five. Walter borrowed $75 from the college administration to attend the funeral, another debt to pay. This spring he graduated from Mennonite Brethren Bible College with a Bachelor of Theology degree. He wrote the publishing agent at Mennonite Publishing House in Scottdale about openings for a novice such as he. The answer was no. Such positions were given to members of the Mennonite Church. However, he was invited to look over the plant, even to stay for several weeks. He decided against that.

Now what? The board of the Yarrow Bible School asked him to return to teach there. I could not agree to that. My memories of Yarrow were still too harrowing. He accepted a teaching offer from Bethany Bible Institute in Hepburn, Saskatchewan.

After a calamitous journey to Hepburn with our heavily packed trailer, we moved into the new dormitory with rooms at one end to house a teacher and family. Our remuneration consisted of housing, $100 per month for the six months the school was in session, all the flour and beef we could eat, and evening milk from a cow. Another family got the morning milk.

In addition, we were expected to eat our main meals in the school dining hall with Walter leading evening devotions and generally overseeing the student body during mealtimes. When after three years a teacherage opened up, I pushed to move into it. I had spent seven years at this time, singly and married, in dormitories. Seven was a complete number in my mind for unsatisfactory living arrangements.

A high point in 1953 was Walter's ordination to the ministry by the Hepburn MB Church. In his usual fashion he debated with himself: "Can I say no? Can I say yes? May I say yes? May I say no? Dare I say yes? Dare I say no?" He said yes. At the ordination service he referred to this call as God speaking to him. He mentioned the lonely walk he took to the altar at a revival service in Coaldale, causing the current to begin flowing in an opposite direction from the one his life had taken during adolescence. He felt humbled by the church's endorsement of his calling to the ministry. He saw it as a "sacred honor." Even as childbirth was a woman's task, ordination was for men.

I had bought a new black velvet hat for the occasion and sat on the platform with him. When I came home that evening, I noticed that the preacher's sweaty fingers had left their imprint on my new hat when he had prayed over us. I had the sign of ordination on my head but no assignment. In those days wives received their identity from their husbands. I was usually introduced as "Mrs. Walter Wiebe." Now I could say I was "Mrs. Rev. Walter Wiebe." Walter's rise up the church hierarchical ladder also took me a small notch higher, something I, in my immaturity, subconsciously treasured at the time. We were moving on up.

Beginning March 7, 1954, Walter began a ministry of pulpit supply at the Laird MB Church, about fifteen miles away. The church was small—about forty members, mostly farmers and their families. He preached Sunday mornings and led the Friday evening prayer service. Early each Sunday I packed clothing and supplies for Joanna and Susan, later also for Christine, for the entire day, because we were expected to remain for the evening service, sometimes a Christian Endeavor program.

Spending Sundays in the Laird church meant a long, wearying, but enjoyable day for me. The people were friendly and comfortable to be with, mostly Kanadier with a few Russlaender. I liked these people. I was at home among them.

My family had attended this church for years when I was growing up, so it meant being with old friends, comfortable friends. For this work Walter received $10 for the morning service, $5 for prayer and similar services. The last time we traveled to Laird was May 27, 1956. Walter made about 175 trips to Laird; I accompanied him about half the time, on Sundays, as expected. A wife was a partner in ministry even if she had no designated job description.

Sometime during this period Walter enrolled in a Christian Writers Institute correspondence course for beginning writers in Chicago. He completed the lessons and received comments from an instructor. I read them on my own time and studied the comments. Somewhere, deep inside, a small seed was sprouting. I felt the urge to write. But I shared my longing with no one. I had no idea what a writer did to succeed.

CHAPTER 6

Following the follower of the Holy Grail

It is in this life story that God's plan may be accomplished. A man in movement, is continually undergoing change, living a history, unfolding from birth until death. The very movement implies meaningful life.
—Paul Tournier

Toward the end of four years of teaching at Bethany Bible Institute, in the tiny "Lotus eaters" community in Hepburn, Walter grew restless again. To stay or to leave? The Main Center (Sask.) MB Church had called him to serve as pastor, but he lacked the joy to accept. That even smaller community was too far removed from a university. The United States, particularly Kansas, near Tabor College, was a possibility, but no doors opened. Kitchener, Ontario, looked promising , but that required a long move. I resisted moving again. Hepburn was beginning to feel like home.

Walter felt pressured to further his education. He had been whittling away at courses at the University of Saskatchewan during the summers. The expanding needs of the MB Conference, where he wanted to serve in an "enlarged ministry," demanded educated leaders. The logical steps were to follow a B.A. with a master's degree My brother Jack was studying at the University of Saskatchewan in Saskatoon, so he mulled that over in his mind. Decisions. Decisions.

True to his nature, he examined each possibility carefully. Some decisions affect our lives significantly, some don't, he wrote. Which tie to wear was an insignificant decision. A vocational choice "to better serve the Lord" was of graver concern. "The big issues of life are sometimes wrapped up in and determined by little decisions of seemingly insignificant points of life. Life's greatest choices are rarely conscious choices," he wrote in his journal.

His answer came when the Hepburn MB Church, where we had been members for four years, called him to be their pastor. They knew him and his preaching style well. He accepted on the understanding he would be free to continue his education as he served the church. Two issues faced this congregation: the pressure to shift from German services to English and to commit more fully to a salaried ministry, especially with regard to a candidate determined to study at the nearby university without time for part-time remunerative work. Walter knew his critics, and he told the church council that if it came to a vote, he would choose furthering his education over the pastorate. They accepted his terms. "Come, be our pastor," they invited. He was only their second salaried pastor. I would be the pastor's wife, an unspoken dream of years ago. I didn't know what to feel.

That spring, Walter and I and our three daughters moved to the parsonage across the street from the Bible school on a former farm. On the property, in addition to a weathered two-story frame house, stood an old barn, chicken coop, and a farm-sized garden plot. Most church members were farmers. The salary was modest.

The congregation expected I would immerse myself deeply in the time-tested activities of a farmer's wife to keep expenses down. I was otherwise inclined after an admirable try. For a few years I brought in the fruits of a huge garden, canned up to 400 jars of vegetables, fruit, and meat in fall; sewed all the girls' clothes, some by ripping and turning old garments. The violent tremors and blood splattering of the first hen I beheaded disturbed me enough to say "never again." I even sewed sport shirts for Walter. He felt most comfortable in a suit with a starched white shirt and tie. Ironing a shirt took me about twenty minutes. I encouraged more casual clothing. I made small booklets for the children to use as writing material by stapling together used envelopes carefully slit open.

I baked, I cooked, I cleaned and polished. We entertained guests. But an inner stirring urged me to shape my life in a less traditional way. I set up my college typewriter on a small table under the staircase in the dining room and wrote. My wastepaper basket filled with drafts of articles. I quit raising chickens. I felt like a toad that has come out from under an old log and joined the human race. My living space suddenly enlarged. I had made myself room to grow.

Years ago I had written a few lines to myself: "I'm afraid to be a writer —I'm afraid to put things down on paper, things I might regret later on, as if these things really applied to me. But then they do. These things that I want to write are my thoughts, the things that keep me going, the things that slow me down and make me wish I was anywhere but where I am. I shouldn't be afraid. I know I shouldn't. No one will ever see these things I write. No one will ever know they belonged to a girl who once had hopes, dreams, but never saw them realized." I now had a small foothold on the side of a rocky cliff.

The challenge to write loomed overwhelmingly. To create with words was for people in books, for men, especially preachers in my Mennonite male-dominated world, for people in other times and places—not ordinary people like me. I had no role models, no encouragement, only a faint nudge within me.

I also felt distressed by women's lack of excitement for their own spiritual and intellectual growth and by the church's unconcern for the tremendous waste of women's gifts unless they were the traditional ones like cooking, sewing, working with children, or in a music ministry. Surely the Spirit honored other gifts.

The work of a pastor's wife had vague parameters in those days in the thinking of both congregation and me, for it was too new. Unpaid ministers' wives, up until now, had been part of the caring function of the whole church, serving as they were able. Under the new system, they sometimes became "little pastors." Husband and wife were identified as a pastoral couple, although her contributions were never defined or compensated. They were her Christian service. And many women found great fulfillment in this role.

For me, being a pastor's wife meant, in part, joining my husband in visiting the elderly, which I soon discovered young pastors had little fondness for. They spoke about this unwelcome task freely when they let down their defenses over coffee and rolls in our living room. When I accompanied Walter for visitation, often with my younger girls in tow because babysitting was as yet a foreign custom, the visit was conducted in Low German. I came home, my jaws aching from making the unaccustomed sounds and not sure what we had accomplished beyond shedding some "sweetness and light."

But no invitations to a specific ministry as the pastor's wife reached me beyond going with Walter on such limited ventures. The forces of church and society were pushing Walter and me in two different directions, so unlike our college years, when we had common academic and social interests. Slowly, the awareness grew that though we were members of the same church, he had first-class citizenship and I had second-class citizenship. The church was a male-determined body. He went to important policy-making meetings. I attended women's gatherings and mission rallies. When we visited with friends, the interesting talk was usually in the men's corner. Women were content to discuss hemlines, new knitting patterns, and potty-training pointers.

As a young married woman, I felt part of me was living in a void, but I numbed myself to the emptiness because I thought I shouldn't feel that way. The problem was with me. I had what every woman wanted—a good, loving husband and three lively, intelligent, and creative girls. I was doing what I had always dreamed about—being married. Why should I ask for more? I couldn't grasp that the spirit, the mind, the imagination, the inner life, must also be satisfied or its hunger pains can lead to another kind of death. The worst aspect of this turmoil was that I didn't dare discuss my confusion with anyone—not even with myself. To do so would reveal a liberal, and worse still, an unspiritual attitude toward life.

A pastor's work in the 1950s meant carrying the burdens of the entire congregation, some of which were carryovers from the previous pastor. Some tattled to the new pastor, a person hired to listen to complaints about other people's "sins." One woman informed Walter that one couple had not attended the Lord's Supper for most of their married life. Another member reported his father had smoked for years. Another member had attended a ballgame in the city with some other young men followed by a dance and drinking binge. And on and on.

A group of new young singers had been brought into the choir about a year earlier, most of whom were not baptized church members, a problem for some members. I never understood the full depth of the problem but lifestyle and disruptive behavior during practice were some issues. A particular concern was a church member dating a non-member. Non-resident relatives had stepped in to churn up the turmoil even more, demanding their relative not be "murdered by gossip." The choir leader quit in disgust.

A second congregational concern was low morality, the issue in southern Russia when the MBs seceded from the mother church. Immorality, whatever form it took, but specially sexual immorality, remained a strong Mennonite Brethren concern. The rumor spread that a married man was regularly visiting a young single woman. About midnight one evening an older church member was searching for a cow that had broken through the fence to see two cars leave the man's yard. He took down the license numbers. This flagrant behavior upset him. He told others.

One late October evening, home alone with the children, I heard a loud knocking at the back door. Before I could answer, several men in winter clothing burst into the kitchen with the words: "We catched J———-in the bush with a girl." A church posse had set up a watch at the man's farm. They wanted Walter to come and do something, pronounce judgment, anything. He was at a church meeting, so off they rushed to church to collect the pastor. With the minister in their possession, they drove to the farm where, Walter later told me, they came to a clearing. He described the scene as dismal. The north wind blew icy cold in the damp fall air. The girl's father had draped himself over the hood of his car, weeping uncontrollably. He had also been called from whatever he was doing. The girl sat dejectedly in her car. A group of men surrounded the culprit so he couldn't escape before the pastor showed up.

Much later that evening, Walter told me how inadequate he had felt facing this group of condemning men and the dispirited young woman. He suggested everyone go home. The matter would be dealt with the next day in another setting. I never learned exactly what the resolution was because it dragged on and on. But that was pastoral work in the 1950s.

An equally tough problem was the pressure from many sources to switch the Sunday morning service to English despite the desperate pleas of older members who understood little English even though they had been in Canada for decades. Some were sure God had said to Adam in the garden, "Adam, *wo bist du?*" Living in small closed communities had made it unnecessary for the older generation to become conversant in English. Church services and family prayers were conducted in High German, but Low German, that much-loved dialect with its many nuances to describe something, was the language of home and hearth. But the time had come to think ahead. Walter preached the Sunday morning sermon in English after a short German devotional. One old man complained bitterly to Walter, "I am starving to death while sitting at a full table." Walter preferred English to German when preaching, so his sentiments were with the progressive group.

He wrote his good friend, Victor Toews, also a pastor, with whom he had roomed the first year at Bible college, "It is hard work, very trying at times, lots of stresses and strains, responsibilities, sorrows and sadness, joys and droll sides. And all of this in a half-year. It is right and rewarding." Walter enjoyed writing to his close friends. His letters were always articulate, carefully worded and often lengthy, frequently about his thoughts about life at the moment. Typing errors were few.

In the fall of 1952, when Walter began teaching at Bethany Bible Institute, he also accepted the editorship of a new publication, *The Youth Worker*, for the Canadian MB Conference Youth Committee. This small multi-graphed publication was sent out eventually to about 400 addresses with ever more requests. Youth work was just beginning in the churches as a separate ministry. As Walter became busier with his teaching and other assignments, I assumed more and more of the editorial responsibilities. I wrote articles and signed his name to them.

In January 1957 he informed Orlando Harms, editor of *The Christian Leader*, that an article reprinted from *The Youth Worker* under Walter's byline had actually been written by me, not him. He was concerned that "one of our capable Mennonite women" would be robbed of due recognition. He attributed my lack of a byline to my "traditional" modesty.

In time, the situation with *The Youth Worker* grew uncomfortable for Walter and me. His role had been reduced to buying the stencils, carrying the finished bundles to the post office, and giving me moral support. But in the thinking of the church constituency he was editor and writer. Which was right and proper in their thinking. The little publication was meeting a need in the churches—and also in my life. It provided me with a creative outlet. But it became a crossroads.

As Walter traveled in the church constituency, he was embarrassed to have to tell inquirers that an article they had appreciated was not his work. We had a few options: to discontinue the little publication altogether or to continue with Walter's name on the masthead only as managing editor and mine as editor. A third option was to reprint all the old material in some permanent form before discontinuing it.

Walter's friend, Peter R. Toews, also a pastor, asked in a personal note if I would take on the work by myself in my name. "I realize that such an attempt might be risky in our conference, and yet the project is great enough to stand such a jolt." Since I had done most of the work in recent years, the character of *The Youth Worker* would not change. The Youth Committee finally agreed to have the masthead read "Walter and Katie Wiebe, co-editors" even though I would do all the work. To have my name stand alone as editor was too big a step. When Walter continued to receive too many comments about "his" good work, he found even this arrangement uncomfortable and we resigned as editors.

Like Florence Nightingale, I had offered the church "my heart, my mind, and all my life, but it sent me to do crochet work in my grandmother's parlor." I turned my attention to freelance writing, picking up an occasional assignment for *The Canadian Mennonite* Walter didn't have time for. Now I wrote news and feature articles under my own name. I dared to sign them Mrs. Katie Wiebe. Kay was long gone. Not literary enough.

Together with a friend I turned my attention to children's work at the church. We started Wednesday evening boys' and girls' clubs to memorize Bible verses, sing, and learn simple crafts. We had a rip-roaring good time. After the first year we were asked to discontinue the crafts because some members found this vigorous activity inappropriate to a church setting.

About this time Walter was appointed to the General MB Conference Publications Committee and to a commission to study publications in the United States and Canada. He also had connections with the Canadian MB Youth Committee. At issue was how to hang onto the young people and shift German publications to English. All these activities meant many meetings away from home and much correspondence in addition to his summer and winter university classes. During the winter he drove to Saskatoon three times a week. But I didn't mind too much. My husband was gaining in importance in the church world, so I was also moving on up. Husbands were their wives' status symbols in a preacher-conscious world. Wives found their identity in their husband's identity. I chuckle to think how important it was at the time and how trivial it seems now. But that is the way it was done at the time. Wives lived in their husbands' shadows, praying these shadows would keep growing.

Walter found it difficult to convey to others how his university studies enlarged his horizons. He felt lonely in his pursuit of higher education. Church members wondered when they would have a full-time pastor, not just a "student-pastor." The situation did not satisfy him or the congregation.

He felt the prick sorely to be called a "student-pastor," which he defined as a young man with limited experience who did only preaching, even though he had taken over the administrative work at the church. Could others do his present task? Could others do the task he felt destined to do in a literature ministry within the wider MB constituency?

It troubled him that if he finished his B.A. in Saskatchewan, the church would expect him to continue as pastor in return for allowing him to study these past years. He planned to resign in April 1958, leaving him free to attend summer school. His friend P. R. Toews advised against leaving so soon—not good for his reputation as a Christian worker. "The air is rather thin at the top," P. R. wrote, "and one must move very cautiously." The MB political situation had its hazards.

I found the decision to leave difficult. I could see immersing myself more deeply in the role of pastor's wife in local ministry but also with the broader women's church organization. Some women were sending out feelers about organizing women's ministries at the provincial conference level. The MB women in B.C. had tried this and the *Prediger* (preachers) had promptly stamped this revolutionary movement out! But we Saskatchewan MBs were going to give it a try.

Secular magazines were publishing articles about the growing pains of women following World War II, but the church remained silent. When I briefly broached the subject to a few church leaders in the broader church community about a larger role for women, some felt threatened and even defensive. Few women had the courage to consider the topic, for it reeked of heresy, even self-betrayal. To accept that all women had to conform to one mold crushed my spirit. I determined to accept myself and my gifts even though others might consider me strange if I chose reading over canning and writing over quilting. To accept myself meant listening to myself. I started to listen to the silence within.

During the turbulent sixties, a conservative church reacted harshly toward anyone who marched to a different drummer. I didn't dare approach a minister for counsel, for intuitively I knew I could not expect understanding. But I am getting ahead of myself.

Shortly after Walter's letter of resignation from the Hepburn MB Church was written on March 30, 1958, I realized I was pregnant again with the baby due in November. I didn't know where this child would be born.

CHAPTER 7

Living in Eden but far from it

Do not be afraid of God. He has a shepherd's heart and skill. He will not overdrive his sheep. He will suit his pace to theirs.
—F. B. Meyer

In May 1958 Walter began negotiations with Eden Christian College, a Mennonite Brethren sponsored high school at Niagara-on-the-Lake, Ontario, to teach there for the 1958-59 school year at a beginning salary of $3,000. Three universities were located nearby: McMaster's, Waterloo, and the University of Western Ontario. By now he had two years experience teaching part-time at the Mennonite Brethren Collegiate Institute in Winnipeg while attending Mennonite Brethren Bible College, four years of teaching a short-term GED high school in Hepburn, and six years of teaching Bible school in addition to public school teaching and pastoral work.

In July he attended the Canadian MB Conference and delivered a paper at the deacons and ministers conference on "The Inferiority Complex of the Mennonite Brethren." I did much of the research. I was increasingly becoming his secretary/researcher.

In mid-August the church held a farewell for us. The sale of our household goods netted about $240. We left on August 26 after a trip to Blaine Lake to say a tearful good-bye to my parents. We had enjoyed their close company for eight years. Joanna was entering Grade Six and Susan Grade Two. The details of the trip and succeeding events are described in my book *Alone: A Widow's Search for Joy.*

Housing at Virgil, Ontario, where the school was located, was limited, so we were offered rooms in the girls' dormitory. We had already spent five years living in a dormitory since our marriage, not including my two years and Walter's one year at MBBC. I did not relish another dormitory experience but acquiesced when I was assured this arrangement would be temporary.

Our "home" included two massive bedrooms on the second floor of what was once Colonel Ball's 1812 estate home, now part of the school campus. Our bedroom measured about eight by twenty-four feet. In a pinch the room could be used as a race track, I concluded when I first saw it, thinking of the much smaller house left behind. The children bounced around in a bedroom measuring eighteen by eighteen feet. We shared bathroom privileges with the teenage female students, who seemed to think the bathroom was society's most important invention. Heating dated back to 1812. Our kitchen, living, and dining room were combined in another large room on the ground floor. The kitchen sink emptied into a pail in the basement, making it important to keep checking to see that it didn't overflow. The rent was $35 per month, including utilities.

I easily envisioned gracious ladies with powdered hair piled high, trailing hoop skirts, moving gracefully down the wide winding stairs, or relaxing with their gentlemen in front of the massive fireplace in the school parlor across the hall. That vision soon vanished when high school girls in white blouses and navy-blue jumpers, undergirded by layers of frothy crinolines, and wearing white bobby socks and saddle shoes, dashed up and down the stairs.

All fall Walter felt sick after having been acutely ill in a motel on the journey to Ontario. He decided it was flu. Physician visits produced no diagnosis other than flu or stress. Walter had never suffered from stress. In late October, in my eighth month of pregnancy, I slipped on the winding staircase and severely sprained my ankle. The children felt lonely and took turns being sick with coughs and colds in the unaccustomed damp, dreary fall weather. Walter continued to meet speaking engagements as well as his teaching assignments, but the joy he had previously experienced in such work was slipping away.He felt ill continually.

On November 23, 1958, James Philip was born at the nearby Niagara-on-the-Lake Hospital at a total cost of $98.16. We called him "*frintel Wieb*," or "friendly Wiebe" because his friendly nature brought a small ray of joy into a trying situation. That whole fall was difficult, nearly impossible, as I dealt with a sick husband and unhappy children, including a newborn. I didn't know how to drive. The community was strange. I had few friends. Money was always short.

After Christmas, Walter traveled to Winnipeg for Canadian MB Publication Board meetings and then on to Hillsboro, Kansas, for General Conference Publication Board meetings. I encouraged him to go thinking that meeting with friends might give him new zest for living. The person I now lived with was not the man I had married. His sparkle and joy in daily life had left him. In Winnipeg, after conferring with a doctor, his better judgment advised him to return home, but the other board members were anxious to have a Canadian at the Hillsboro meetings and urged him to go.

On New Year's Eve in the morning, I had been mopping the huge upstairs floors feeling a little more upbeat. Life looked a little more promising. Maybe we could pick up the threads of life again in this new year. But a voice inside insisted, *Deeper, still deeper.* The almost audible words startled me, but I dismissed them. In the evening as I was putting Jamie to bed, the phone rang. In Hillsboro Walter had collapsed, having run out of antibiotics. Emergency surgery revealed that his appendix had burst, probably as early as September when he first became ill. Death seemed imminent.

The next day, New Year's Day, I was downstairs alone pondering the whole situation when the words *This is the will of God concerning you* impressed themselves upon my mind. What did they mean? The ensuing flood of promises of prayer, cards, letters, even money, was overwhelming as I packed to leave for Hillsboro. My mother flew from Saskatchewan to take care of the girls and bake them comfort food—cinnamon rolls. A young woman who had lost her baby at birth when I was in the hospital took newborn Jamie to her home.

After four weeks Walter returned to Ontario only to have a relapse. Anything we had experienced up to now seemed easy compared to what I experienced next. I had a very sick husband and the children a very sick father, a newborn infant, three miserable girls, and no money. I found myself in a dark tunnel steadily slipping downward with no light to guide me.

The school lacked money in the budget to give Walter sick leave, so we were without income for about three months with huge expenses. Walter told me to use money in the Lord's treasury but to keep careful record of what I took. That purse was hidden in his underwear drawer underneath his socks. He was always a strict tither, even of small amounts of income, and the one who did the actual giving. Money gifts found their way to our address. Local people brought us what they could spare, so that winter many a car backed up to our door to unload jars of tomatoes and peaches. We ate peaches for breakfast, lunch, and dinner when there wasn't much else. I was reminded of the children of Israel in the wilderness eating manna daily. For years I couldn't eat a canned peach.

We lived life one day at a time, one hour at a time. The girls went to school. I looked after Walter, little Jamie, and our lowly dormitory rooms. He spent time catching up on correspondence, long neglected. We rejoiced when word reached us of a sweeping revival in the Hepburn area with about one hundred people signing commitment cards. Some church problems that had originated before Walter's tenure which had plagued his pastoral work were finally being cleared up.

Walter and I had time to talk together and pray about the future. I thought he would make a good pastor if he could yield himself to this ministry. I desperately wanted a more settled life. As a pastor's wife I could see myself moving more into freelance writing. He, as pastor, would have time to develop his teaching, preaching, and writing skills. I was convinced he enjoyed preaching and teaching too much to make a good journalist, the Holy Grail still leading him. I lagged in my zeal to follow. He admitted he should have stayed in the Hepburn pastorate. He was giving up high school teaching and found it humiliating to do so.

The Canadian MB Conference had many mature men who had come into the ministry after the war, eager for work but also for more visible positions after spending years in some isolated conscientious objector camp. Pastoral work as a professional salaried ministry was in its infancy. The MB church had begun as a "brotherhood" in Russia with its roots in congregational fellowship. Ministers/preachers had been financially independent, often with an agricultural background. In Canada the trend was steadily moving toward a trained and salaried pastorate. Walter debated whether to accept another pastorate.

He received an unofficial invitation to accept an editorial position in Winnipeg with the Christian Press. He declined for now. Another invitation offered him a position with Canadian MB publications in Winnipeg.

The state of Mennonite Brethren publications at this time was in flux. The entities involved were *The Christian Leader*, the English MB publication for both the United States and Canada but not widely accepted in Canada; *Der Zionsbote,* a German language periodical for mostly Canadians, especially new Canadians who had not yet learned English; the *Konferenz-Jugend-blatt*, ostensibly a youth periodical for Canadian readers, mostly in German and published irregularly. The American churches had dropped German worship services a while ago. Part of the mix included the two publishing houses: Mennonite Brethren Publishing House in Hillsboro, Kansas, and the Christian Press in Winnipeg, acquired about 1960 from private owners.

A number of boards and committees were involved in trying to reorganize MB publications: Canadian Board of Publications, General Conference MB Board of Publications, Unification Commission (an advisory board to the Christian Press, Centennial Celebration Committee, General Conference), Canadian MB Youth Committee, and later on a Literature Commission. Walter was a member of most of these entities so that meant much travel.

His voluminous correspondence sets out his philosophy of publishing, which foremost aimed for a higher level of writing excellence. He decried the "chaff produced under the caption of sound evangelical literature." He declared that some of it was neither literature nor evangelical in the best tradition. He was appalled at the lack of emphasis in MB educational institutions on higher standards of written expression and facility with the tools of written language. Basically, he supported that the Canadian entities work together with the United States in publishing, while the popular trend was toward separatism. None of these board activities had a salary attached them.

As soon as the news was out that Walter had finished at Eden Christian College, he received an invitation to join the staff of the MB Bible Institute in Clearbrook, British Columbia. He was also in contact with the MB Publishing House in Hillsboro about a staff position in literature development. The Ebenfeld Church near Hillsboro indirectly offered him the position as pastor. Walter declined all offers. He needed more education. But that seemed like an impossible dream. He now had a wife and four children to support.

Walter's word to himself was that "some people are born thirty years too soon. Their ideas are ahead of their time. Every man is made by his past experience, advantages, heredity, and environment—and by the future he entertains in his breast." He continued to dream, but the doubts caused by the buffeting of life crowded the dream. Had he been deluded? Perhaps his goal to serve Christ was merely a mirage on the horizon of his life.

The struggle within him continued. He had once set his hand to the plow to prepare for a publications ministry in the

MB church. I had supported him in that goal. Could he step back now? (For a fuller discussion of his concerns, see *Born Out of Season: A Short Biography of Walter William Wiebe,* by Katie Funk Wiebe, 1997).

After completing the school term at Eden Christian College, we moved to Kitchener in fall 1959. Walter planned to teach at the Ottawa Street MB Bible School and attend Waterloo University. The light of the Holy Grail still beckoned. We left behind staunch friends developed over a short time.

As if sensing that his life would not be long, he wrote in his journal on September 1, 1959:

> "And I will restore to you the years that the locust hath eaten"(Joel 2:25). A year has passed since our coming to Ontario. A great sense of this swiftly passing life has come over me during this year. It seems that so many years have been "eaten" by the locust . . . cankerworm . . . caterpillar . . . palmerworm. What are those insects in our lives which "eat" away our lives and jeopardize fruition? Has it been indolence, sloth, lack of perseverance, failing to continually press toward the mark? God forgive me.

We rented a house at 25 Bournemouth Ave. for $100 a month. The children enrolled in school and I remained at home with Jamie. Employment outside the home was not an option for a married woman in a conservative church. Joanna was in Grade 7, Susan in Grade 3, and Chrissie began kindergarten. Jamie was crawling. He remained a constant source of joy.

Life seemed to be stabilizing. In winter 1960 I took my first writing course, Effective Writing, at the University of Waterloo in the Department of Adult Education and started looking for freelance writing assignments. We had decided that after Walter finished his M.A. I would begin university classes.

In 1960 Walter edited the Mennonite Brethren Centennial publication, *A Century of Grace and Witness,* spending some time in Hillsboro in spring of 1961 to develop the publication and again in fall to see it through the press. A manuscript we (mostly me) had been working on for several years, *Youth Worker Program Helps*, in spiral binding, was published (500 copies for $709) by the Canadian MB Youth Committee. Our stipend was $300. The Hepburn MB Church invited us to attend its fiftieth anniversary, but we declined. Walter was attending summer school—back to his usual pattern. He was feeling somewhat better.

CHAPTER 8

Living apart for the Lord

A brook, sheep bells, mill wheels:
"all these they took. . . .
"But that green blade of wheat,
"My own soul's courage, that they did not take."
—John Masefield

The children adjusted to life in Kitchener. Eden Christian College moved further and further into the background, although we still ate donated canned peaches and tomatoes from those difficult months. Walter was teaching at the Ottawa Street Bible School and attending Waterloo University.

The dream was back in focus. If a dream dies, so does the person's sense of aliveness and focus. Life for us as a family had moved toward a more even pace once again. With one course left to complete his B.A. requirements, Walter considered attending Syracuse University in the religious journalism sequence. It was the only school in North America that offered a program of studies leading to a master's degree in religious journalism, aside from a Catholic school.

In September 1960, he visited the Mennonite Publishing House in Scottdale, Pennsylvania, "to see and to learn" about church publishing. He reported being overwhelmed by all he saw at this well-established enterprise operated by the Mennonite Church. The administration gave him VIP treatment and opportunity to ask questions. He spoke of his time there as the Mount of Transfiguration and the MB Publications Board meetings at Hillsboro, Kansas, that followed as the valley where the disciples felt powerless to cast out the disturbing spirit from the lunatic son. At issue was whether to make *The Christian Leader* the official publication for both the United States and Canadian congregations or to start a new Mennonite Brethren periodical in Canada. Walter continued to support a joint paper although Canadians supported a Canadian publication, fearing they would lose influence in oversight with just one periodical published in Kansas.

Joanna enrolled in an enrichment class with special teachers and curriculum. She thrived under more academic stimulation. Susan loved doing homework above and beyond what her precious Miss Adamson asked of her. She faithfully carried her speller home each evening and carried it back the next morning without having opened it. She knew all her spelling words. Her refrain that "good students get special privileges" pushed her to get all privileges available for her superior work.

Chrissie remained our placid, gentle butterball. She trudged to and from Rosemount School kindergarten with friend Judy from across the street in the cold winter, coming home to a mug of hot milk and honey and some special time with me.

Jamie found keen interest in leafing through all of Chrissie's library books, page by page, nearly every night, until they had to be returned. As he grew older he noticed that his father was gone a lot, especially later, when Walter was attending Syracuse University. I had begun to work outside the home. I don't remember any major objection from Walter. It was now a necessity. As I came and went to my little secretarial jobs, Jamie's concern when I so much as moved toward the door with my coat on was always, "Who will take care of me?"

I took another small step toward freelance writing by joining a Christian Writers Club. My college roommate, Vera Isaak Janzen, lived across the street with her husband and children, so we looked after one another's children as needed. I was elected to the Junior Church Committee at the Ottawa Street Mennonite Brethren Church and helped reorganize the church library.

In February 1961 Walter and a Kitchener friend, Elroy Belbeck, also interested in religious publishing for his denomination, traveled to Syracuse University in New York state to investigate whether the program of studies there could be useful to a church publications ministry. Walter came back convinced it could and applied to Syracuse University to attend during the 1961-62 school year in the religious journalism sequence.

Two weeks later, his physician, Dr. Helmut Matthies, discovered a mass in his abdomen. Surgery was scheduled for when the Bible school term ended. Despite this setback, Walter met with Orlando Harms of the Mennonite Brethren Publishing House in Hillsboro, Kansas, to search for a "spiritual" basis for publication work in the MB constituency, for he saw the problems confronting the church as primarily spiritual, rather than financial.

After completing the semester's teaching responsibilities at the Ottawa Street Mennonite Brethren Bible school on May 28, 1961, the next day Walter took the street car to the hospital. I wanted him to take a taxi but he figured it was a luxury he could still do without. I didn't have a driver's license. I had failed my first test, disheartening me completely. The children clamored to be taken here and there to their various activities but I had no license.

The surgeon removed a large cyst of about three to four pounds from his abdomen. I didn't quite make it to the hospital by street car until after the surgery was completed. Nor did I know what to say to Walter when he recovered from anesthesia. This mass didn't have a name nor did Walter receive a prognosis, but the thought of that huge mound of intrusive material inside his body cavity terrified me.

After spending the day at his bedside, I had to leave. I was torn between two responsibilities. I wanted to stay but at home four children waited. I could only cry to God for strength for what lay ahead.

I returned to Bournemouth Street by street car again, a long journey with transfers, my heart growing heavier by the minute. I stepped off two blocks before my stop to go to my friend, Mary Dueck's home, and weep. This new burden was too heavy to bear. I couldn't face the children without having shared with someone that the doctor feared some malignancy with the primary cause being the appendix that had ruptured nearly three years ago.

On July 5, 1961, Walter had further surgery to remove the appendix. The pathologist's reports in both surgeries indicated no malignancy because his illness (jelly belly, in lay terms) was rare and there weren't enough similar cases on file to make a prognosis. The doctor called it a pseudo-cancer with the possibility of recurrence.

In August we took a four-week trip to Saskatchewan and Alberta by train and car to visit relatives, returning to Kitchener on September 1. The children had long begged for a train ride and I was homesick for my parents. For the first time in years Walter did not attend summer school. In September his health had improved sufficiently for him to pack a few bags and move to Syracuse University, borrowing money from a relative to pay for fees and living expenses. He weighed 189 pounds and was gaining. I was working occasionally for a temporary office help firm and also as a school secretary when I could arrange child care. We had no fixed income.

We faced an uncertain year. Once again the issues before us were health and money—and courage to continue. But I had conquered one huge barrier—I passed the driver's test. Walter left the car with me, now a licensed driver. I and the children were mobile.

Those years missionary families were expected to sacrifice life together for the kingdom of God. Didn't missionary David Livingstone live alone in the heart of Africa for twelve years? I could point to examples of famous people who sacrificed for the sake of the task they felt called to. Missionary kids as young as six were sent to distant boarding schools because the mission compound lacked schools. I wonder now why I didn't question our strange living arrangements with Walter 300 miles away in the United States and I, alone with the children, living on a very limited income, augmented by occasional secretarial jobs. I didn't murmur. This was God's will. Submission and more submission was the key. I knew that self-pity meant instant defeat.

Walter encouraged Orlando Harms, editor of *The Christian Leader*, to ask me to write a women's column for the magazine. "I personally would wish that she could be ushered into this work," he wrote. He knew my longing to do more writing. I had earlier volunteered to write such a column because I was disappointed in the current column, "Pots, Pans, and Patter." I wrote Orlando Harms that the church needed clarification as to the status of women's work and contribution. I hoped my writing would provide information and inspiration. It had long been my conviction that as women we were subject to too much patter over the radio, television, and the dozens of women's magazines. Women also needed to think. I was only dimly aware that by writing about women's roles in the MB church, I was moving into virgin and dangerous territory. But Orlando Harms didn't reply to my letter. Had I been too forward?

In Syracuse Walter roomed at the Literacy House owned by Dr. Robert Laubach, son of Frank C. Laubach of literacy missions fame, with Luckson Ejofodoni, a Nigerian, and Larry Lin, a friendly young Chinese from Taiwan. Walter enjoyed his studies. He was in his element buried deep in his books. His world opened up in new ways by rooming with interesting people of other ethnic groups. He had grown up in isolated farming communities in Saskatchewan and Alberta. The other two men often had visitors and when Luckson was invited out (he was well known in evangelical circles), Walter was invited also.

Yet his letters revealed that he felt like Ezekiel with his wheels within wheels, only with him it was term papers within term papers. His grades were the occasional A and Bs, which satisfied him. Phone calls were too expensive so we wrote often. His letters remained cheerful; he was doing what he had always wanted to do—study full-time. He had gained weight and now weighed 193 pounds.

His first visit home was at the American Thanksgiving in November. At Christmas, he brought Larry with him. Together we all went tobogganing on a large hill using big pieces of cardboard, one of James' few memories of his father, a carefree one. Later in Syracuse, Larry told Walter our home's atmosphere deeply impressed him. Something he couldn't quite identify satisfied him deeply. That Walter could leave all that behind to get an M.A. puzzled him.

Jamie was the most vocal child about his father's absence. "I wish my Daddy would come home–with a present." Once when playing with the Janzen boys across the street he forgot to go to Vera if he needed help. Chilled through, with wet pants, he opened the front door to find the house empty. "I wanted a mama at home to look after me," he told me later tearfully. Chrissie loved to write letters to Walter but had great problems with verb tenses. If she wrote "tomorrow" and Walter received it "tomorrow," wouldn't that be a problem?

I wrote my parents in Saskatchewan: "This winter without Walter has been quite a winter for us all—although there have been the difficult times, I see it as a winter when the things that are important in life begin to stand out more and more. And I often realize that you have helped to produce that in me." My parents always stood by me through any trying time.

A huge event that fall was the sale of my first article to *Christian Living*. Editor Dan Hertzler had held the article so long I had given up, but he finally wrote he planned to publish about two-thirds of it. He returned the scraps he didn't want. Payment was $5. I wanted to frame the check, but I needed the money for expenses. I kept the scraps. Joanna wrote Walter that I was so excited I kept dropping things and doing things wrong.

Walter wrote from Syracuse that he wished I could take some university courses in summer. He would take care of the children and household. I longed for an editor to give me assignments. Freelance writing was too uncertain, yet I began to have a few sales. I was still writing articles for *The Youth Worker* in 1961, which provided a small stipend. We were no longer editors.

Walter envisioned research projects related to the Mennonite Brethren world. He analyzed Mennonite periodicals and met with other Mennonite students. He encouraged J. B. Toews, now executive secretary of the MB Board of Missions, to send missionary candidates to Syracuse for religious journalism training. He continued to be amazed by the strange ways of providence, living with a Nigerian and a Chinese, who both opened doors for him in cross-cultural experiences that he had never thought of entering.

Like me, living in Kitchener with the children, Walter was meeting new people, such as the world-famous literacy missionary Frank C. Laubach, whom he described as a warmhearted, sincere old man, who carried his listeners into the presence of God when he prayed.

To make Walter's work lighter, I did as much of his research as feasible, getting a course in religious journalism by default. In his course in readability testing, I analyzed about ten books, fiction and non-fiction, for each decade beginning with 1921 according to the Flesch formula for readability and human interest. This entailed locating the books in the library and then counting words, syllables, personal pronouns, and so forth. I spent many late evenings with a counter doing the repetitious work so that Walter could compile the results. I also did readability studies of three prominent MB ministers' writings published in *The Voice*, organ of Mennonite Brethren Bible College (Ewert, Toews, Peters). Only much later, when I wrote more myself, did I realize how much this work enabled me to recognize good writing.

We had joined the Ottawa Street Church, very German, very traditional. We were among Russlaender again, a majority of whom had belonged to the Allianz Church in the Ukraine, a church group that served as a bridge between the Mennonite and Mennonite Brethren churches in that country. The German language became a big barrier—the children spoke no German. Church life, not satisfactory for me or the children, became a battleground. The girls objected strenuously to attending non-intelligible services, so Walter brought them home after Sunday school during the years before he left for Syracuse, and he and I attended church alone. Even Walter, the half-Russlaender, found the congregation somewhat elitist in its approach to outsiders.

Individual people were warm and friendly, but the theology that seeped out of the cracks and crevices created strange reactions from me and the girls. Joanna was probably more honest than I was about church life. She rated it "poor." I agreed that the preaching was hard to go into raptures about. It was like chewing on dry crusts.

The ultra-conservative theology of some preachers, as well as members, dismayed me. One highly recognized visiting minister, who held a series of meetings, proudly told the congregation that in all his married life, he and his wife had never subscribed to a daily newspaper. I thought of how I hungered for reading material and devoured anything I could get my hands on. He did subscribe to a daily newspaper for a while, but when he saw his children's attraction to the comics, he discontinued that. He censored issues of *The Reader's Digest*, cutting out all references to sex and other possible offensive material. I found it hard to endorse his God-as-policeman attitude, which dared people to step over the line, only to get swatted back.

When the pastor suggested young people pray on dates, Joanna laughed. In a lectures on do's and don'ts for young people, he never got close to the subject other than speaking of "moral lapses" and thereafter referring to these lapses as "it." She thought she was ready for dating at age thirteen, when a Grade 13 student asked her out. I thought she was too young, and the young man too old. Bringing up children alone was a challenge beyond my wisdom.

Some members were concerned about letting "the ideas of other churches get into our churches." You kept sin out by building walls around the church. Adult Sunday school was frowned upon. Some men brought their children to Sunday school and sat outside in the car until the adult service started. I offered to teach a mothers' class for women with infants and toddlers as I had in Hepburn but was turned down by the superintendent because "women were not to teach." Communion was closed to everyone but members. I was lonely for a less literal approach to Scripture..

During the year Walter was gone, I risked attending lectures by important speakers such as Robert Walker, editor of *Christian Life*, and Ella Mae Miller, a Mennonite women's radio speaker on Heart to Heart talks. Seeing a woman in ministry gave me a wonderful treat—and example. After the children were in bed I read as voraciously as they did before I went to sleep. I had felt intellectually starved for years. Now I had access to books upon books. We made weekly visits to the local library, each child returning with an armful of books. I had begun reading more daringly, especially books about women's role in the church. I read biographies of women and books by them. Dr. Marion Hilliard's books, *Love Without Fear* and *Women and Fatigue* as well as *Christ and Modern Woman* by Argye Briggs nurtured my soul. She wrote the kinds of reading I had been longing for.

Slowly I found it more productive to write articles than to work part-time for $1.50 or less an hour. In fall of 1961, while Walter was at Syracuse, Orlando Harms wrote him asking whether I would write a women's column for *The Christian Leader* beginning January 1962. Why hadn't he written directly to me? I swallowed my pride and accepted his offer. He had probably seldom negotiated such an assignment with a woman before.

In spring I gave my first speech, knees shaking, at the *Gabenverein* (women's circle) at the Kitchener MB Church and consequently was invited to speak at the MB Ontario women's rally at Leamington, for which I received $5. I commented to a friend that I was too inexperienced to speak to women. Mary replied, "Who has more experience?" All of us women were newcomers to women's ministry. The same week I received $10 for two of my new *Christian Leader* columns, $6.85 for a *Canadian Mennonite* article, and a $5 gift from a relative. I felt rich. Money in my pocket.

I worked part-time at McLean Peister, as school secretary at Shepherd and Rosemont schools, and at Teperman's Wrecking—anything to keep bread on the table without dipping into our bank reserves too deeply. That money might be needed for more urgent needs. In the back of my mind, at least subconsciously, I feared Walter's illness might return.

I learned other ways of coping with financial shortages. I attended my first "rummage" sale sponsored by doctors' wives. When my friend Anne and I entered the room crowded with tables piled high with mounds of used clothing, I wanted to turn and run. Turning my family's used clothing into dresses and skirts for the girls was one thing, but diving into those huge piles of other people's castoffs seemed too much. Had I actually come to this? I swallowed hard. I belonged here. We were poor. I found some great bargains in sweaters, blouses, slips, and even a raincoat.

But we were not as poor as some. Late in summer of 1962, I gave one of Chrissie's sweaters to an outgoing missionary for his little girl. I gave a coat to a home missionary who wrote she was still wearing it after several years. We had not yet reached the bottom. I still had things to give away.

I learned the hard way that cars need attention. Once the brakes gave out. Another time the battery died. I had it charged but it froze and cracked. Fortunately I had a friend in mechanic Hardy Klassen who advised me.

Orlando Harms was putting out feelers whether Walter would consider coming to Hillsboro, Kansas, to work at the MB Publishing House as the first book and literature editor at a salary of $400 per month. Walter accepted. If he finished his M.A. degree at Syracuse, he would be the first Mennonite Brethren with an advanced degree in religious journalism. I received a tentative offer to work for the Board of Missions office, also in Hillsboro, as a research assistant. This offer turned into bookkeeping, but I accepted.

In May Walter finished his studies at Syracuse for the time being and brought his roommates Larry and Luckson with him again for a few days. Larry was again much impressed by the atmosphere in our home.

In late June, Walter noticed another growth in his abdomen. After a lot of testing, the doctors decided not to operate again because the mass did not directly involve the bowel or intestines. They also decided against radiation because of possible danger to his bowel. He was instructed to watch his diet (low residue) to avoid bowel obstruction. Dr. Matthies said that the tumor or mass looked discouraging, but it was also important how Walter felt and was getting along. He advised against giving up and waiting for his health to deteriorate. God sometimes worked in matters of health differently from the way the medical profession had evaluated them, he told us.

We discussed the matter. Was this just an obstacle God had put in our way to test our faith? What now was the will of God? We had felt called, had prepared for a literature ministry, and had waited upon God for light. Walter wrote: "In the darkness I put my hand out for the hand of God—and it is resurgence of strength to my soul."

He decided to keep working to get immigration visas to the United States and for health insurance in Kansas, without which he was not prepared to leave. He tentatively contemplated summer school should our departure for Hillsboro be delayed. For years now, summer had meant summer school whatever our financial circumstances. We took a short camping trip to Algonquin Park.

In August 1962 Walter and I had the wonderful opportunity to attend sessions of the Mennonite World Conference held in Kitchener and entertained guests in our home. This was my first introduction to the wider Mennonite family, coming from many countries and branches of the church. I heard speakers of the caliber I had not experienced before. I attended a woman's session. I opened myself to this generous unexpected outpouring of blessings. This was a mountaintop experience, but the dark valley lay just ahead.

Orlando Harms and Walter agreed to try every possible door to enter the United States. In August 1962 the medical doctors at the United States Consul in Toronto decided they had no reason to hold Walter back for health reasons even though the Canadian doctors had said the tumor might recur. He had developed piles and his abdominal muscles had become weak from the surgeries. I gave him one of my stretched-out girdles to wear. The mainstay of a woman's wardrobe those years was a girdle to which she attached her hose. Pantyhose had not yet been invented.

We reserved a moving van to take some of our better items of furniture. Leaving Kitchener was a step of faith, if a faltering one. What would life for me and children be like in Hillsboro? Walter would soon find his niche. Once again we were moving into the unknown.

CHAPTER 9

The ending before another beginning

Life ultimately means taking responsibility to find the right answer
to its problems and to fulfill the tasks which it ultimately sets for
each individual.
—Viktor Frankl

We packed our 1953 brown Chevrolet and crossed the United States border on my birthday, September 15, 1962, at Port Rowan, Ontario, and arrived in Hillsboro a few days later. I was thirty-eight. We had four bright, lively children. The sign beside the road leading to this small city described it as "The land of milk and honey." The children cheered when we saw it. From a long distance we could see the lights of this new community twinkling in the darkness. What lay ahead?

We moved into 308 West Grand, an ancient two-story frame building with huge trees shading nearly all sides. Rent was $60 a month. The furnace boomed frighteningly whenever the fan came on. When I flicked on the kitchen lights, a huge army of cockroaches scurried into the cracks. I didn't know what they were.

We began attending the Parkview MB Church, formerly a Krimmer MB Church, because we needed the fellowship of a small group. We decided against the "big" MB church, also in Hillsboro—too big and elite-ish. We needed something small and close.

Walter began work at the publishing house, a few blocks away and I, part-time, as a bookkeeper at the Board of Missions office, where the bookkeeping system dated back almost to the board's organization at the beginning of the century. The girls attended school and Jamie spent afternoons with Gretchen Faul while I worked. He enjoyed the Faul boys, especially their grandparents. Grandpa Faul, a wonderful human being, gave his complete attention to the three little boys, something Jamie hadn't experienced for a long time. "I like this grandpa," he told me. He had not learned to know my father, and Walter's father had died before he was born. Jamie found the adjustment to our new routines the hardest of the whole family. Why didn't he have more children to play with? Why was Daddy with us now only to leave for work every day? I found a cat which let Jamie fairly tear it apart before it fought back.

We attended our first football game, a dirty, muddy, violent sport. I didn't understand it. And still don't. We soon found out that Americans spoke a different dialect of English resulting in many amusing misunderstandings. My name once again underwent a change. Kansas Mennonites had long ago forgotten about unstressed German vowels, or schwas, at the end of words. "Wiebe" in Hillsboro was pronounced with two distinct syllables. These new friends leaned hard on the second syllable to make it rhyme with the first—Weebee! Vocabulary, spelling, and punctuation had to be relearned. As a family we were introduced to pizza, sloppy joes, and five-for-a-dollar hamburgers. We were immigrants, strangers in a strange land, just as my parents had been forty years ago when they arrived in Saskatchewan from the Ukraine.

The first few weeks of work went well for Walter as he planned long-term goals for the MB Publishing House, a schedule of publishing, board responsibilities, style manual, copyright rules, and so forth. But soon he was feeling ill again. On October 15 some local ministers and deacons laid hands on Walter and prayed for his health. He continued to feel ill.

About three weeks later, he phoned me from work that he felt sick and wouldn't pick me up after work at the missions office. At home, before I took him to the hospital, he drew three-year-old Jamie closely to himself and murmured, "My dear little boy." At our last family devotions, we all sat beside him lying on the living room couch and sang, "When we walk with the Lord in the light of his word, what a glory he sheds on our way." I wish I could write about strong, vibrant faith at the time, but I can't. Where was the glory? Would we recognize it if we saw it? Now? In the future?

In the hospital, it seemed as if, now that we were in the United States, the tumor had received permission to grow wildly. Walter's abdomen increased rapidly in size, exerting pressure on his heart and lungs. An attempt to tap the tumor proved unsuccessful because all the doctor could extract was a jellylike substance. Walter suffered considerably at first, but with the help of hypos, the pain was controlled. We called a specialist who told us bluntly there was no hope of recovery. I immediately called Walter's sister Susie Martens in Coaldale if she could come. My sister Frieda Schroeder also came a little later.

The last night Walter's mind became quite clear toward evening, and we talked together for quite a while. He was hard to understand without his dentures, but he accepted he was dying and was ready "to be with the Lord." At one point he told me that the way ahead was all golden. What should he do? Unhesitatingly, I encouraged him onward. I would not hold him back. "Walk toward the light," I said.

New friends brought food, money, and love to our home. Susie helped greatly with hospital care. She was overwhelmed how the Hillsboro people turned out to ease our burden. John C. Ratzlaff, Parkview MB minister, spent much time with Walter in the hospital, relieving me when I went out for meals. The entire MB General Conference constituency was made aware of Walter's condition, so that meant thousands of prayers were offered for his well-being.

Walter had lapsed into a coma. Susie and I slept in easy chairs until about two in the morning. She awoke to notice that the end was near and woke me. Together we watched him take his last breaths on November 17, about seven weeks after arriving in Hillsboro. The autopsy showed that he had died of *pseudo mucinous myxoma peritonei.* Dr. Peter Enns told me that the strength and dignity of Walter's dying had affected the entire hospital.

Much of the fifteen years we had been married, Walter had been studying, preparing for a literature ministry. I had supported him in every way I could. His death hung like a huge heavy curtain between me and the future.

The news of Walter's passing quickly reached friends and relatives in Canada and the United States. All his ten siblings except two sisters (Helen and Erna) came for the funeral. For two days we were nineteen people around the small table.

The funeral service on Tuesday, November 20, was simple and beautiful. I planned very little of it. The weather remained clear and sunny, although a little cool. My fear that the church would be nearly empty didn't materialize. The children's school classes had been dismissed for the funeral and many Hillsboro supporters also attended. John C. Ratzlaff, Orlando Harms, and Henry R. Baerg officiated. Burial took place in the Gnadenau Cemetery, two miles south of Hillsboro, underneath some aging fir trees, later cut down, to my dismay. The church women prepared a lovely meal of stew, jellied salad, coffee, and cookies. I opted for a closed casket and no photos of the body to the disappointment of some Canadian relatives, who expected I would follow traditional customs.

By Wednesday morning most guests had left. Sister Frieda was the last to go, having taken control of the household for ten days. Letters, telegrams, and cards came in almost by the bushel from relatives, friends, former colleagues and students, congregations, church leaders, and organizations with lists of signers.

The children were brave through it all, with no hysterics. They were too brave, I see now. They knew Walter's death was coming. Christine never fully understood what was happening. Until she died in 2000, she was troubled that she had wanted to see Walter in the hospital and the rules refused her admittance. Both she and Jamie had birthdays during these days and received gifts, confusing the matter. Celebration mixed with mourning created a strange atmosphere. In a few days Jamie asked, "Why haven't I got a daddy anymore?"

As much as possible I grieved in private, for the children had enough to deal with. We should probably have talked about Walter's death more, but I knew too little about the right way to handle grief, either my own or my children's.

Some people have the luxury of making a life plan and then following it. I had had no life plan for fifteen years other than supporting Walter in his endeavors. My immediate concern was how to support my family. Returning to Canada wasn't an option because I had no place to go. Ontario had been a temporary stopping place to allow Walter to study at a university. My parents were planning to retire and hadn't decided where. Only if it was impossible to earn a living in Kansas would I return to Canada, but if God opened a door to rewarding work and service, I planned to stay in the United States. Both the Publishing House and the Board of Missions offered me a position. I opted for the Publishing House. At least for the time being.

The children found the new routine with me gone all day a hard adjustment. The first morning I got up to go to work, Jamie couldn't grasp that now he also had to leave his warm bed in the darkness to go to the babysitter. "I don't want to be baby-sitted," he wailed. The children said they enjoyed the Hillsboro schools, the church, and the friendly people.

Only later I learned how out of place my Canadian children actually felt in this new learning environment. School did not challenge them. Joanna, a freshman, finished first in a reading aptitude test the entire school, except seniors, took. She had been in an advanced class in Kitchener. Now she had to adjust to her class. Christine, who had always stood when the teacher addressed her, cringed when her classmates laughed when she rose to answer a question. The children were outsiders with their Canadian ways.

Walter had always promised us a meal in a restaurant when he finished his studies. He wasn't there to enjoy the wonderful meal an older couple P. B. and Hannah Willems treated us to at the Ramada Inn in Newton with mashed potatoes piled mountain high and rivers of gravy. And soda pop to drink. With refills. And ice cream. More than one scoop.

The immediate financial situation looked hopeful. Gifts totaled well over $600, not counting a substantial gift from my parents, always ready to help. A burial policy covered funeral and medical expenses. Dr. Matthies in Kitchener canceled the balance on his account. The money loaned to us was in an insured account, but the relative who had advanced it to us graciously forgave our debt.

Little things boosted my spirit. The trash man noticed the children burning trash on the ground and donated a barrel. At Christmas our family was remembered by many families. Mail kept coming from all over Canada and the United States. By the end of December I passed the Kansas driving test after failing it once. "God has given me courage for the daytime when the task often seemed mountain high and sleep at night when I needed it," I wrote my parents. My task now was to make a family without a husband and father at a time when one-parent homes with young children were rare.

Life was too short for Walter to work out all the ideas he had generated. His life lacked completeness. The wheel had been broken at the cistern. I had no good answers to the enigma of life. I now had to begin anew.

Part II

CHAPTER 10

Mother goes to work

Hope can be neither affirmed nor denied. Hope is like a path in the countryside; originally there was no path. Yet, as people walk all the time in the same spot, a way appears.
—Chinese poet Lu Xan

Family life without a father soon took on a new daily structure. On January 15, 1963, at eight a.m., I walked through the Mennonite Brethren Publishing House door at the north end of Main Street to work as an editorial assistant from eight to five each day and half days on Saturdays, a long week away from the children. The church community accepted my working outside the home because I had a family to support. They even praised me for being able to support the family. The taboo had been lifted—only for me, not for all women. Orlando Harms, manager, soon allowed me to stay home Saturday mornings with the understanding I would write my biweekly column at home. I was grateful for his leniency. I had completed one year of writing *The Christian Leader* column "Women and the Church" under the name Mrs. Katie Wiebe.

Jamie, now age four, attended morning nursery school through the kindness of new friends, and then spent the afternoons at the home of Gretchen and George Faul. The girls ate their noon meal at school. Susan picked Jamie up after school while Joanna went home to begin the evening meal. Before I left each morning, I wrote in the little black book what to make and exact times to start each dish. Our neighbor, Grandma Hiebert, became our friendly backup sitter when a child became ill. She enjoyed having Chrissie lie on her couch all day until the rest of us came home, and Chrissie enjoyed the extra TLC. A new friend picked up our dirty laundry each Wednesday and returned it Sunday after the evening service, neatly folded, ironed, and sometimes mended. What unexpected love!

Life was lonely. If there is a word stronger than lonely, I would use it. We were well known in the community because of Walter's sudden death but not part of it. Friends invited us, often when the father was absent, prompting one daughter to ask, "Aren't we ever going to be invited to a family with a daddy anymore?" They keenly felt being set aside as a one-parent family.

I remember from those first years desperately trying to find interesting activities for the children to numb the emptiness. For a while, on Sundays, we wandered through cemeteries in outlying areas, investigating, especially the Orphan's Cemetery near the original Krimmer Mennonite Brethren Church, about two miles south-east of Hillsboro. "Fresh-air children" from Chicago who had lived in the Orphan's Home were buried here. The KMB Church cemetery was a little distance away. We puzzled why there were two cemeteries, one for orphans and one for regulars.

My heart raced the first time a tornado siren pierced the atmosphere. Was this a fire alarm? Surely not a tornado? The children and I rushed outside to locate smoke or an unfamiliar spiral. We learned to deal with power outages, torrential rains, strong winds, and a flooded crawl space. Because we had no basement, a few times we rushed to the nearby stone Lutheran Church, a designated tornado shelter, to find ourselves the only family frightened enough to look for more adequate shelter.

We experienced 100-degree Kansas heat without an air conditioner or fan. We tasted our first homemade ice cream. In a few years we bought our first new car, a Ford Comet, on time payments. I felt more secure in a vehicle with good brakes and tires even if it meant monthly payments, which I abhorred. I bought a different house when I found the mortgage payments equaled my monthly rent. But I hadn't considered the many repairs I'd have to make.

Throughout those first years I struggled to maintain faith in God. Had God let me down or had I let God down? I debated that if God's power to heal was all-powerful, why hadn't that grace been extended to us? God promised to be with the widows and orphans. That verse from the book of James was quoted to me often. I quoted it to myself also. Why then was life so difficult? Was it really God's will for my family to grow up without a father? Didn't God want wholeness and fullness? Yet I recognized our earlier faith in Kitchener that God would heal and which kept us pursuing the goal of getting to the United States to begin a literature ministry was a gift from God that carried us through a difficult time. Without it we might have folded our tents and silently stolen away long ago.

I debated that first spring what to do with the children during the summer when I was working. I finally accepted my two sisters' offer in Edmonton, Alberta, to keep the three girls with them. Anne took her daughter Nancy, along with Joanna and Christine, to church camp for the summer where she was the cook, with the idea Chrissie would stick close to her older sister. Susan would spend the summer with my sister Frieda Schroeder, whose daughter Peggy was close to Susan's age. The plan looked good on paper. I was grateful for such caring sisters. Jamie would stay with me.

Only years later did I learn how lonely the girls had been without Jamie and me. Even the trip to Canada, so carefully planned, had had its hazards. They traveled by car to Winnipeg with a Canadian nephew attending Tabor College. At the border the officials had separated the girls from Don, in his early twenties, and questioned them whether they were traveling on their own volition. From Winnipeg they traveled by bus to Saskatoon, having to find their own food at rest stops, with Joanna responsible for the trio.

Here my parents picked them up. After a few days in Blaine Lake, Anne and Wes took them to Edmonton for the summer.

Henry and Frieda Schroeder brought them back in August before school started to the overpowering buzzing of cicadas and blistering heat with no air conditioner or fan in the house.

Four-year-old Jamie and I spent the summer alone, he with a babysitter and I at work. The first evening as we sat down to our little meal in the kitchen, he commented, "We're sure lonely now." In the evening he sang to himself, "The girls are gone away and my daddy is buried and I am going to heaven." My heart ached for him.

I have written in *Alone: A Widow's Search for Joy* about the issues we faced those early years and the wonderful response of new friends to those needs.

I continued writing my column in *The Christian Leader*, airing my concerns and joys about the church, especially as they related to women, as a rank amateur. I saw these columns as essays, testing an idea. I soon learned that when you write for the public, you are expected to be knowledgeable and skilled in all aspects of your subject matter. My first speaking engagement was at a mission circle gathering of three churches, followed by an invitation later in spring from Clarence Hiebert, that all-time champion of women and minorities to use their gifts, to speak to a group of high schoolers on "Facing Life's Tensions." I knew the questions but not the answers. I spoke at a Christian literature emphasis event at a local church.

Over time I allowed myself one evening out a week to accept speaking invitations. Jamie was still unready to have strangers looking after him, needing the stability of my tucking him into bed every evening with a story or song. Well-meaning visitors arrived in the middle of the evening to inquire about our welfare, and then seemed disturbed when my young son grew restless. What was wrong with him? This was his time with me. He wanted it. At times he demanded it. Motherhood was at the top of my priorities, not politely conversing with well-intentioned strangers.

Eventually I became a clearing house for requests from leaders of MB women's organizations needing better materials for organizational structures, program planning, devotionals, and information about women's roles in the church. I also fielded questions about the duties of the pastor's wife, an emerging role. Pastor and wife came in one package—a two-for-one deal. My long-ago dream to fill that role had vanished. My task was mainly to earn a living and keep a household happy.

In a few years reader requests included copies of plays and skits I had written or had on file as well as talks I had given. I had no time to retype material. Photocopying had not yet been invented. The implication was that if I was writing a column titled "Women and the Church," surely I had material to recommend. Unable to answer the requests, I ordered materials from larger denominations, like Presbyterians, to glean information about the broader church world. I discovered that women's work was not a new thing, as in our congregations, but a long-standing ministry. I clipped and filed everything I could find and buy inexpensively about women in the church. My file soon bulged.

Another file automatically filled with material about the ways God deals with suffering, although I had to postpone a serious study of it until I had more time. Right now I had to find my way in this new country, new work, and new people. F. B. Meyer in his devotional study of *Christ in Isaiah* writes that in early life our path seems clearly defined. I agreed. I had accepted at marriage, not without difficulty, that my role in life would be as wife and mother in the home. I had never planned to work outside it. Now my steps took me in a different path, without footprints in the sand to guide me. Meyers adds: "When the way forks. . . , when the expanse of desert lies in front without a beaten pathway—stand still; take an observation; hush all voices in the presence of Christ; ask what He would have done; ask what He would wish you to do." I had no time even for standing still.

I was only thankful I had a job, although not one of my choosing, but still a way of earning money. My children would be fed, clothed, and loved as long as I had health and strength. We would survive. But beyond that I saw no light. I didn't see a fork or a path in the road.

Subconsciously, however, I cherished two other goals: to become a better writer and to clarify for myself my role as a woman in the church. As I wrote column after column, I seemed to be fiddling with a radio dial to bring in a station more clearly. What was I trying to say? Did I have anything to say? Often I asked myself, *Are these true words?* I struggled with writing what I thought was expected of me—great answers to prayer, successful mothering, wonderful insights into suffering like the great writers I admired, fulfillment in church life. I could not speak to any of that, only to a slow slogging through the days.

I had not expected reader response. But letters arrived with comments like these: "Your articles reflect an insight and awareness beyond most MB women I know." The writer described my *Christian Leader* column as "meat for her spiritual diet." Another reader found in my writing truths she had sensed but not thought through. As the years sped by, I became aware that wrapping words around thoughts readers were struggling to articulate was my greatest gift. Other women were also striving to find answers to questions they didn't know how to formulate. I was no different except that I had the opportunity to think openly about them.

The notes and letters encouraged me: "If the article has your name written over it, I read it every time." "Your column has lifted my day many times." "Your articles should be published separately and publicized."

Dimly I acknowledged that women's role in society was changing. I was helping women in their relationship with God in view of this changing role. Many had never found their own identity as a woman. It had always been submerged in someone else's—a husband's, a father's, sometimes even a child's if that child was a missionary or other prominent person. I wrote that the apostle Paul had high regard for women in the work of the church and entrusted us with responsibility to find out what it was.

I corresponded with a number of editors of Mennonite publications who had shown interest in my writing. I wrote the late Frank Epp, editor of *The Canadian Mennonite*, that "I would like to see our Mennonite papers slanted more to women, not as homemakers and housekeepers—they get enough of that in other papers—but as individuals responsible before God for their way of living. We have many educated, thinking women who are not finding their place in relation to the church." They were being recruited outside the church.

I responded to Waldo Hiebert, former Mennonite Brethren Biblical Seminary faculty member, that "it seems to me that society as a whole is opening its arms wide to receive women, but the church still feels their only place is with the missionary society." I wrote a woman student at Syracuse University that "Too few of us are free to act from within. Too many of us, and I am thinking of women, in part follow the approved religious patterns, rather than striking out in God's way for us."

I encouraged women to do more reading—and writing. I wrote one reader in Chilliwack, B.C., "We need more writers, and I am convinced that this is one area where women could do more, especially housewives, who can spend more time thinking while engaged in housework." I longed for the days when I could spend time thinking while I ironed or washed the dishes.

I wrote Hedy Durksen of Winnipeg, responsible for getting a new column "Wayside Inn" started in the *Mennonite Brethren Herald*, that "Women have been neglected far too long in our church periodicals—other than to provide recipes and poetry." In another letter to the editor of *Christianity Today* I mentioned that women today spent too much time with "marshmallows and Jello." I was pushing in a direction possibly clearer to my reading audience than to me. I didn't know what I was pushing for or against.

And the responses kept coming. One reader wrote, "I am continually amazed how you write on topics that I have mulled over, and what's more, seem to have come to the same conclusions."

Another woman wrote I had helped her "think out many problems that confront us, but I hesitate to voice a negative view. You have a maturity that makes it possible for you to write and not be embarrassed about it several years hence." Maturity? I felt very young, inexperienced. and ignorant at forty.

I was amused when I spoke publicly to find women in the audience show surprise at how different I looked from the image I projected in my writing. One woman, not in agreement with my views on women, had sent a daughter to check me out. She was sure she would see a dark-haired Gestapo-type woman, with iron will and sharp tongue, only to find a rather mild-mannered person attempting to look feminine and attractive despite the odds. Another response was predictable: Mothers at home had a full-time job. They didn't need encouragement to become involved in anything else. My encouragement for them to identify their gifts was wrong.

Another writer included affirmative phrases like "tremendous thinking, contemporary outreach for the constituency." Where did my boldness suddenly come from? Had it been simmering beneath the surface all these years since I left college?

My interest in Mennonite Brethren church life had subsided or, more truthfully, been set aside in light of pressing family needs. But my interest in writing and women's roles was rising. I echoed Walter's often-expressed words that the MB Conference needed a higher standard of writing. I proofread adult Sunday school materials written by church leaders, dismayed at the profusion of theological abstractions and generalities, almost impossible for the ordinary layperson to grasp.

Christmas of 1963 became a defining moment for us as a family. We had survived one year without a father and husband. I chalked it up as a victory of sorts. Finances were tight, but we were not broke, only thinly stretched. A financial advisor's advice had been "Pay God, pay yourself, pay your bills." So I started tithing again but without Walter's rigid approach. I also deposited a small amount in the bank each month so that I always had one month's salary ready for emergencies. The Internal Revenue Service questioned the amount I had donated to charitable institutions one year. It seemed more than a widow with four children could or should give, but I produced my paid checks to prove my case.

The children joked about their "famous mother who went around speaking at women's clubs." I felt the lack of a "wife" to help with housework, and after a few years at the Publishing House, I felt stifled by my work mostly proofreading and copy editing. I had begun sighting Walter's Holy Grail. I had come to *The Christian Leader* with great hopes of moving into editorial/writing work but ended up writing obituaries and congregational news.

I was an employee of the Mennonite Brethren Publishing House, a commercial printing firm that did a great deal of job printing, not just publishing *The Christian Leader*. I wanted to attend conference meetings and interview people, but I was needed to proofread print jobs. Some mornings I forced myself to go to work. Eight hours of proofreading emptied me as surely as a strong dose of laxative. I was tied to words that weren't mine and didn't inspire. My horizons fenced me in. Orlando Harms, managing editor, promised me more challenging work, but I don't think he saw me as Brenda Starr, MB church reporter

I don't know the exact moment that I grasped I was working at a job only to put bread on the table, not one that affirmed and used my gifts. I faced an identity crisis most men face in high school and college. Our culture expects young men to look into the future and to pursue a career image they admire. They choose a trade or profession and move into it with the encouragement of family and friends. In my youth, women worked outside the home at a job, any job, treading water until they married. It is called "circling the airport."

I had once chosen marriage and family as my calling and dabbled in writing. At age forty-two I had to choose a career because I couldn't go back to homemaking as a full-time occupation. I needed an income to support the family. But the children would not always be with me. Joanna was soon ready for college. What did I want to do with my life for the next twenty-five years? What did I want? Money? Power? Love? Fame? Security? What did God want of me? That was the bigger question. I had to be responsible for my intellectual, spiritual, and emotional growth until I died. I wanted an identity I could respect. I wanted to create with words.

In the silent night hours, by myself, I pondered other possibilities, such as starting a secretarial and ghost-writing service. I had found people in Hillsboro who needed such a service. I was already doing that for men aware of my secretarial skills. Mature women were returning to school, but with uncertainty. I considered that but backed out. Too risky. Fear ruled. One woman who had started studies as an adult told me, "I don't know whether I am doing the right thing." She needed the stamp of approval of someone or some institution to go ahead. These pioneers in adult education had few encouragers. They were moving into new patterns, disturbing the old ones.

I wrote Helen Alderfer, editor at Mennonite Publishing House, that I agreed with Elizabeth Achtemeier, author of *The Feminine Crisis in the Christian Faith*, that there was such a crisis. Women were abdicating responsibility because the challenges before them didn't resemble the tasks mothers and grandmothers faced. I found it easy to write such words but harder to push myself into the front lines.

I wrote the editor of the *Mennonite Brethren Herald* that women were flocking into the work force without church guidance or support. Their letters to me showed their turmoil. No one felt comfortable dealing with women's roles except to remind them of limitations, not opportunities. In some Canadian MB districts the organizing of women into provincial or district organizations was viewed as anti-biblical. I wrote that if the church didn't accept all of women's gifts, society would. Editor Harold Jantz admitted that he was grappling his way through the question of women's roles in church and society. His writing revealed it was a struggle between heart (what he felt was right) and his head (what seemed logical).

The next few years at the Publishing House had a number of highlights. With the permission of managing editor Orlando Harms, I attended my first weekend writers' conference at Moody Bible Institute in Chicago in 1964 attended by 125 would-be writers and twenty editors. I was introduced to the broader religious publishing world. In 1966 I traveled to Green Lake, Wisconsin, to attend another writing conference, where I heard many well-known editors and writers in the Christian publishing world and made contact with about fifty Mennonite writers and editors. Here I caught the vision that effective writing for the church needed to be of superb quality. God didn't bless mediocre writing because it was done in the name of Christ. I left Joanna, now age sixteen, in charge at home. Later, the girls told me that the red splotches on the ceiling had been created when the cook for the day had dropped a large pan of cabbage rolls in tomato sauce I had prepared before I left.

I dared moving my books and papers to Walter's large oak desk, feeling like an intruder. My desk had always been only big enough for my typewriter. I bought some books for my use, beginning my personal library.

Dr. Roland Wolseley, one of Walter's professors at Syracuse University, critiqued an article, stating I was given to making big statements without proof. I used too many weasel words like "perhaps" to avoid saying what I meant. Humbled, I accepted his advice. I also took a correspondence course in writing from the University of Wisconsin yet never took the final exam. I was too afraid I might fail; I hadn't taken an exam in years.

About this time my brother-in-law Harold Kruger urged me to return to school, enrolling in one class. I would have no problems keeping up with college students. He was working on a master's degree following his and my sister's return from the Congo (for a time known as Zaire), as MB missionaries. The answer to my future lay in more education. I considered his advice.

In June 1966 I reviewed *The Feminine Mystique* by Betty Friedan for *The Canadian Mennonite*, at the request of Frank Epp, editor. This review was a daring venture into the feminist arena. I first discussed it with a women's group and also a college sociology class. Some women timidly agreed with Friedan's findings, a few more openly. The book shook me thoroughly.

I kept writing to church leaders. To a religious education leader in the U.S. MB Conference, "Women in our churches are in desperate need of leadership training for work among themselves. The men are not giving women much leadership along these lines. . . . I personally have often wondered why the women's work is in no way connected with the conference like youth work or educational work. Our women's work exists, but sort of like a conference running parallel to the other conference, not fully integrated. Perhaps I am wrong in this." There was that weasel word *perhaps* again.

In fall 1966 I bravely asked church leader Marvin Hein what the conference leaders had planned for the women for the upcoming General Conference sessions. If I had hit him with a bat, I couldn't have surprised him more. He confessed they had never considered the women at all—but would rectify the matter. At the time women were not yet accepted as conference delegates but observed proceedings from the left back corner of the auditorium. At lunch the male delegates ate first and then the women. The conference theme was going to be "Conflict about Commission," but commission did not include women.

In an exchange with the editor of *Journal of Church and Society*, I urged him to consider an article dealing with a "practical discussion of the place of women in the church. . . . Most articles deal with the topic in terms of women's limitations to service rather than what is open to them." He offered an apology for reading the "Women's Section" of *The Christian Leader* and enjoying it.

Men were trespassing boundaries to read my column in *The Christian Leader* because the subject matter did not limit itself to women. A lengthy letter from a former Sunday school student, now at one of the eastern universities, discussed his discomfort with the MB Church and its insistence on a particular kind of salvation experience. Had he spotted my own uncertainty about spiritual formulas like the Four Spiritual Laws and rigid theological systems in my writing?

I reviewed well-known writer Elizabeth Elliott's book *No Graven Image,* about a missionary without a "happily everafter," ending for *The Canadian Mennonite.* Elliott was one of five women whose husbands were massacred by the Auca Indians in South America. In this novel, she hoped to bring people to a higher faith by showing God as sovereign rather than as the bellhop of missionaries. A reader in defense of God criticized the novel as being written in a deluded and frustrated state of mind. Readers responding to my review were quick to ally themselves with this writer: God always jumped to the rescue of someone in trouble. No one should question that God answered prayer. Elliott later mentioned that her speaking engagements dropped considerably after the publication of this controversial book about a God who was with us through a trial, not by removing the trial.

One morning, in 1966, Wes Prieb, acting dean of Tabor College, came to my little cubicle at the Publishing House and offered me the task of teaching one section of Freshman English at Tabor College for the coming year. Enrollment was higher than expected; they needed someone to teach one class. I had no degree, no teaching experience, but after discussing it with Orlando Harms, I agreed to teach during my lunch hour so that the other employees would not feel I was being favored. I faced a major turning point, unexpected yet welcome. I might not have to spend my days proofreading for eight hours for the next twenty years.

CHAPTER II

Student and teacher at the same time

*An adult crisis becomes a religious event when the person recognizes
in the experience the challenging and supportive presence of God.*
—Evelyn Eaton Whitehood and James D. Whitehead

At a Wiebe family reunion in the 1990s in British Columbia, I made three points in my short sermon: Heredity is
powerful; you can't get away from your DNA. Pain is always
present; living brings with it many upsets, sorrows, and agonies.
Grace is ever-abundant; the hand of God reaches into families
to bring healing, peace, and forgiveness. I had witnessed all of
that in the large Wiebe family. My late husband had nine living
siblings, some with large families. I saw the same pattern of pain
and grace repeated in my family.

The same is true of an institution like Tabor College, a four-
year Christian liberal arts college situated in the small city of
Hillsboro in central Kansas and affiliated with the Mennonite
Brethren Church, where I spent the next twenty-four years. An
institution, especially a small one like Tabor, is like a family. It,
too, has its own DNA, passed on by a process of osmosis
through generations of students, faculty, parents, alumni, and
supporters, holding the entity together.

Living in close proximity, one class of students overlapping
another, and some faculty staying with the school for almost
their entire working life even as others came and went, strong
links were forged between students, alumni, and faculty. Traditions, attitudes, and values were handed down from student to
student, faculty member to faculty member, and administrator

to administrator, to become its DNA. Students graduated from Tabor to return to teach after they had achieved advanced degrees and teaching experience. They had forged values in their years at Tabor and now wanted to pass them on. Admittedly, at times pain and misery abounded in that wonderfully complex maelstrom of people of different generations, backgrounds, education, and worldviews. But so did grace.

When I became a member of the faculty in fall 1966, I knew little about that Tabor DNA except through hearsay. The post-World War II students who became teaching faculty in the 1960s and 1970s formed a strongly bonded group, hard to break into. All I wanted was the opportunity to equip myself to teach and to earn a living for my family. I had no formal entry into teaching with the usual interview procedures associated with new candidates. I stumbled into the school when I agreed to teach one class that fall of 1966. My work at the Mennonite Brethren Publishing House was becoming more and more disappointing. I knew I would be working a long time because my children were all young. I clutched at straws. This Tabor straw looked the strongest. I reached for it.

I knew little about American higher education and how important a college education was in this new country. In Canada relatively few high school graduates went on to university when I completed high school. Church-related colleges were few, Bible schools many. Tabor had been founded by the Mennonite Brethren Church in 1908 because early leaders believed in education, a value brought with them from the Ukraine when Mennonites migrated to Kansas in the 1870s. This was a different branch of the Mennonite Brethren church than the Russlaender group in Canada. Most of these Kansas Mennonites had come to Kansas in the 1870s due to threats that their Mennonite schools in the Ukraine would be russified. Terms like *Russlaender* and *Kanadier* didn't exist here in Kansas.

I had little understanding how church-related institutions of higher education such as Tabor operated. My experience was limited to my years at Mennonite Brethren Bible College in

Winnipeg, and Walter's teaching at Bethany Bible Institute in Hepburn, Saskatchewan; Yarrow Bible School in British Columbia; and the Ontario MB Bible school in Kitchener, all unaccredited institutions. I knew little how curriculum was determined or what students expected of an instructor and an instructor could expect of students. The Canadian public educational system, patterned after the British system, demanded higher standards than the American system. My children found this to be true at the lower educational levels. I was soon known as a demanding teacher, unaware that in the United States I might be more popular if I dropped my expectations several notches.

My twenty-four years at Tabor spanned many changes in the school and in me. I began in 1966 teaching one course, no degrees, feeling like a rabbit running aimlessly in an enclosed field with coyotes lurking on the other side of the fence. Yes, there were a few coyotes nipping at me when with the years I became more forthright in my views, but mostly kind, friendly colleagues, ready to give me a hand up. At first students called me Mrs. Wiebe but with the push in the 1970s for more personalization, I became Katie to students, a name that bothered me at first. I didn't expect to be called "professor" because I wasn't one, but where was respect for one's elders?

When I resigned in 1990 I had finished two degrees (B.A. and M.A.) and was head of the English department and chair of the Faculty Personnel Committee. I had enjoyed two sabbaticals and served on various committees, including faculty representative on the Board of Education and Administrative Committee. I had beens awarded the Professor Emeritus position, an unexpected honor, and later in retirement, the Distinguished Alumni Award. And I was known, and I hope respected, for my staunch support of women.

When I started teaching, American church college life was in flux: required chapel, hours for freshmen women, no cars on campus for freshmen students, dress codes, and no football. All were subject to change. The Tabor student body stood at a new high that year with a record enrollment for a few years in the late 1960s. Students came from all parts of the United States and Canada and many denominations, with the largest percentage from the supporting Mennonite Brethren constituency.

I didn't expect to have difficulty with teaching the writing courses that first year because I had been seriously studying the craft of writing for years. Whether I could pass that passion on to others was debatable. The college needed an instructor for an extra section of English Composition 101 in 1966 to accommodate the large incoming freshman class. I looked like a possible candidate. Two weeks after Academic Dean Wesley Prieb asked me to join the Tabor faculty, I was in the classroom three times a week over the noon hour, spending the rest of my time at the Publishing House. For weeks I wrote out every word I would say in class, fearful the words would elude me.

When the following spring, in 1967, the Tabor administration offered me a full-time position as Publicity Director at Tabor, with the opportunity to finish a B.A. degree in addition to teaching additional sections of Freshman English, I accepted. The contract offered me the huge sum of $5,783. I had little to lose and much to gain. I would be home when the children had vacation, a major incentive, although that time soon was eaten up with summer school. I shifted to Tabor College full time in fall 1967. My days of proofreading were over. I thanked God. The days of hating to go to work each morning were in the past. My horizons had lifted.

My first assignment was publicity director (including being chief photographer), editor of the *Tabor College Alumni Magazine*, advisor to the *Tabor College View* (student paper), and instructor of several sections of Freshman English Composition, that most lowly of all required general education courses on campus, which students took "to get it out of the way," not to learn anything.

My Tabor years were some of the most mind-stretching, enriching years of my life, but also some of the most challenging, fearsome, and at times shaky. I watched Tabor dip and rise in enrollment, finances, and morale. The school vision faded some years as conflict within the administration and between administrators and faculty dragged on with no one admitting to any fault. Yet the school was too important in the hearts of loyal MBs to allow it to stagger to a close as occurred in the 1930s during the height of the Great Depression, so the vision was carefully re-polished to a new brightness after each dip. The first years I juggled teaching, taking classes to finish a B.A. degree, acting as publicity director, and keeping a home going. I clung to my biweekly column in *The Christian Leader*. It was a lifeline to the bigger world.

Tabor had few faculty women to serve as role models. With no academic degree, not even a B.A., or teaching experience, I felt overwhelmed. In my book *Bless Me Too, My Father*, I wrote: "I gradually became aware that I carried with me the intense fear of being considered a fraud . . . I read in a newspaper that this feeling is common to women moving into new arenas of work and thought in this age. It's called the impostor syndrome. Women can't quite accept they have the authority to do what they are doing because they have never been officially blessed for the task. They can't bless themselves because they see themselves as trespassers in uncharted territory. It is a form of guilt women carry unnecessarily." I was certain I was a trespasser at Tabor and in my writing ventures. An advanced degree would have been an academic blessing, but I lacked that.

I was sure I had come to Tabor under false pretenses. My *Christian Leader* columns, the way most people knew me, might have given off the aura that I knew more than I did. I couldn't accept that I had gifts, skills, and strengths to offer students and faculty. I felt as insecure as a sow on ice. It took years to find a new identity and confidence. Family needs took a huge toll on my emotional and spiritual strength as the girls struggled through adolescence and young adulthood.

People who know me now don't usually think of me as a timid person. They don't know how I inched through a forest of fears. The easiest way out would have been to avoid decisions that propelled me to my ultimate goal– to become a thinking, contributing person. I could simply have drifted.

Even at Tabor I was tempted once again to assume the traditional Mennonite women's stance by hiding behind male colleagues and letting them do the thinking, planning, and deciding in committee and departmental meetings while I sat silent and submissive. I echoed to myself the words of Dr. Marion Hillyard, Canadian writer, whom I had read years ago, that from the time a woman is born until she dies, she is not only a woman but also a person. The basic need for every woman is to have a central core inside herself, a center and a strength that is entirely her own. Without this she's going to be whatever turns up, whatever the economy asks, or what men think beautiful, or what the children want to make them happy. My core was knowing I was a valued person in God's eyes, on a personal pilgrimage with God, not obligated to a society (or a college) attempting to funnel every woman into the same mold.

My new life brought me more and more out of my home and into the public sphere to which I had previously sent my husband and children. I now had to decide issues I had accepted as predetermined for the Christian when I didn't have to test them personally. The pat answers I used to give my children about what to do when they collided with moral and social issues now needed more examination and a stronger underpinning because I personally needed answers.

My experiences at Tabor College are colored not only by what happened in the classroom and in my office but also by what was happening in society at large and in the MB constituency. My theology was being tested without my knowing what theology was. Society in the Sixties and Seventies wrestled with serious socio-political issues. Paradigms were shifting. Colleges were challenged to confront these issues in the classroom and on campus. Students pushed the faculty into the fray. As faculty sponsor of the student newspaper, I soon encountered firm demands for a free student voice. No faculty oversight. Students could decide for themselves which articles were worthwhile or which words were obscene or vulgar.

At the same time, in the U.S. MB constituency, school leaders saw the solution to years of little or no growth in student population by developing a closer relationship to the National Association of Evangelicals constituency. The Tabor Board of Education recognized that the Mennonite Brethren community was too small a constituency to provide enough students and funds to keep two schools flourishing, one in Hillsboro and another in Fresno, California, as well as some private academies. The answer lay in reaching out to other evangelical denominations with their vast untapped student population. Parents in Christian evangelical homes were aggressively looking for conservative schools to which to send their sons and daughters because of the social climate.

Leaning more toward evangelicalism meant shedding Mennonite ethnic accretions, a comfortable identity to a number of MBs. Ethnicity hindered evangelism, I heard repeatedly. You can't win souls to Christ if you like eating *vereniki* and borscht. Kansas Mennonites, on the Great Plains since the 1870, had brought with them some generalized antipathy to other kinds of Mennonites, from whom they had separated in Russia. They saw these other Mennonites as not quite as "spiritual." Anything tinged with the word *Mennonite* was considered ethnic. Anabaptism was as yet a foreign word. So Tabor College leaders positioned themselves closer to the evangelical community than to other Anabaptist groups or schools although two other Mennonite church-related colleges (Bethel and Hesston) existed within a radius of thirty miles.

The years 1965-75 were boldly declared as the Decade of Enlargement in the U.S. MB Conference with "Double in a Decade" as the slogan. The program began with great enthusiasm and hoopla with Rev. Elmo Warkentin, conference evangelist, as cheerleader. This same emphasis on evangelism and missions became part of Tabor's mission through President Roy Just's influence.

Dr. Just, one of twenty-one men who signed the Double in a Decade declaration, was a man of enthusiasm, with a measure of charisma and great zeal for evangelism and missions. He urged cross-cultural concerns as a means to grow the college, a worthwhile goal in itself. The United States MB Conference population never doubled in the decade, and I don't know how much this emphasis affected Tabor. After a few years the entire puffed-up program sort of faded away. But the pressure to get close to the evangelical world remained.

In the classroom I taught narrative writing, grammar, and sentence structure. But in chapel and faculty meetings and in the Parkview MB Church where we attended, I had to sort through the theology of this vigorous, almost fundamentalist, effort to become more like evangelical churches. The pastor, a zealous former missionary, was not beyond having an altar call after every service while the congregation sang through a dozen verses of "Just as I am."

At the MB Bible College in Winnipeg we students had been introduced to modern evangelism in classes like Personal Evangelism where "cold turkey" witnessing—talking about your faith to everyone and anyone (the person next to you in the airplane, your neighbor, your grocer) was encouraged. The deeply committed person lived with persistent guilt for failing to speak that word of witness at every encounter with a stranger. That same pressure was reaching me in this new Kansas environment with its strong focus on numbers of people being reached for Christ.

Dr. Just and students were involved in Probe 72 and Expo 72, both large interdenominational or inter-Mennonite evangelistic efforts. Operation Wichita was a big exciting effort on campus, with a large group of students going to Wichita every weekend to take part in World Impact activities, an inner-city ministry, just as the Gospel Light radio ministry had been at MBBC. World Impact survives in expanded form to this day in successful ministries to minorities. Founder Keith Phillips was Roy Just's close advocate in such matters, a frequent visible presence on campus. But a few students also went to peace conferences and organized a local chapter in the late 1970s when John E. Toews, who urged a stronger Anabaptist emphasis, arrived on campus.

In the fall of 1966, when I joined the Tabor faculty, sixteen Gospel teams had organized on campus, a sizeable proportion of the student body. Students with musical talent, on reaching campus, rushed to join an ensemble of some kind because it meant travel and excitement in the form of ministry. Churches invited these teams to present programs and recruit students. They gave Tabor that much desired spiritual aura to combat rumors of worldliness in student life.

As a new faculty member, I struggled with how much to expect of students in the classroom who were out "witnessing" instead of doing their class work When I talked to one student about his incomplete assignment, his candid response was that his responsibility to spread the gospel was more important than an insignificant English essay. A division on campus between "Christian" students and the others became noticeable. A coffeehouse was started to bridge the gap.

Student lifestyle was a major concern at a time when the prevailing philosophy was *in loco parentis*, the college standing in for parents. During my early years male students flaunted hair to their shoulders and women resisted being held to dorm hours if the men had no restrictions. The original reasoning behind this rule was that if the women were restricted, the men had no reason to roam at night. Naming of the campus queen was important enough to be mentioned in *The Christian Leader*. Some drinking occurred on campus and off, a major concern. Once some students held a dance on campus to the president's consternation. The administration's concern always in that era before the Internet and e-mail was to keep negative news from reaching that all-important constituency that held the keys to Tabor's future in its financial hands.

Some students recruited from Florida and other southern states solely for the new football program were not a good fit for

Tabor. They had not been informed well enough about life in a small rural laid-back community of 2500, sixty miles from the nearest large city and their favorite forms of entertainment. Hillsboro lacked a theater and beer parlor. Not a few had difficulty with academics and the Tabor lifestyle code. These left after one year, sometimes after one semester, necessitating that more money be spent on recruitment.

Over the years the growing percentage of students with weak language skills made teaching English difficult. In the English department we moved toward remedial work as student language skills slowly declined. At times I wondered if I was teaching at a college as I drilled students on subject/verb agreement and comma splices, material I had learned in grade school. My dream of large numbers of students becoming passionate about creative writing vanished. I had to settle for a few. A few students had never read a whole book in their lives. Teaching at the lower levels became a tough assignment, upper-level literature my delight.

African-American students taught me a lot about the simple joy of living. Often more open than traditional students, they seldom hesitated to express their views. On the other hand, women, especially those from conservative denominations in rural areas, hesitated to offer their views on any topic, a result of a long conditioning regarding women's roles in society.

Big changes in grading also took place over the years. The traditional Bell curve no longer held. In my latter years, instead of a few A's and several B's, the bulk of students received A's and B's. During this time the college instituted a learning lab for students lacking strong language skills to make it through college.

During Dr. Larry Feil's tenure as academic dean, he became enamored with Glasser's learning-without-failure philosophy of education. He introduced competency-based learning which stipulated that students could retake tests until they had mastered the subject. Faculty were expected to make a series of tests over each aspect of the subject. Some students soon got smart and tried the first test without studying to see how hard it was. They knew they could come back for another try next week without penalty. For us in the English department to produce several tests over each section became a major headache.

In the later years I taught at least one or two experimental courses on writing with computers. To have a student come to class with the excuse, "Someone tripped on the cord and I lost everything" was not unusual.

Turf warfare between academics and the growing athletic program presented a challenge to a new teacher. Athletes had excused absences for field trips. The athletic program was seen by some, including administrators, to be ultra-important because a winning season in any men's sport boosted morale on campus more than anything else. Teachers were expected to be lenient with athletes when it came to assignments. A colleague was pressured by a coach to "just give him a little work for extra credit" to raise his grade so he could play. Mastering the material wasn't the concern. Another time several athletes had spent a night in jail for drinking. The coach picked them up from jail in the morning and without penalty took them on a road trip. I was glad to see that several faculty members were greatly disturbed.

But these were exceptions. Memory brings back recollections of many top students who worked zealously and achieved in writing and literature and went on to advanced degrees in English, linguistics, and other fields.

A highlight of my first years was the first interterm sessions in the early 1970s, an experimental approach to college work introduced by Dr. Abram Konrad, originally from Edmonton, Alberta. For four intense weeks in January the first year all students and faculty grappled with how to relate to a temporal, changing world in an academic setting from a Christian perspective.

The overarching activity for the entire school during the interterm was the daily convocations with outstanding guest speakers from beyond the academic world or even the Mennonite constituency. Konrad brought to the Tabor campus speakers like Haddon Robinson, Colin Jackson, M.P., from London, writer Warren Kliewer, theologian John Howard Yoder, church musician Mary Oyer, as well as an African-American social worker, a translation consultant, a television music director from Hollywood, a seminary president, and many more in a short four-week period, all speaking to the topic of "Christian Responsibility in a World of Change."

Certain broad themes kept cropping up in convocations and seminars: United States involvement in Vietnam, racial discrimination, pacifism, New Morality, existentialism. Tabor found itself in a new position of leadership by offering this type of academic program together with the other schools in the Associated Colleges of Central Kansas. To hear a topnotch speaker every day for four weeks was memorable in expanding my intellectual horizons. I had never experienced such a plethora of new ideas before. I wolfed it down. My mind came alive. Life was good. I had made a good decision to shift to Tabor College. Some evenings I could hardly contain myself because of all the new ideas I had fallen heir to that day. Today I value the opportunities to grow intellectually at Tabor even more than the opportunity to teach.

Faculty and staff came and went during my twenty-four years on campus. However, in the late 1970s and early 1980s, one senior faculty member pointed out that thirty-six teaching faculty had left in the last ten years. Why? The buzz-word during this time became "marketing" and, a little later, "integration of faith and learning." But many faculty stayed on as I did because they enjoyed the class work and students, survived the stringent evaluations, and valued the camaraderie of other faculty members and the Christian stance of the school.

A painful resignation was that of Cal Redekop, vice-president, later a personal friend. He left after two years. His influence on campus was growing too fast to suit some. The personality clash between him and the president could not be hidden. He introduced a Committee for the Future of the College with an enlarged vision. The solution to the conflict of ideologies was to eliminate his position, thereby eliminating him. I recall one emotional and painful evening in the local bank basement meeting room, a neutral site, when the president explained to the faculty the reasons for the position elimination. The tension in the room was so thick, it was hard to breath. This kind of conflict-resolution meeting was new to me.

Admittedly resignations were sometimes due to low faculty salaries. Not enough donations were coming in to raise salaries. One professor admitted his family was using food stamps. I thought of D. H. Lawrence's short story "The Rocking Horse Winner," in which the house murmurs to the little boy, "We must have more money," over and over. The college was whispering the same words. Sometimes the board called for a budget freeze toward the end of a semester, which meant no more spending except for contracted expenditures. Eventually I learned from more experienced faculty members to spend my English department budget early in the year before it was frozen. How to meet the demands of the tight operating budget remained a constant concern.

For a decade in the 1980s Tabor and also Fresno Pacific College became entangled in a money-raising project, generally known as the Antelope Valley project. Faculty and alumni, including ministers, many without pension plans, were encouraged to invest in real estate in California, Colorado, Oklahoma, and Hawaii; and then later, when the land was developed, share the huge profits from the sale with the schools. The leaders of this investment program had unbridled optimism and heavy pressure to fund the college's programs. Surely God had sent the organizer of this scheme to save the schools from financial ruin. The development director and President Roy Just both saw this scheme as Elijah's cloud bringing financial deliverance, especially when it netted some profits the first few years.

The spokesman pushing this investment scheme on campus wore a shining halo around his head as he strode the Tabor halls. People were flown to California to look at land and entertained with banquets. The mood was upbeat. Dozens of people were persuaded to invest their savings in a sure thing not only to earn money for Tabor but also make a financial killing themselves. I kept my distance from the whole affair and was never approached. When the venture folded, the mood on campus turned grim. Many faithful supporters lost much money, some who could not afford to lose even a dollar.

The view of investors had been that a Christian institution was offering investment possibilities with Christian principles. Surely God would bless. As faculty representative on the Board of Education, I drove with Vernon Wiebe, acting president, to a meeting at the Buhler MB Church and listened to Vernon, in his calming way, pour oil on troubled waters. Troubled investors aired their thinking: The outside leaders of the project used the Christian concept of "fellowshipping together. We've got a good thing going. Don't you want to join us?" "Investors were guaranteed a gain of ten percent. The project was over-sold."

One investor made the telling comment, "The reason I was gullible was because it was for Tabor, a Christian institution. It couldn't lose. It's my own fault. Where would one buy land and not go look at it? I had the confidence that Tabor was behind this, and I thought it would turn around."

Despite the huge losses of some, some leaders admitted gullibility and investors offered forgiveness. Tabor would overcome this dark blot on its history. My files don't show any public disclosure or how the debt was met. One faculty member's wife told me that her entire paycheck for the next years went to pay off their loan on this empty investment. I learned a great deal about gullibility and the power of strong, charismatic leadership.

But there is a brighter side to the Tabor story. I was privileged to be at Tabor during a period of strong growth. The little college on the prairies began emerging from its isolation. The Tabor College Foundation began and a development director was hired. Marketing continued to be the magic word. The col-

lege was encouraged to "position itself" in the academic world
and find its unique role as a four-year Christian liberals arts college. The Mathematics and Science department bought a computer to stay in line with the growing new technology. The
library grew in its holdings. Enrollment kept increasing. Dormitories were built. Tabor hired its first psychological and ad-
missions counselors. Chapel was no longer a five-day-a-week
requirement but was changed to an optional chapel and assem-
blies, partly to meet government concerns about accreditation.
A director of alumni affairs was appointed.

The Center for Mennonite Brethren Studies was organized
in 1974, and I became a member of the first board and remain
on it even now. Tabor began registering its first non-traditional
students, the root of its adult education program in Wichita.
School terms began with freshmen/parent orientation, a new
approach to student retention.

Tabor joined the Associated Colleges of Central Kansas in
1967 for the purpose of inter-library loans and data processing.
A number of church-related colleges were situated in fairly close
proximity, three of them Mennonite church-related schools.
That affiliation brought together faculties of all these colleges
for meetings and joint teaching projects. Tabor became a member of the Tri-College (Tabor, Bethel, Hesston) Band, the Tri-
College Cultural series, Christian College Coalition. The
annual MB Basketball classic began in the 1960s. Tabor became
a visible presence in many arenas.

Faculty were earning and/or being encouraged to get advanced degrees. In time, new faculty without a terminal degree
in their discipline were expected to finish that degree within the
first seven years or face dismissal. A few kept postponing the
completion of the degree and were dismissed, to their chagrin. I
was grandfathered into Continuing Employment with only an
M.A. degree. I had been going to school for years and didn't see
that a Ph.D. degree would benefit me a great deal.

Faculty were evaluated by colleagues and students after a
specific number of years for promotion/continuing employ-

ment as they are at all institutions of higher learning. Tabor did not have a tenure clause in contracts, only continuing employment. Notice was given the faculty member of the impending evaluation. The faculty member under scrutiny selected students and faculty to evaluate her or him as did the Faculty Personnel Committee. Although we were told such evaluations were undertaken to help us improve our teaching, I found them terrifying. I thought I knew what it felt like for the early Christians to face the Inquisition. As I relaxed and became more confident of my teaching, I found student evaluations of me rose.

Thinking students in those decades were looking for a leader to guide them through the many ideologies being thrown at them. John E. Toews might have been that person, but he, like other male faculty aiming for greater influence in the MB constituency, had more sensitive antenna to the possible fallout than I did. Unless you promoted the party line, you remained silent until you moved on to another school.

When the popular basketball team was no longer a winning team, certain team members, particularly one player, who had an important father in the evangelical world the college was currently wooing for funds, agitated for a new coach. The coach, who had many previous successful years, was given the choice to submit to an evaluation, often painful, or leave. He chose to resign.

The same student who exerted pressure to get rid of the basketball coach also complained about my choice of literature for a Christian school, demanding that stories or novels depict nothing negative to the Christian life. The story I had asked the class to read was mild to say the least but did mention a husband letting his eyes drift toward a young babysitter. That students be asked to widen their horizons, explore ideas, and have exposures that went beyond those they had experienced in previous communities and school was not his prime goal. I was learning fast what the real world was like.

Eventually this student almost caused my dismissal. I resigned as head of the English department in 1976, although I had never been officially appointed to the position and left the struggle for academic freedom to someone else. I felt bereft, deserted, for even faculty members who had promised to see me through this disagreement kept silent. I was reappointed to the position again in 1985 when a new administration took charge and continued until 1990, when I resigned from Tabor College.

At times while I was at Tabor the administration became a top-heavy bureaucracy for a small school. Too many presidents and vice-presidents and not enough followers. On the other hand, the student body demanded more power, to the point that some faculty thought the tail was wagging the dog. They accused the administration of being a student-managed school. What students wanted, they got out of fear of offending some student or constituency member and decreasing financial support.

Accrediting teams pointed out that the English faculty carried too heavy a load because of large class sizes and amount of paper work. However, I usually entered the classroom with enthusiasm for what lay ahead. I had a clear idea of what I wanted to cover and how I wanted to do this. I was an organized and disciplined teacher which led to the criticism of being inflexible.

Always I tried to uphold high standards of language. It gave me much joy when the editors of *The Mennonite* in 2000 awarded me the honor of being one of the most influential Mennonites of the twentieth century. The others on their list included John Howard Yoder, Robert Kreider, Mary Oyer, Vern Preheim et al. The citation listed among other points that I had "raised the creditability of Mennonite writing." I hope some of that passion for language rubbed off on some students. I think it did.

CHAPTER 12

Everything I know, I learned while teaching at Tabor College

When you go out in the world,
watch for traffic, hold hands and stick together.
—Robert Fulghum in *All I Really Need to Know*
I Learned in Kindergarten

What did Tabor mean to me? What had this small school on the Kansas prairie given me? What had I given it? What was my greatest accomplishment as a faculty member? The answer to this last question is probably for others to say, but in my retirement years it made my day when a pastor phoned from Alberta Sunday morning to thank me for helping him with his writing skills. A former student told me that his supervisor had commented on his language skills. "I have you to thank for that," he said. I recall the time a student rushed to my office to tell me he had passed the Iowa Language Skills tests needed for a teaching certificate. I had been tutoring him. I gave him a big hug.

I had entered the work world as a naïve widow, meek, eager to learn, fearful to risk, ready to please, wanting to be liked. Women had been socialized to act out the theme of helplessness. Fortunately that has changed. I had never learned to confront issues or deal directly with personal conflicts.

Tabor gave me a chance to start a new life after being forced into the work world and, especially, an opportunity for personal and intellectual growth. I have sometimes said that college is wasted on young people. When an education comes at great personal cost, it has greater value. More people should wait until they are forty-four like I was to begin such studies. A number of summers I left Hillsboro at 6:30 a.m. to attend 7:30 classes at Wichita State University, fifty-five miles away. The children were still sleeping. I trusted them to get themselves up and find something to do before I returned about 1:30 p.m.

Those summers I allowed myself fifty cents for lunch at McDonald's for a hamburger and a milkshake. Free hours were spent in the Student Union studying. The hit song one summer was the poignant, heart-wrenching "Lara's Tune" from the movie *Dr. Zhivago*. As I listened with half an ear, my mind returned home. What were the children doing? Did they resent my studying the way I had sometimes resented Walter's regular enrollment in university courses? Was I neglecting them? My heart ached for them and the way the older girls were pushed into responsibilities beyond their age. Where was this strange shift in my life leading? When I finished a B.A. in 1968 and a M.A. in 1972, the children were genuinely pleased with my accomplishment.

During the years I taught at Tabor all four children attended two or more years. James and Christine graduated from Tabor. Joanna transferred to University of Kansas at Lawrence to finish a degree in journalism and later a master's degree in distance learning. Susan transferred to the University of Nebraska at Omaha to complete a degree in psychology and in midlife finished an MBA and M.D. degree. James became a successful entrepreneur.

In a personal evaluation to the Faculty Personnel Committee, I wrote that feedback from students, workshops, Sunday school teaching, and so forth told me I had teaching abilities, even though I had never planned to teach. I had come into the academic world with fears and inhibitions but now rejoiced to recognize my confidence, initiative, and drive. I enjoyed working with the world of ideas. I enjoyed seeing growth in students and their awareness of where they fit into life. I believed I had considerable competence in the areas of writing and language.

I had lazy students and zealous ones. In lower level literature classes I expected students to memorize twenty-five lines of poetry of their own choosing. I wanted them to have one classical poem in their memory bank. They could recite it in my office before a deadline or in class thereafter. One student recited his selected poem in my office at great speed. I monitored him in the text. Suddenly he stopped. I prompted him. "That was twenty-five lines," he said. He was four short lines from the end. Another student memorized all of Richard II's speech in prison, much more than I had assigned. And then, after he married, he named his first son William in honor of Shakespeare.

When the accrediting association demanded literature courses with more ethnic content, I designed and taught Black Literature for several years until it became an integral part of American literature courses. I also taught a course in Mennonite literature and several Bible courses for the Bible department, such as Wisdom Literature, Psalms, and Devotional Christian Classics. After studying at Wheaton College one summer under Dr. Leland Ryken, I designed and taught "The Bible in Literature," which I enjoyed immensely. I became increasingly aware that students missed many allusions in classic literature because they didn't know the Bible.

I also saw myself with some latent leadership ability, which emerged when I was elected chair of the Associated Colleges of Central Kansas English Committee, my first committee position ever. A number of individuals personally thanked me for my efforts during my two-year term regarding the projects I tried to complete.

During the first years I was head of the English department by default (no one else stepped up) I worked at strengthening the major, had a style sheet accepted for use by the entire school, became a member of the editorial board of *Direction* and the board of the Center for MB Studies, attended all ACCK meetings, usually the only person from Tabor present. I taught a few classes at Bethel College in Newton, Kansas, about twenty-eight miles away, for two years at great inconvenience to allow someone from the Bethel campus with a Ph.D. degree teach on the Tabor campus during accreditation proceedings. I worked with the ACCK Creative Arts magazine as advisor and the *Tabor View*, attempted to establish a publications board and write a constitution for it, looked after all freshmen English placement and testing, and generally supervised the department (scheduling, budget, etc.) without extra load credit.

In my self-evaluation I admitted I was not a remedial teacher even as the number of Tabor students needing remedial help increased. I regret my impatience with such students. I recognize my standards of excellence were probably too high. I had received my education in the British system, where comprehensive exams and essay questions were the norm, not the exception. I became upset with students who felt that half an hour should be enough to prepare for any Tabor exam or that essay questions were outdated, at least anything more than a paragraph of three sentences.

I had been accused of being prejudiced against football players, even though I rarely went to games or knew who the players were. I tended to forget how much a student's attitude toward the teacher was a reflection of the grade earned. So in a period of inflated grades (though it went against my better judgment) I acquiesced and handed out A's and B's like the leftover candy from last year's Halloween trick or treating.

The English department had serious weaknesses: heavy course loads (I spent most evenings reading students papers— sometimes a thousand a semester, making careful comments on most papers), too rapid academic innovations such as competency-based learning and grading, heavy emphasis on faculty evaluation that resulted in competition with other faculty for popularity votes, and that insidious political factor (stroking the right person at the right time). It hovered over everything, looming larger than Christian integrity.

At Tabor I learned about friendships. The bonds between some faculty members were strong. My strongest memories are of Alma Schmidt of the English faculty and me drinking coffee with the science and math department faculty at the end of the teaching day in the cafeteria. Those times brought closeness and understanding—and lots of heated arguments and laughter as we unwound from a day's teaching. We talked about everything from the Irish wars to planting tomatoes.

Another good remembrance was of meeting at regular intervals Sunday evenings in homes during my latter years at Tabor with other faculty members. For a few hours about seven or eight of us—a philosopher, psychologist, theologian, nurse, musician, scientist, educator, and others—became lay theologians. Those hours gave me a new understanding of what it means to be a Christian and disagree yet remain friends. None of us had deep roots in Hillsboro, which gave us time to find such friendships. I cherish those moments and those friends.

While many faculty were leaders in their own discipline, Clarence Hiebert was probably the one with the widest campus influence through his classes, responsibility for chapels, and cross-cultural trips. He risked readily. He was first to ask women (faculty and students) to speak in chapels and experimented with worship styles. He introduced student body communion services on campus, frowned on by some constituency leaders, who saw it is a congregational ordnance only. He remained a personal friend and encourager until his death in 2005.

Over the years I recognized that change in attitudes comes slowly. I was changing so fast myself, I expected my world to do the same. The Tabor academic world, birthed in the conservative Mennonite Brethren Church, though intellectually invigorating in some areas was stifling in others, such as women's roles. At a time when few women had public roles in the MB church, some faculty, administrators, and students felt more comfortable with male leaders. Women were to do "feminine" things like make coffee for faculty meetings and serve at receptions. Men were to head departments and divisions.

At a faculty meeting a motion before the body asked for a change in the names of several General Education courses from

Man and Society, Man and Nature, Man and Values, Man and Literature to something less gender-definite. The air was heavy with emotion. Some couldn't see the point. *Man* was a generic term. It was not unusual to have married students referred to as Mrs. Joe Jones. But the motion passed. Accrediting organizations were concerned with Tabor's low number of women and minority faculty.

In 1983, the Faculty Advisory Committee, of which I was a member, undertook a study of sexism on campus after the Diamond Jubilee speaker showed obvious lack of respect for women in the audience. His jokes were at their expense. Dr. John Lee of the Psychology Department acted as chair.

In our report to the administrative committee we listed ten areas where we saw positive change: greater use of women in public events plus change in language and course titles as well as course content. We also recognized that this was a time of transition regarding men's and women's roles. Women students needed help in knowing how to survive professionally and how to combine a professional life with a healthy personal life. Male students needed to be educated to see women differently than they had been raised to see them. Men had the psychological advantage of having more access to information, political skill, and experience, which meant women had to overcompensate to keep up. Women needed encouragement to become involved in productive politics and develop leadership skills.

We listed areas that needed improvement, especially the need to increase the number of full-time women teaching faculty, to re-examine men's and women's salaries and health insurance benefits, to deliberately aim for greater women's participation in committees and boards, and opportunities for advancement. The Student Personnel Committee was asked to encourage women to think about becoming doctors as well as nurses, managers as well as secretaries, superintendents as well as teachers, to prepare them for the reality they would probably be working outside the home a good portion of their lives. This was a daring statement.

The Administrative Committee responded in a lengthy document concurring with some of our statements. They also said: "Although our goal is to provide equal opportunity, it may not be possible to require equal participation because of other significant factors needing to be considered when making personnel decisions." They urged that the Bible be the first source of inquiry and highest voice of authority. "We urge that sensitivity be exercised toward diversity in biblical interpretation but that our goal be unity in finding and practicing what we as Mennonite Brethren understand to be biblical."

Anyone familiar with the conservative MB stance on the role of women at the time knew the direction such a study would probably go. The Administrative Committee voiced particular concern about using terms like "working women," which they saw as demeaning to women who were homemakers. I don't know what came of this exchange of thinking, but at least we had talked about it in the academic setting, something the church was not yet ready to do.

At that time for men, power, and politics, even in a small academic arena, was an accepted approach. In my Tabor days men expected women to support them and their structures and therefore hesitated to encourage them to take big risks on their own. I learned in time that to fail in the workplace is often due to having failed "politically" rather than to weak work skills or habits. I watched with awe the way some men barreled into a political fracas headfirst. I also witnessed men resign because they held onto principles. I was dismayed when some men bowed out of the decision-making process to keep themselves untainted and free of frustration. They simply refused to play the game. I rejoiced when I saw others, servant-like, pass on power and privilege to those without either.

Once an acquaintance from Canada met me in the halls of Tabor. Pleased to see me, he asked if I was a Tabor secretary. I said, "No, I'm on the faculty." He was visibly embarrassed.

Five years later, in March 1988, after a faculty discussion on the matter (the issue of women's roles wouldn't go away), Academic Dean Stanley Clark asked me to record my thinking about what could be done on campus to further the equality of women and men. I listed among my thirteen points greater consciousness-raising of the issue and promotion of inclusive language, particularly in the academic area. Women should be seen and heard at public gatherings. Too often a public gathering meant a row of black suits on stage. I mentioned that women might need more moral and emotional support than men because most (not all) women faculty came into college teaching as a second career or late in life. Women students needed strong female intellectual models. It was inevitable that as new faculty joined the staff they brought with them their thinking about socio-political issues. Concerns about the role of women in church and society moved in strongly with new faculty.

Work means consciously imposing an order or pattern on one's life. To be satisfying it can be either paid or unpaid. Work comes in many varieties. As a homemaker, I imposed pattern, order, and harmony on my family life. Sometimes I succeeded, sometimes I didn't. As a teacher and writer, I chose to impose another kind of pattern upon ideas, so that students and readers could trace the pattern and use it if need be. And it is that creating of something new that gives life satisfaction. The reward of work comes when young people move into these patterns.

I learned at Tabor that if you want to have a lasting influence, stay with an institution a long time. At times the temptation was strong to look elsewhere for a way to earn a living. Teaching, working, trying to keep a home going, was tough climbing. But I stayed at Tabor for twenty-four years and have never regretted it. I am glad to have been connected with this institution. I felt humbled when the Tabor Centennial publication mentioned me as one who influenced the struggle to define Tabor's ethos during the years I taught there.

Part III

CHAPTER 13

How my world lost its boundaries

If you have ever had the vision of God, you may try as you like to be satisfied on a lower level, but God will never let you.
—Oswald Chambers

Our exercise class instructor always began with stretching exercises before we moved into the sweat-breaking stuff. Stretching loosened tight muscles and prevented injuries, he said. I found stretching exercises boring even as I recognized their value to extend my physical capacity and endurance.

Life is like that. It offers stretching exercises, yet we resist. We subconsciously prefer to keep our worlds small, secure, and safe. We're afraid stretching might hurt. Often it does.

In the middle 1970s our European tour group visited an ancient castle now a museum of Middle Ages torture instruments. We looked at old handcuffs, balls and chains, spiked collars, spiked belts, tongue pinchers, guillotines, and stocks for gossips. I stood a long time before the rack and wondered about the men and women who had been stretched on it, ripped limb from limb, until they died.

My inner stretching didn't come on a rack, but sometimes it felt like it. While growing up in my little immigrant community, a secure place in the middle of nowhere, I sorted out what I believed, like most children do. What my parents believed was right and true. What everyone else believed wasn't quite as good. We were on the inside and everyone else was on the outside. I didn't think there were Christians outside our small Mennonite Brethren world.

Then, when I went to the city to work, a boyfriend invited me to attend Inter-Varsity Christian Fellowship meetings. I listened to young people my age sharing their faith in Christ. What? My little denomination didn't have a claim on the truth? People like the Baptists and Presbyterians also worshiped Christ as Savior and Lord? One day I took courage to reach out to draw these believers and others who weren't Mennonite Brethren into the family of God. This little bit of stretching didn't hurt a bit. In fact, it was strengthening.

But I still had unspoken reservations about other kinds of Mennonites. My father's family came from a group called the "General Conference [GC] Mennonites." They never said grace at meals audibly, just bowed their heads. Faith was a silent private affair between them and God. Marriage by a Mennonite Brethren to someone from this church sometimes resulted in excommunication. My father had been ousted from the MB Church in the Ukraine when he married my mother, a member of the *Allianz* church, similar to the MB Church, but with a few differences.

I had a hard time bringing these GC's, even if relatives, into the kingdom of God. They weren't like me and my friends who could pray openly at the drop of a coin. I'm not sure it was always a well-thought-through prayer, but it contained God-words. Mennonite Brethren were better, I was sure. We were going to sit in God's patio some day and have a special barbecue with him because we did church the way God wanted us to.

I also had reservations about those labeled the "Old Mennonites." None of them lived in Saskatchewan, but we moved into a nest of these strange creatures in Kitchener. They wore head coverings, plain clothes, and sometimes beards. Some painted their car bumpers black.

In my push to become a freelance writer, I accepted an assignment to write an article about entrepreneur Dorothy Swartzentruber of the (Old) Mennonite Church, who managed a freelance secretarial service for ministers and other church workers. Few ministers in those days had their own secretaries.

She wrote letters and prepared Sunday worship folders for a fee. After the interview she turned to me to say, "I'm so glad to know there are Christians among Mennonite Brethren also." I felt stunned. She felt about me the same way I felt about her. God said to me, *Now you know. Reach out and draw her in. God is no respecter of persons. Whoever calls upon the name of the Lord shall be saved.*

So I cautiously reached out and drew her in and with her all kinds of Christ-believers who called themselves Mennonites. And they drew me into their midst, and, in later years, became one of the main audiences of my writing and speaking ministry. Herald Press published several of my books and Mennonite church editors accepted my articles for their publications.

A friend told the story about traveling in northern Minnesota with his family in a heavily loaded station wagon when the engine quit. The sun was setting. They were a long way from the nearest town. What to do? Cell phones didn't exist. But then a car drove up. He told the driver his quandary. The other man hemmed and hawed. It was late. He had farm chores to do, etc., etc. In the ensuing conversation the man discovered my friend was a Mennonite. At once his countenance changed from grimness to a big smile. He reached out his hand in friendship. "Why didn't you tell me you were a Mennonite before?" He packed up the family and drove them to the nearest garage. Only Mennonites fit into his category of neighbor, people who needed to be helped. Mennonites were in. Anyone else was out.

As Christians who are also Mennonites, we may confuse two kinds of church membership: one as a people of God with a spiritual history and the other as a member of an ethnic group with distinct food, language, sometimes dress, names, and customs. A Mennonite pedigree is always a plus in some Mennonite circles, yet the spiritual identity should be the stronger one.

My stretching journey hadn't ended. Years later, while teaching at Tabor College I attended an English conference in Houston, Texas. In the elevator I recognized the name tag of a former high school classmate, now in a priest's clerical garb. After forty years, he remembered me at once even though he had been in a lower grade. He was now teaching in a Catholic college in Saskatoon, Saskatchewan. Over tea, a very Canadian custom, we enjoyed a wonderful time sharing memories of growing up in that quaint little village of Blaine Lake. He told me how as a child he often wondered if only his family had true Christian faith or if other parents also read the Bible and prayed with their children as his did.

A few years later when my daughter Christine converted to the Catholic Church in Chicago, I had to stretch some more. I knew what she believed. I knew also she was looking for something more worshipful and spirit-enriching than the services she had encountered in traditional churches. I blessed her in the path the Spirit was leading her. She became a parish nurse and also much involved in Young Catholic Worker activities. Later, when her failing health caused her to move closer to family in Wichita, she couldn't find the same kind of free-spirited Catholic congregation here that she had enjoyed in Chicago, so she became as associate member of the Lorraine Avenue Mennonite Church. At her funeral in 2000 after a lengthy illness, our mutual friend Father Tom Welk preached. That stretching didn't hurt a bit. God is the judge of faith, not me.

Although I have never had many contacts with African-Americans, my attitudes toward the poor and discriminated against were molded to a large extent by my father's attitudes. He grew up on the Russian steppes as a descendant of the thousands of Mennonite settlers who moved there in the late 1700s at the invitation of Catherine the Great. She needed good farmers. The Mennonites of northern Germany had a strong reputation as good farmers. Yet they lived in closed settlements in the Ukraine, thereby preserving their own distinct culture successfully.

The poor neighboring Russian peasants, not as successful either materially or culturally, became the objects of Mennonite discrimination. My father, himself the victim of misunderstanding as a boy because of his left-handedness, told bitter stories of how Russian stable boys were denied the privilege of even a bed in the house attic. They were sent to the hayloft even on cold winter nights. They ate poorer food in the kitchen of the large Mennonite estate owners who dined on full-course meals in their spacious dining rooms. He shared their misery of being an outsider. All my life I watched him help those being stepped on by others—the poor families, the men without work, social outcasts, and widows—with the few resources he owned.

It was, therefore, a simple transfer of his sympathies in spirit, at least, from the exploited Russian peasants to the discriminated Negroes of the slave era. Mother had read Harriet Beecher Stowe's *Uncle Tom's Cabin* in a German translation. Her account of the slave girl Eliza's flight over the ice-floes with hounds and hunters in full pursuit couldn't be equaled by living color TV production. Yet I do not think I felt full empathy for the blacks at the time because, in our little northern Saskatchewan community, we lived far removed from the race question. Or did we?

I recall driving slowly through the nearest Indian reservation on a Sunday afternoon gaping at the tiny hovels in which the First Nation people lived. Mother often donated clothes we had outgrown to a Metis family in Blaine Lake. When one of the girls showed up in school wearing my old dress the same day I was wearing my sister's hand-me-down made of the same material, I was incensed. My prejudice showed.

African-Americans, as we were to eventually come to know them, were objects of jest. The only Negroes we knew were the jolly minstrels, faces darkened with burnt cork, who gave our recreation-starved community an opportunity to laugh. Then one autumn day a strange-looking family moved into the shack at the edge of town: A white man whose youth had long left him. A younger white woman who looked old, tired, and unkempt. And an assortment of children—one white, two Negro, dark as night. Their presence in school was both a novelty and a source of curiosity. As a high school senior I taught them about the love of God in the United Church Sunday school. One early evening, my friend Mona and I, in a moment of righteous guilt, visited them. I recall a small dark kitchen, a pan of dark bread dough sitting heavily on top of the stove. What were we doing there? I don't know. In early spring when the snow melted and roads opened, they were gone. I think we were glad.

At age twelve I attended a United Church girls' summer camp. One leader was an African-American student from Trinidad who taught us the meaning of the word *prejudice*: Being down on what you are not up on. She also taught us her name: Wilma Samlallsing. After seventy years, hers is the only name I remember of more than 100 people at that camp.

But I remembered her definition. When Walter attended graduate school at Syracuse, New York, he shared an apartment near the university campus with a Chinese student from Formosa and a young Nigerian, both in America under the sponsorship of the Laubach Literacy Foundation. Walter told me the unique experiences of this "little United Nations" in their apartment. Both young men were intelligent, outstanding individuals, exhibiting a caliber of character I had seen lacking in some white American students.

Lucky, the Nigerian, more so than Larry, the Formosan, suffered from the blight of racial intolerance. One summer he motored with friends to the West Coast to find summer employment. En route he was denied admittance to restaurants because the proprietors identified him as an African-American. This was 1961. With the hurt rankling, he tested a hunch on the return trip. He traveled the same route and stopped at the same restaurants. This time he was decked out in the outstanding *agbada* of a Nigerian, a long full-flowing gown of brightly checked cloth, embroidered and closely fitted around the neck. The result? All doors swung open before him.

During the early 1960s, at the height of the race riots in the United States, I studied books about the equality of all humankind before God. Had the church spiritualized the matter too much, relating only to the eternal destiny of people of other colors rather than present relationships? My sister Susan and husband Harold Kruger and family spent about eight years in Zaire, formerly the Congo, as missionaries. In the rebel uprising of 1963, they lost all belongings and escaped only with their lives. I read both church releases and newspaper accounts of the events. They usually emphasized one thing: whether white people, missionaries, business and corporate people, and government agents were safe. The thousands of Congolese who died in the struggle didn't seem to matter. Whites were on top of the heap in matters of life and death, and other races at the bottom.

The full seriousness of the race issue in the United States overwhelmed me when we moved to Kansas in 1962. In Canada we heard only faint rumblings of racial unrest and discontent, but now it was a real thing of marches, riots, bombings, and killings. Every time I saw an African-American on the streets of Wichita, I took a second look.

When I traveled to Chicago to attend a writers' conference in the early 1960s, a large black man sat beside me on the bus. I had never been that close to a person of color before. Someone had told me that as a child she had heard if you touched a person of different skin color, you would break out in a rash.

To learn more about the race issues I attended a large open-air meeting in a nearby community at which Rev. Vincent Harding, a Mennonite African-American, related his experiences while traveling in the Deep South, similar to those our friend Lucky had told us. He was denied the use of rest rooms, restaurants, hotels, and other public services. The report was a straightforward account of what he had encountered.

At the close of the service, he taught the audience the civil rights song, "We Shall Overcome." Slow, dirge-like, we sang it but without the depth of feeling I have heard it sung by African-Americans. I sensed a strange restraint in myself and others in that almost completely white audience. The restraint seemed to say, "Blacks should have civil rights, but must I, a white person, identify myself completely with them to help them achieve their freedom?"

I ached with a Nigerian student at Tabor who confided in me that the checkout clerk in the local store had taunted him about his heavy accent. I knew I needed to know more before more stretching could take place. I volunteered to study and then teach Black Literature, one of the most mind-stretching exercises I have been through. With the blacks I walked through each period in their American history from slavery to the present. I felt good when a student told me after reading Margaret Walker's *Jubilee* he finally understood what racism was about. Travels to India and Central America kept breaking down the barriers in my thinking. All people are children of God. Skin color has nothing to do with it.

It hurt when at Tabor College I was accused of racial prejudice even as I worked hard to combat it in myself. African-American students were recruited for the athletic program. Some came without a strong academic background. When I didn't give these the social pass they were accustomed to, I was deemed prejudiced. One day the issue came to a head. The college counselor called a meeting between the students and me. I distributed copies of essays written by the student making the loudest noise to my accusers. Later, one black student confided to me, "I didn't know his work was so bad."

God's stretching experiences never end as long as we are alive. Plants grow, anything with life grows. Only rocks don't grow; they only erode. I had always known that men were the mainstay of the family of God. They stood up front and preached and waved their arms and pounded the pulpit, declaring, "Thus saith the Lord." Women never did that.

Over the years I sorted out all Scripture passages dealing with costly discipleship and labeled them Men's Tasks. I left the women sitting on the sidelines, not using all the gifts God had given them, not permitting them to become involved seriously in fighting God 's battles.

I allowed women to become missionaries and ministers' wives, but beyond that I didn't see them serving in the church much—maybe a little Sunday school teaching, singing in the choir or working the sewing circles. I was content to hide behind my preacher husband and let him do the serious thinking, praying, and doing for Christ.

The hardest stretching I had to do was to quit sorting tasks and admit that discipleship was for everyone, male or female, single or married or divorced, not just a few male leaders. God was rattling my hiding place. He asked: "Katie, are you using the talents I have given you?"

My response was "A woman isn't expected to do much in the church, is she, other than pray and be nice?"

The answer I received from the whole of Scripture disagreed with my glib answer. The first time I spoke before a mixed Sunday school class, I trembled with fear. Would God cause hail and brimstone to fall on me because I was not heeding the word for women to remain silent? It was a small first.

I admitted I wasn't using my gift of writing. I was letting others be responsible for my service while I coasted. I hugged myself hard as I told myself, *God loves me as I am—as someone who wants to write*. I began to write. At the time I didn't know that God also wanted me to move into public speaking and teaching.

CHAPTER 14

How I received shoes as a writer

You are created for more than just existing. While we have redefined mediocrity as normal and far too often expect nothing more than that for ourselves, God will not have it."
—Erin McManus

My Russian-born father understood the meaning of shoes as a symbol of belonging. He grew up wearing *Schlorre*, a wooden sole with a leather band over the toes. As soon as he was old enough, he made his own footwear, usually from willow wood. Younger children inherited an older sibling's Schlorre. In that socially divided Mennonite world in south Russia, the *Anwohner*, or landless, wore Schlorre; the landed gentry, or wealthy, wore shoes. All the time. To call someone a *Schlorr* was an intentional slur.

As a young boy, my father yearned for a pair of shoes. One long summer as he herded a relative's cattle, he dreamed about buying shoes with his earnings. At summer's end, his relative gave him only one small ruble. He ran home crying about the bitter end of his dream.

His stories about shoes surfaced at other times. As a medic in the Russian army during World War I, he was issued boots, real leather boots, which he buried near the family home in Rosental after the Russian Revolution to keep them safe. Good footwear was unobtainable. One day a revolutionary soldier forced him, at gunpoint, to dig up whatever he had buried. He dug up his boots. That ended his hopes of wearing shoes once again. Back to Schlorre.

I look down at my own feet. I am wearing shoes. In child-hood I often went barefoot but now I always wear shoes. I es-chew the modern flip-flops because they remind me too much of my father's Schlorre. An old African-American spiritual con-tains the line: "I got shoes, all God's children got shoes, and when we get to heaven we're going to put on our shoes; we're going to walk all over God's heaven." Hubert Brown in *Black and Mennonite* writes, "To the black person, shoes symbolized acceptance into the . . . forever family of God. And with shoes on the feet one can walk, jump, run all over God's heaven. One can be jubilant and rejoice."

I see myself in those black slaves who longed to wear that symbol of acceptance as equals in American society. I see myself in my father who longed for leather shoes instead of the unre-lenting Schlorre. He wanted to be a fully accepted member of Russian Mennonite society, highly socially stratified at the time. As a young woman I longed to wear the shoes of a full-fledged writer in the Mennonite world so I could walk, run, and jump freely and joyfully. But I had to be content with wear-ing Schlorre for a long time.

I grew up in a Mennonite Russlaender home, but because we lived across the river from the Mennonite settlements in Saskatchewan and touched base with them only occasionally, never in winter, the full influence of Mennonite life and culture never affected me. In the small white, frame building where the Mennonite Brethren congregation across the river gathered, I was introduced to Christian Endeavor, which we children loved because it was a variety program like the Major Bowes Amateur Hour but without the gong. I attended revival meetings, heavy, heart-throbbing affairs. I learned about church disciplinary ac-tions indirectly from my parents when they discussed an ex-communication privately, unaware how acute my hearing was at such times.

I memorized German Golden Texts. I sat crowded on benches behind green curtains strung on wires dividing the Sunday school classes. I watched the occasional rituals of riverside baptisms, counted the nails in bench backs as I knelt and waited for the prayers to end. I endured day-long missionary conferences with speaker after speaker, held in huge tents erected for the occasion. Yet in this amalgam of experiences, I heard voices calling me to a faith life and to become a disciple of Christ.

Sunday evenings when our family returned to our small, mixed, mostly Slavic immigrant community, I heard other voices whispering, even calling. Sometimes, while lying on a blanket spread on the backyard woodpile in the warm after-noon sun, these voices invited me to another world—the world of the imagination. The prisoner of Chillon reminded me that "stone walls do not a prison make, nor iron bars a cage." The poet Shelley cried to the West Wind for a renewed spirit and op-portunity to let his words fly like leaves over the world. I cried with him, "O wind, if winter comes, can spring be far behind?"

This world of the imagination dared me to let go my inhibi-tions and move into it. But I didn't, because the voices never de-clared openly, "You can be a writer." When I left Blaine Lake after high school to work in Saskatoon, I silenced these voices that had awakened my consciousness to that other world but never revealed how to join it. They didn't show me how to pay my way while I wrote. A weekly income remained high on my list of priorities at the end of the Depression. Furthermore, how could I reconcile the two sets of voices—one to a life of faith that looked for certitude in doctrine, the other to using my creative gifts that accepted ambiguity?

Deep down I considered writing a pleasant hobby, a frill, not necessary for regular people. At the time, women were cau-tioned to stay out of any field that brought them into competi-tion with men or where they might critique male fields of endeavor. I could not grasp writing as a reality for me. I knew no writers. No one encouraged me to creativity, although no one discouraged me either.

Vaguely I sensed that the mystique of writing offered a sat-isfaction I wanted, but I needed a tutor to show me how to line up words and sentences and paragraphs into meaningful prose. Writing was for people in books, like the Brontë sisters in England, or Jo in *Little Women*, or poets like Elizabeth Barrett Browning, who lived an exotic life in Italy. I was much too ordinary. I wore long underwear in winter that showed up in embarrassing creases under my lisle stockings. I rolled those same stockings into fat brown doughnuts around my ankles in summer. I wore heavy galoshes in winter that made me feel like a Clydesdale horse. Me, a writer? Never.

What barriers kept me from wearing writer's shoes? When I started freelance writing in the early 1960s, writing and publishing in the Mennonite world was a male-dominated profession. No woman served as editor of a major church organ, only children's publications. Although women represented the majority of readers, all other positions like publishers, editors, and writers were filled by men. When I discussed the possibility of becoming editor of *Rejoice!* an inter-Mennonite devotional magazine, years later, a board member said, "I don't think it will matter that you are a woman."

I thought my experience of being rejected for the editorship of *The Youth Worker* in the 1950s was unique to me but I discovered other women had the same experience. Virginia Hearn in *Our Struggle to Serve* writes that there is "too much prejudice against a woman's having authority over men or teaching men for it to be otherwise." 1 Timothy 2 set the tone for all discussion about women in church ministry. Writing and editing were teaching. Often a small corner of a periodical was reserved for women and their special interests in the home.

It didn't take long to notice that men were asked to write for the church press with no other credentials than that they were ministers, preachers, and theologians. Some had no writing skills whatsoever, only good intentions. I groaned as I edited their material when I worked at the Publishing House. Their writing was often wordy, abstract, pious, and general, directed only toward other ministers—their peers—not the general reader. I sensed the tacit mutual understanding of early editors that women were not interested in church life beyond the children's department, certainly not in thinking through theological issues. Yet I often thought of my own mother whose great joy was attending those church conference sessions at which the delegate body discussed theological issues of life and faith.

It took years to learn that some editors believed there was a big difference between a male writer and a female writer and their audiences. Although men could write for both genders, women did not write for men. In the 1960s William Lederer advised in an article on "The Women's Magazines" to write to fit the audience: Write significant, thought-provoking things for the men. Write fluffy, soap-sudsy things for women. Their mental needs are not alike.

At writing workshops children's writers were encouraged to write stories for boys to insure maximum sales. Boys did not read stories about girls, but girls read stories about boys or girls. Write to make a buck.

To succeed I had to change my thinking about the role of women in the church. I had to accept that I, as a member of the body of Christ, like all other members, had the responsibility to define for myself the nature and teaching of the church. I had to accept that I had the obligation to test its doctrine and theology against the Scriptures with the goal of growth of individual members as well as the body as a whole. Which meant venturing into areas of thought and life not usually open to women.

To be a church communicator I had to prove my seriousness about the Christian life, about the church, and about writing without letting down on home duties. Men could place church ministry ahead of family responsibilities without being criticized. Homemakers couldn't. I couldn't lock myself into a room, even the bathroom, if it was the only room with a lock. Writing could never be a first. In the early years I wrote with my typewriter on the dining room table where I could keep an eye on the children. Gifted women dropped out of writing before they found out if they could make it as freelance writers. The public encouragement was absent.

And they feared being offensive. Women have been conditioned for decades to be pleasing in appearance, dress, manner, and relationships. Topics dealt with on a women's page were not expected to be handled in a hard-nosed way. Novelist Erica Jong wrote to would-be women writers that one voice said, "Be like mother and be safe." Another voice said, "Be like Daddy and make your mark."

Often I asked myself, *If I write this thought down, will I ever be able to live it down—or live up to it?* When men spoke up boldly, they were considered forthright and bold, fearless for the truth. When women spoke up, they were shrewish, denying their womanhood. It took a long time until I acknowledged to myself that I had the right to speak about the church simply because I was a member.

I didn't recognize until much later in life that I never accepted the shoes of a writer because I lacked a strong woman-teacher-intellectual model who could give me the permission to write I couldn't give myself. When my husband accepted his first pastoral position, a wonderfully wise older man in the church, Rev. H. A. Willems, mentored him. The two men spent hours together. Many men have achieved because some older man has made room for them in a vocation. Older women have done this for younger homemakers, but mentoring for women in the professional world was not a concept well-known when I was starting out. I longed for someone to encourage, stroke, coach, give support to my dreams, and help me put them into effect. I found writing models in my reading of authors like A. W. Tozer, F. B. Meyer, Marion Hillyard, and others.

I needed a mentor, someone close by, to show me that an immigrant's daughter could wear the shoes of a writer. It just wasn't done. Who in my limited world had ever written anything? Blaine Lake was a cosmopolitan community of Scottish, Irish, British, German, Russian, and Doukhobor immigrants. Completing high school was already a great accomplishment for most children, including my family's. My role models were loving, generous women who made excellent *Zwieback* and borscht and sewed fine stitches in pillow cases, but understood little of my yearning to give myself away on paper.

And being a woman, did I even dare try on a writer's shoes? In the Mennonite Brethren constituency they only came in men's sizes. The message reached me that women's place was not with thinking. Not with dreaming. Not with making decisions like whether to stay or leave Russia. Not with declaring or proclaiming. Not with discerning sin or binding and loosing. Fear of both success and failure haunted me. Fear sat close to me every time I opened my typewriter: Why do you think you can write with authority? Mennonite women aren't an authority in any matter except cooking and cleaning. The poetry of living had no real attachment to the poetry of words.

If fear sat close on one side, guilt moved in on the other. Shouldn't you be baking another batch of cookies for the children? What will the family say if they get casserole again tonight? A woman's place was at home kneading soft dough with strong hands; with stripping milk from soft, warm udders; with serving *Prips* and *Schinkefleisch* to tired men when they came home from the fields; with cradling children into quietness; with loving deeply without spoken words; with praying silently, head bowed.

When I started writing it could seldom be a first for women who were wives and mothers. Mothers didn't have a secretary as my husband had in me. They didn't have a wife. They could be interrupted by children, husband, plumber, and paperboy. Walter could say, "I need some time to prepare my sermon for tomorrow, so please keep the children quiet." I couldn't. So some women were eased out of writing early, unless they made peace between family concerns and writing. For decades I struggled with the inner debate: Were motherhood or teaching to earn a livelihood being shortchanged because I couldn't give up the need to write?

Whatever flicker of interest in writing I had had in my youth was never quite extinguished as I moved into adulthood.

I made a renewed commitment to Christ and joined the Mennonite Brethren church, attended Bible college, married, and began family life. The first years of our marriage, my husband Walter and I spent many hours sorting through what we thought God wanted of our life together. One evening we knelt besides our kitchen table and committed our lives to a literature ministry within the church. How this would work itself out, we didn't know.

It took years before I heard the inner voices again. We were living in the small Mennonite community of Hepburn, Saskatchewan, population about three hundred. That might be an overstatement. As I cooked, cleaned, canned, sewed, and helped Walter in his pastoral work, I wondered what to do with my renewed cravings to be creative, to write, to teach. I felt like a ship at sea without a rudder. I finally took a small step forward. I placed my college typewriter on a small table under the staircase and began to write. Crumpled paper filled my wastepaper basket. I wanted the shoes of a writer but didn't know the first step.

As I have already written, Walter was soon given shoes for his writing ministry. And I, in my zeal to be part of what seemed to be a needed and opening field in our denomination, dogged his footsteps. They were big. After all, he wore size twelve shoes. And hadn't we made the commitment to serve the church together? But the journey toward my wearing shoes was a long one.

He took a correspondence course in writing for Christian publications; I studied the same course on my own. He was given an assignment to edit the denominational paper, *The Youth Worker*. I did most of the work because he was too busy. Even when the committee in charge knew this, they didn't have the freedom to appoint me as editor. I had the wrong body shape. At that point my Schlorre began to feel uncomfortable. What was wrong with me? Had God made me a misfit?

Walter was asked to write for *The Canadian Mennonite*; I picked up the assignment because he was busy. Editor Frank

Epp affirmed my work with a letter I still have in my files. It was my first step toward wearing the shoes of a writer. I could see myself wearing them. Leather ones, well-polished. But it took a long time before I could discard my awkward wooden soles.

I took another step forward when I decided to work at finding the steps to becoming a writer. I read everything I could find about writing, especially for the religious press. Freelance writing was in its infancy, especially for women in the home. I studied all forms of the craft. In Kitchener I took my first writing course at the University of Waterloo. I joined a writers' club and offered to write book reviews for a local minister who had made a commitment he had no time for.

In Hillsboro, while working at the Mennonite Brethren Publishing House, I attended two national Christian Writing conferences in Chicago in 1964 and at Green Lake, Wisconsin, in 1966. I met real editors, real writers, and heard about real opportunities for writing. I took each writing tip to heart. I learned editors wanted seasonal material in spring. I had sent a story to Canada's national family farm magazine, *Family Herald and Weekly Star*, only to have it rejected. When I came home from Green Lake, I rewrote the same story and inserted a Christmas emphasis. In two weeks I received a check for $125. And in a national periodical at that. Now I was at least in the shoe store.

I recall Sherwood Wirt of *Decision* magazine telling us in Chicago that any article or book with the word *woman* in the title in the next few years would be a best seller. From his perspective as editor of a national magazine, he was aware of a new social movement soon to sweep the nation. I took his words to heart.

For a while every time I sat down to write, a jury of twelve solemn men in dark suits with large black thumb-indexed Bibles open to 1 Timothy watched me work. It took years to realize the barriers to women's greater involvement were not divine interdicts but human concoctions, deeply embedded in me. My goal was excellence, so I practiced. To revise a *Christian*

Leader column six or seven times was not unusual. I often re-typed book manuscripts up to four times in the days before computers. I accepted assignments and fulfilled them. Editors learned to depend on me. Later when I did some editing, I found out why they appreciated my promptness. Writers who commit themselves to an assignment only to beg off the day of the deadline are an editor's nightmare.

I analyzed articles written by professionals to find out how they were put together. I looked at leads, transitions, support-ing proof, and so forth. One morning, as I was grading papers at Tabor College, I read the same article I had just analyzed and set aside on my desk—now handed in by a student under his own name.

I accepted assignments I didn't know how to complete. I was lured into writing *Alone: A Widow's Search for Joy* by the book editor of Tyndale House Publishers with frequent phone calls and suggestions. For several months I resisted. Fourteen years had passed since Walter had died. I had just recently packed up his remaining papers. I was no longer in the "widow" frame of mind. One snowy March weekend, after several more persistent phone calls, I toyed with a possible outline. I was hooked. The hitch was it had to be done by the end of summer. And on top of that the publishers had a problem with my name. "Funk" was not acceptable as part of a published author's name. In the end we compromised on using the initial *F.* But I wasn't happy about that. Part of my identity was gone once again.

I had also accepted a proposal from Herald Press to com-plete a manuscript on Mennonite Disaster Service started by another writer. It too had to be ready for the press by early fall. Two books in one summer. Could I write every day for six to eight hours? I wrote that summer without one smidgen of in-spiration, sometimes feeling a terrible emptiness, hating the bondage of writing I had longed for. Those days I realized that most good writing is not mere accident or the result of high in-spiration. Usually it comes by work—hard work, and lots of it. Deadlines are unyielding slave-masters, and the act of writing can be tedious and painstaking, sometimes so wearying I wished I had never started.

In early October on a trip to a Mennonite Central Committee Peace Section meeting in Ottawa, Ontario, I dropped off the manuscript for the widow book to the Tyndale House book editor at the airport. The other manuscript was also finished on time. Herald Press had no problem with the name *Funk*. This branch of Mennonites had many Funks.

A writer friend told me he doubted whether there was any such thing as a talent for writing—only pressures, which the person has to apply to him or herself. But in the end I was glad to have accepted the challenge of two book contracts. I had tested myself and won. *Alone: A Widow's Search for Joy* by Katie F. Wiebe sold thousands at once as it rode the crest of the new emphasis on widowhood. Baring my life in print gave me huge rewards as readers wrote to express their identification with my experiences.

People handed me the shoes of a writer long before I looked down to see what I was wearing. Even after I had written hundreds of articles, columns, and eventually books, I couldn't say, "I am a writer." I had every right to call myself a college instructor. I had a contract to prove it. But a writer? What legal contract authorized me to write? In creative writing classes in later years I had students make themselves a I AM A WRITER badge to get them past this hurdle.

Over time I was invited to conduct writing workshops. I taught at People's Place in Intercourse, Pennsylvania, and at writing conferences in Manitoba, British Columbia, Alberta, Oregon, California, and Kansas. Some would-be writers are attracted to writing contests like flies to honey. One woman, eager to win a *Guideposts* magazine "your most inspirational moment" contest, wanted help to slant an article about an accident to show how her husband had been profoundly converted through it. Her husband's muttering of the words, "Thank God we weren't hurt," made her hope an experienced writer could turn them into a breathtaking account of conversion.

Would-be writers told me they had invested in books, type-writers, separate office, all equipment necessary. They were looking for glue to hold them to the task. I couldn't give them that. I could only tell them that writing is a job like any job. It requires commitment.

People tell me I am wearing the shoes of a writer. I see many books, articles, curriculum material, devotionals, on my shelves. What allowed me to wear those shoes?

First, I believe I had something to say. Call it a call of God. I saw certain areas of the Christian life not being spoken to. Often someone on the outside looking in has a better under-standing of what is going on than those in the center of the ac-tion. As someone outside the power circles of church life, I saw that the church had developed into a strong institution but had lost its sense of being an alternative witness to current culture.

I have a deep basic faith in God, sometimes quite simple—a sense of God's existence in a dimension beyond the natural. I believe in sin and evil. I believe that we struggle not against flesh and blood but against principalities and powers in high places.

I have wanted to be known as a thinking writer, not a con-veyer of hackneyed words and sentimental thoughts. I don't necessarily expect readers to agree with me, but I aim to make them think about the issue again. I have always found the com-ment "You made me think" to be a compliment, not a criticism. Somewhere we have perpetuated the myth that faith requires little thinking and that God is more on the side of those who do not think seriously than of those who do.

I am willing to acknowledge that aspects of my worldview have outlived their time and should be yielded up for some-thing nearer to truth. To change my theology has been most dif-ficult, for to do so makes some readers believe that God and the Bible are variable with the times. I knew that life would become increasingly difficult unless I changed my mind and kept changing it about what I accepted as God's Word for humanity as the culture around me changed. I wrote about this in my book *Bless Me Too, My Father.*

I often think of the patriarch Abraham, who was asked by God to sacrifice his son on Mount Moriah. He was convinced that God wanted him to commit this horrible act. Yet at the critical moment a ram appeared in the thicket and a voice told him to kill it instead of the boy. Abraham changed his actions to suit God's new instructions. Did he debate with himself whether the new voice was that of the devil in disguise and not an angel's? Why didn't Abraham stick to his original convictions? The devotional writer Oswald Chambers that writes Abraham didn't make a fetish of being consistent with his earlier convictions. So I tell myself that faithfulness to God is more important than faithfulness to tradition.

I am wearing shoes because God gave me the courage to risk exposing my views in print. Writing is a form of giving oneself away, of standing in the public square without clothes. A writer has to be willing to say, "These are the things I think about deep inside me." Writing is often an exercise in self-revelation. I have told many writing workshop participants that the more personal the writing, the more universal.

Being persistent in my calling over the decades helped me break down the barriers. With the help of editors, friends, and children, I moved toward the barrier again and again. Bumping, blundering, blustering, battering, bluffing, and blessing, I crossed over. I cherish the opportunity to share my stumbling through life with others. After I have lived it, why hang onto it? Granted sometimes my vision was blurred by personal circumstances, at other times it became a little clearer. Yet each time I sat before my computer I faced the question of integrity. How honestly could I write about apparent contradictions between the church's official say-so that all is well and the murmurings from the underside?

I found the Tabor College academic setting a great place to look at ideas a first and then a second time. Being in the academic world was like having a left-handed person sitting at my right side jabbing me in the ribs with every forkful. Ideas I had long held sacred were up for grabs. I had to speak to questions that concerned me but not with catchall phrases. If I did, I could bow out of the writing world as contributing thinker.

Elise Boulding, author of *The Underside of History*, writes that when she first approached the subject of women's social history and discovered account after account of rank injustice toward women in many countries, she felt angry. Until this anger subsided she couldn't write. I waited fourteen years to get a perspective on the subject of widowhood, an event that changed my life, before I wrote my book *Alone*. I struggled with anger, hurt, confusion, in addition to grief and guilt. I wasn't in a loving mood and was tempted to lash out.

At present I am not as fearful of life's ambiguities as I once was. I am not as afraid of not coming up with either-or answers. I am more ready to allow the mystery and glory of God to remain and not codify the teachings of Scripture into three points and a conclusion. I am weary of the absence of artistry in sermons and the dullness that sometimes permeates corporate church life. I long for a wave of wonder, beauty, and joy to sweep over our congregations. And to hear the poets sing.

One evening, several decades ago, my young son came rushing in with his usual "Mom, come see!" I followed him outdoors. In our backyard, for our private viewing—at least that's the way it seemed—freshly washed, colors bright and gleaming, arched a complete rainbow, a full 180 degrees, without a wisp of cloud to obstruct our view.

We stood together for several moments silently enjoying the fragile beauty of the moment. We stood and wondered. Surely Noah saw this kind of rainbow as a token of the covenant between him and God. I can't explain a rainbow, or why there is beauty and meaning in the world. I only know there is a mystery and beauty to godliness. And the writer who uses her imagination allows the mystery of God to remain without feeling compelled to push everything into formulas and boxes.

Characteristics of this age are complexity, fast pace, and emphasis on specialization. Specialists, those who bring us bits and pieces about a limited field of study, are a danger to society, said one college president. They must be ever confronted by the lay person who asks, "So what?" I wear shoes today because I have asked, "So what?" What is the significance of that?

I have tried to write so that ordinary people can understand. I often whittle at an idea first in my mind and then on paper until it is clear to me. Readers can handle difficult concepts but not vague abstractions that wander around like spilled milk and can mean anything.

I heeded Oswald Chambers's words in *My Utmost for His Highest*: "The author who benefits you most is not the one who tells you something you did not know before, but the one who gives expression to the truth that has been dumbly struggling in you for utterance." When I first started writing for *The Christian Leader*, letters from readers pointed this out to me again and again. As I clarified an issue for myself, I helped the fog to lift for readers. That column became a journal of my life and concerns. In it I can trace my interests, ups and downs, periods of growth and stagnation. Grappling with a problem in my own life by putting it into words helped me find myself. I am grateful for the opportunity to write this column for thirty years. It taught me the discipline of the deadline, the joy of creating with words, and especially the stewardship of ideas and words.

I wear the shoes of a writer because of editors who encouraged me and gave me assignments. Among them are Daniel Hertzler, editor of *Christian Living* and *Gospel Herald*; Frank H. Epp of *The Canadian Mennonite*; Orlando Harms who first asked me to write a column for *The Christian Leader* and those who followed him: Wally Kroeker, Don Ratzlaff. I risk mentioning a few other names knowing I am leaving others out: Paul Shrock, Harold Jantz, Michael A. King, and others.

There is another factor that summarizes why I wear a writer's shoes.. Years ago I wrote an article for a college textbook titled "The Barriers Are Not Real." I told readers that you don't have to wait for someone to take down the barriers to become a writer. I didn't quite believe my words. Yes, I was writing, but I was always waiting for someone to measure my feet and ceremoniously hand me the shoes I earnestly coveted. I wanted someone to give me the authority to write. I wanted someone to bless me. That was a key issue for women seeking greater involvement in church ministry.

One evening I sat at my kitchen table reading Steinbeck's *East of Eden*. The novel closes with the Chinese servant Lee begging Adam, the protagonist, on his deathbed, to bless his son and release him to move on with his life. I found myself crying as I recognized that all my life I had waited too long for the church to bless me.

Although this official loosing of people for ministry is important, there comes a time when one must accept God's blessing and give a blessing to one's own life, to use Erik Erikson's words. I had to bless my life because God's blessing was on it. I had waited too long to acknowledge I had been freed by the Spirit of God to serve Christ and the church. Until I willingly named my gift and made myself responsible to God for it, I would never wear shoes. I would always blame someone for having to wear Schlorre. That was an "Aha!" experience I wish had come earlier. I have written more about this in *Bless Me Too, My Father: Living by Choice, Not Default*.

Now as I move into the last decades of my life, I struggle with the compulsion to speak out in opposition to my own need to keep life more evenly spaced and paced because of the diminishments of aging. I see more mellowness, but I also am more aware of the tremendous responsibility of the wordsmith and word-warrior in an information age. When readers write me in appreciation of words I have written or show me a book heavily underlined, I stand humbled, but I am also afraid. Are these true words I write?

So what is next? I want to keep walking in my writer's shoes. I want to keep making the truth of God's love great with as much wonder and joy as I am able to bring to it. And I want to help young people find their calling to get out of their Schlorre into real shoes.

CHAPTER 15

Confessions of a
woman ~~preacher~~, no, *speaker*

Have faith that words last longer than the moment in which they are uttered, that the other person will still sometimes come back to them, that they will sometimes still examine your arguments and their own.
—Mieczylaw Malinski

As I sat on the church platform about to give a talk (I never called it a sermon even if it was Sunday morning at 11 a.m.), I asked myself what I was supposed to do until then. I had seen preachers, head bowed, Bible open, obviously in deep communion with God before they rose to preach the Word. I had seen some bounce up the steps to the platform ready with a joke. Still others stalked to the pulpit solemnly to begin with a thunderous prayer. Should I use men as my models? Or find my own way as a woman speaker?

I always wanted to be a writer. I never considered becoming a speaker, let alone a preacher. "Woman speaker" was an oxymoron. Public speaking moved into my life slowly, like the early morning fog lifting. I accepted first one invitation, then another, always amazed that anyone would want to listen to my stumbling words. Speaking extemporaneously was not my forte. I had to seek each word, fearful I might speak in error.

Did I even belong behind a pulpit? I had seen missionary women give reports standing to one side of the pulpit, one hand gently holding onto it, letting the congregation know they knew they did not belong behind the sacred desk.

And then I had to deal with the pulpits themselves, all built for good-sized men. Some were too tall, some too flimsy, some just a music stand, so I avoided leaning on them. Some had an odd shape, like the outspread wings of an airplane with a deep trough in the middle, causing my notes and Bible to drift to the center. Another kind without a front ledge sent my notes sliding to the floor. With trifocals I was not always able to find my place in my notes. Once the metal buttons on my suit coat rattled the microphone every time I moved my arms. People may have wondered why I stood there like a soldier at attention.

But there before me sat an audience looking up at me, expecting me to say something. I didn't know what to sound like. Should I thunder like Tony Campolo (if I could) and strike the pulpit for emphasis (if I dared) or speak in modulated tones like a therapist (if I knew how)?

My travel speaking experiences didn't take off until the children had left home or were attending college. The time away from teaching or home duties was always a main consideration. If the entire trip could fit into a short weekend, I considered it.

In the early years I sometimes lugged half my library along on the assumption I would have time to prepare en route or at my destination. I had watched men lugging over-packed attaché cases. One day the man sitting beside me in the plane opened his, and I glimpsed only underwear and shaving equipment in it. But it looked expensive and full of important files from the outside. From then on I left the books behind. I slimmed down to a few file folders, an outfit I could comfortably wear for two or three days if my baggage didn't make it (this happened several times), and personal items. Often if a man picked me up, he insisted on carrying my briefcase while I gently insisted I would carry it. I and my speech were not soon parted.

Never having taken a homiletics course or even public speaking, I learned by trial and error. I had only one chance in speaking. I could revise an article as often as I wished. Readers could return to an article to reread it. Writing and speaking are dialects of the same language. The spoken word should not sound as if it was written to be read. Writing uses different ways to emphasize—punctuation, sentence structure, choice of diction. I listened to political speakers to find out what techniques made them effective—repetition of words and phrases, parallelism, short sentences, emphasized words, pauses. I learned to memorize my opening words with my head up, eyes on the whole audience. If I had a good time, I knew my audience would also. I found it was important to go with the flow. At one morning service the flow included so many preliminaries it was time to quit when I began. I should have prayed and said, "That's all, folks!" The congregation would have blessed me.

One of the first times I gave a public talk, I felt satisfied with my presentation and was sure the woman barreling her way down the center aisle toward me was going to commend me for the pearls of wisdom that had fallen from my lips. Instead she blurted: "Katie, where did you get your dress? Or did you make it? Where can I get the pattern?" So much for thinking my words had lasting effect.

After the opening session of an Elder Hostel in a neighboring state, a woman told me she had heard me speak a number of years ago at a women's retreat. "I don't remember a thing you said except for one joke," she gushed. What was this unforgettable joke?

Decades ago in the horse and buggy days, a farmer and his wife were producing baby after baby and didn't know how to stop the process. They agreed the husband would drive to town to discuss their concern with the doctor while she waited at home with the children.

Hours later she heard the horse and buggy clip-clopping down the lane. "What did the doctor say?" the wife asked impatiently.

The husband hesitated a minute before he replied, "He said I should go sleep in the barn."

The wife thought for a moment before replying, "Well, if that helps, I'll go sleep there also."

I had told that story?

At a book signing breakfast I took my designated seat toward the front to realize all eyes were turned to another author gliding into the room wearing layers of flowing pink chiffon trimmed with gold ruffles, hair piled high, and strumming an autoharp. No one had told me this was a dress-up affair.

In a northern state I was told to meet four men, not Mennonites, at the baggage claim area in the airport to travel by limo to the outlying community for the workshop. They had been told to watch for a "Mennonite" woman. I'm not sure what they had in mind, but when I showed up in my usual pantsuit carrying a Gloria Steinem MS tote bag, they weren't convinced I was the right woman. In Wyoming, I arrived at Laramie to find the airline to my next airport had gone bankrupt. In Colorado the driver drove through a fierce whiteout, quite unconcerned, while I clung to the sides of the Jeep hoping the deep snow alongside would not be my final resting place.

In Bellingham, Washington, I arrived at the airport to find no welcoming person to drive me to Abbotsford, British Columbia, across the border to a Mennonite Central Committee Arts Celebration. The MCC offices were closed and I had no other numbers. I hitched a ride with strangers to Abbotsford, where I phoned relatives and left a message on the answering machine of MCC headquarters to let my hosts know I had arrived. Everyone thought someone else was picking me up.

Another time when I was in frigid Manitoba for a fall Sunday school convention, a friend offered to drive me from Winnipeg to Steinbach, a distance of fifty or sixty miles. Before we left she commented that her car needed new tires. On our way home late after the evening service, one tire blew and we chugged to a slow stop. The air was bitterly cold and I was not wearing Canadian winter clothing.

Almost immediately a large semi-truck pulled up behind us. The driver jumped out of his cab. He was a short, heavy set man with a bull neck and too much belly fat, wearing a too-short shirt and too-low pants. A small black toque topped the untidy dark hair on his small head. I admit to some terror. But he was all warmth. He checked the spare to find it was also flat. Next he drove us about twenty miles into Winnipeg to buy new tires, returned, and put them on the rims. Good Samaritans come dressed in various garbs and body shapes.

In Pennsylvania I stepped off the train at a flag stop and could find no familiar face. The sun had set. I longed for a safe well-lit depot to wait in. But I stationed myself bravely near the dark overpass with my suitcase close beside me until a policeman spotted me and encouraged me to move a few blocks into the nearby town. Not a safe area, he said. I moved closer to the well-lit business area where the person designated to pick me up found me.

In Ohio after picking me up at the Cincinnati airport my hostess drove to the designated church in an outlying community to find it empty. We checked our correspondence and brochures. A maintenance man told us the meeting had been relocated ten miles away to accommodate the expected crowds. Someone forgot to tell us.

Sometimes the problem was mine, all mine. I am directionally challenged. I've gotten lost in huge buildings where every hallway looks the same, while driving to a rural church in Kansas, while trying to find my way to my cabin in a large conference center in total darkness.

I always asked for a mike but sometimes didn't get one. "Can everyone hear?" the emcee would boom out. Of course heads nodded, but when I started speaking, they shouted for me to speak louder—and louder. One time, the meeting stopped while someone brought a public address system. Even then sometimes in a large auditorium the speaker system was inadequate for the size of the room. "I couldn't hear a thing you said," was the comforting comment when I had been shouting as loudly as possible. Early public address systems were not made for people with soft voices.

I never knew what inviting committees expected of me. Were they expecting an Aimee Semple McPherson who would wow 'em with exuberant oratory and then have to make do with an ordinary woman? At one meeting I removed the obligatory corsage I always was given in the early years and sat down with a group of women at lunch after I had spoken. One woman smiled warmly and asked, "Are you a visitor here today? Tell us your name and where you are from." I had been too ordinary.

Where would I be staying? Most of my hostesses were kind, generous, and friendly. In one home I waited in the living room for my hostess to arrive. One by one three young sons came home from school and stepped into the living room to introduce themselves and shake my hand. I was impressed.

I also remember the home in which husband and wife were not on speaking terms and used a child to convey messages to one another. I watched another hostess carefully measure out two scant six-ounce cups of water for morning coffee—one for her and one for me. No more. As she shut off the coffee maker I thought about the three or more cups of tea I usually drink for breakfast.

The husband of one hostess clearly thought I didn't merit his attention. We ate our evening meal while he had one eye on the TV and a radio on his lap to not miss any action in the football game. Another woman told me she invited widows only when her husband wasn't home because she wasn't an interesting person. I understood from her words I didn't deserve an interesting person. In another home I turned on the bathroom faucet to have the showerhead explode full force on my head, and I hadn't brought a hair dryer. Another time my hair spray can leaked over my skirt in my suitcase and I spent the weekend knocking my knees against a huge stiff shield with each step.

Beds varied from place to place, but I remember clearly a few nights I nearly froze, once because I didn't recognize I was sleeping under an electric blanket. I doubt hostesses knew that heat turned on in a room only an hour before I arrived in the middle of winter meant I slept on a block of ice all night. It takes a good six to eight hours to warm a spring-filled mattress.

I usually asked for a single room only to find several times that because beds were limited, I was partnered with a woman who snored loudly all night.

Some hostesses thought they had to entertain me every minute of the day when I wanted silence and solitude. I learned why guest speakers prefer motels. People ask the same questions again and again. I don't mind talking about my family but I also like to discuss ideas. One woman wanted to know if I was nervous before I spoke. Would she have asked a man that? Another found it hard to understand that I worked in my home office most mornings in summer. "You mean your office at the college." "No, at home," I replied. "I begin work at 8:30 and work until noon at my desk at home." She looked perplexed. Good Christian women began the day in the kitchen scrubbing the kitchen sink, not in an office.

Yet other times, with the right group of women, we talked into the early morning hours sharing concerns and joys. One pastor explained how her mother laid out her position against women's ordination—at her ordination. Another pastor told us how her mother had asked her in deep pain, "What do I tell my friends about your ordination?" The shame at her forwardness in receiving ordination was too great for her to bear.

These women mentioned fear of congregations having a woman pastor because she might preside at their funeral and comfort a grieving husband. I learned about different modes of worship—not all followed the traditional pattern of hymn, Scripture, and prayer. At one gathering, a Quaker woman said she felt uncomfortable calling that worship or even a devotional. Yet I knew I felt uncomfortable if a service started without prayer.

Many Sunday evenings I came home late to a dark, cold house. I was tired. I lugged my suitcase into the house, sometimes heavier than when I had started out. I carried home plant cuttings, Lebanon bologna, corn on the cob, books, brochures, lemons, oranges. The mail had piled up. The dryer was still broken. The lawn was standing knee-high.

But it was worth all the discomfort and weariness. Why did I continue? You come alive as a middle-aged person when you are convinced that the range of possibilities is not fixed by tradition, that you are capable of more. But how to convey that encouragement to growth?

After one widows' retreat, the image of the women present that I took home with me haunted me for days. They resembled cardboard figures made by an amateur, stuck in place by tradition, unable to create new lives. I had tried to convey the idea that I was no longer a widow. Legally I might be but emotionally I was now single. There was life after being widowed. Their questions told me that idea was difficult to wrap their minds around. They thought they had been condemned to being set aside for the rest of their lives.

I learned that women need open-minded pastors to give women opportunity to speak. I came across many leaders who said, "Katie, come share what you are thinking these days." Women are rejected for ministry because many people have never seen them in active ministry. My early roles models were pioneers Ruth Brunk Stolzfus, Lois Clemens, and Ella Mae Miller of the then-(Old) Mennonite Church. I traveled around the country to allow men, women, and children to see a woman in ministry with all her flaws and follies as well as strengths.

On one occasion this modeling happened unwittingly. I had come to Pennyslvania to speak at the annual Women's Missionary Service meeting of one of the more conservative conferences merged that year with the annual church conference assembly. When I arrived I found I would be giving the main sermon of the day standing behind the powerful revivalist George Brunk's pulpit in his huge tent extending from his large trailer. He was strongly opposed to women preachers. I gulped and plowed ahead with my sermon, hoping the spirit of the great preacher would not swat down every word as soon as it left my mouth. The WMS had been given permission to select the speaker on this day which coincided with some celebration they were promoting.

I had asked for help from the executive of the Mennonite Brethren Board of Missions and Services with planning my itinerary in India. I was flatly turned down. I was puzzled. Later I found out from one of the mission board executives that the main objection to my attending the All-India Mennonite Women's Conference in 1978 was that it was not evangelical enough. Always that concern.

In India at the close of one large evangelical church conference, John Richards, national pastor, asked me to pray. For a moment I felt stunned. Didn't he know women in America are not asked to bless the assembly at the close of big gatherings? This is a tribute given to the most respected experienced leader present—not to lesser persons like myself. I went forward and prayed as the Spirit led me. When I returned to my seat my missionary friend's eyes were moist with tears. "You blessed my soul." Why in India and not in America? In the fifteen years I have been a member of the Mennonite Brethren church in Wichita, I have been asked to speak to the congregation once.

In 1987 under pressure to be more progressive in their views regarding women's ministry, the executive of the General Conference of Mennonite Brethren Churches asked me to be one of the speakers. Always these main addresses had been called "sermons," but this year they were termed "devotionals" even if forty-five minutes long. Still it was movement.

Other groups made up for my own church body's lack of affirmation. A memorable occasion took place at a women's retreat in British Columbia. In an impromptu moment, the women at one session laid hands on me and blessed me when they discovered my church had never done that for me. I traveled home rejoicing.

Over the years I realized how church women were growing in spirit and mind and in their teaching and leadership. They had great gifts; they only needed experience and opportunity. Devotionals, those darlings of women's circles, changed from gentle little readings from *Chicken Soup for the Soul* to more independent thinking. Women were becoming more involved in church work, locally and nationally. Once coming home to Wichita, at the baggage carousel, I noticed we were four women from different Mennonite branches who had all been away in some kind of ministry.

I always expected to have my expenses paid, even if the inviting group had no money for an honorarium. In Florida when I presented my expense sheet the committee admitted they didn't have enough to pay my airline fare. They hadn't checked fares beforehand. "Always get a contract," said my practical daughter. Once when I had a contract for travel and honorarium to speak at a large retirement center event in a huge Canadian city, the expected check didn't come, week after week, even though I wrote several letters. When my complaint reached board level, I was sent a check for three times the amount I requested. They apologized without explanation.

The payment I valued most was not money but notes of appreciation. I was disappointed when the week after I returned home I received only a check in an envelope from the treasurer. I had expended time and energy, but for some this was just a business transaction. At a large national older adult conference with many speakers and workshop leaders, I sensed it was truly a business proposition. I flew in one day and out the next to keep expenses down. Several standing ovations over the years at various places kept me going for weeks thereafter.

I learned why preachers quit. Some keep speaking after the source is exhausted. Sometimes I offered dry crumbs from that empty place. On the other hand, I asked myself, as probably many public speakers have, at what point do you overstep integrity when you realize you have the power to move a crowd to tears or laughter and you milk that source just to hear applause?

After a presentation on aging in Goshen at which I had read my prayer-poem from *Prayers of an Omega,* "I sure liked to drive my car," a woman told me that the man next to her had cried. He had just given up his license to drive. Several times I felt the hush in the audience when I told the story of how my father had found my mother's parents and siblings lost in the Russian

Revolution. What a tremendous responsibility was mine. But sometimes I felt my words were dry leaves tossed into the breeze.

I learned that people responded differently to what they heard according to their own experience. At one workshop I had stated that older people can change. In the discussion period, one woman denied that statement. Older people remained static. "Then why are you at this workshop?" I asked her. At another on widowhood I admitted to often being lonely. A widow nixed my comments by sharing she had overcome her grief after six months and remarried. Loneliness was for the birds.

At Chambersburg, Pennsylvania, where I had a series of eight speaking engagements in 2007, God answered my prayers for physical and spiritual strength beyond expectations, for I was recovering from surgery. I felt as if I had been carried on angel's wings throughout my days there. I thanked God for his mercies.

Public speaking has not been my choice but God's choice for me. May God forgive me for words I misspoke. May his name be glorified through words I uttered in good faith. Public speaking has been a stretching experience.

CHAPTER 16

Into the arena of change

The modern woman must choose, for the vistas of life have opened for woman with a startling and often overwhelming rapidity.
—Argye Briggs

Beginning about the 1960s our society found itself amid a massive human potential movement. The thrust of it was that each person, man or woman, was entitled to and should develop his or her personal potential to the utmost. This human potential movement forced changes in all women's roles, church as well as society. Young women welcomed birth control with the introduction of the Pill and moved steadily into the work force, despite the misgivings of some. I was pushed into the boxer's ring by my husband's death in 1962.

In some religious settings, self-actualization for a woman was portrayed as a secular goal. A Mennonite woman's goals, always spiritual, were expected to be modesty, submission, humility—and yes, silence, especially in church settings, certainly not self-actualization. Her place was in life's private areas, the men's in the public world. Moving into the world outside the home to work, to exert influence as an individual, was stepping too close to the line. It forebode disaster in relationships. But I was now alone. I had no husband who would be affected by my inner and outer adjustments. I had to change to survive.

During the Fifties and Sixties motherhood was enshrined as the great calling of all women as Rosie the Riveters returned to the home from factories and offices after the military left their war duties. Mothers were encouraged to use all their time and energy in fulfilling their mothering role. Christian mothers aimed to become the"Super Christian Mom," which sometimes meant "smothering" children. The bad word during that decade was "momism" coined by Philip Wylie in *A Generation of Vipers*. Because of their over-possessiveness of children and emasculation of men, he blamed moms for nearly all the social and psychological ills of the world.

In the decades after World War II, stay-at-home moms (and there weren't many of the other kind) were encouraged to clean, polish, and launder with a different product for each task. I had extra time after I finished my housecleaning duties, but that extra time, according to current popular thinking, should be used in the home in some way, cleaning and re-cleaning and re-laundering something even if it wasn't dirty.

When we lived in Hepburn, I re-polished the floors on Monday even if I had waxed and polished them on Saturday. Someone might come to the house and see scuff marks. There were standards to maintain. Respectability was the keyword, upheld by sentimental actions rather than sacrificial love. Betty Friedan attacked this issue strongly in *The Feminine Mystique*, a writing that affected me deeply.

I only saw years later how this drift toward gentle niceness that dominated the Silent Fifties was being countered by the women's movement and strengthened by the human potential movement. The era of the commercial greeting card had begun. I saw a society drowning in greeting-card sentimentality and dying for real relationships. You could be sentimental safely at no personal cost, no misunderstanding, no risk of rejection if you sent a card with someone else's carefully crafted words above your signature. Now with an e-card you can do it even more simply, cheaply, and impersonally.

As women gradually moved into the work force, they had less time for church volunteer work. Attending another meeting after a long day's work for the sake of keeping a nearly outdated organization going seemed too great a sacrifice. Mostly gray-haired women were supporting church circle meetings, women's traditional main avenue of church service. During these years I heard women respond too often to "What do you do?" with "I'm just a housewife." They had difficulty valuing their lives and their work in light of this human potential movement. A friend reminded me that in the 1960s I had told a class of women that marriage and parenting should be a calling, not just something they drifted into because of their hormones. She had never forgotten that.

Women of the church, as I knew them, did not take their responsibility in home and church lightly. But to decide whether it was God's will to remain at home or to go to work to ease the financial burden on the husband was the biggie. Absentee fathers were acceptable, but absentee mothers were not. Could you be a good mother and work outside the home? This question was settled for me when Walter died. If people had commended stay-at-home moms at one time, now they commended me for being able to support a family of four children by working as an editorial assistant at the MB Publishing House. That incongruity bothered me.

As the women's movement gained strength, women's organizations, whether loosely structured or more organized, struggled to stay alive. They were old-fashioned according to women in the new fast-growing women's movement. In 1962, when I began my column "Women and the Church" for *The Christian Leader,* readers thought I had answers. As mentioned earlier, women's leaders wrote me for material for programs, devotionals, and organizational helps. I had little to offer except personal experience, observation, and reading. This new thing happening to women of the church had me asking questions also.

When I first spoke to groups, I wanted to roar like a lion of the forest. I was convinced I had something to say. Other times, I felt like a timid mouse unable to find the hole to her nest as I encouraged women to rethink their role in today's world as servants of Christ. The idea was too new to me. Society was telling us to be pretty, be nice, look young. Don't think too deeply, avoid serious issues. Don't show yourself as anything less than adequate. Always appear to be the abundant Christian, over-flowing, never hurting, never insufficient for the moment, never a real woman who bleeds. My widowhood experiences had shown me how much of what people saw as important to life was actually chaff. Inwardly I was bleeding, but at first I could not find words or voice to describe my need.

As I studied women's roles during the 1960s and corresponded with readers, I sensed tremendous tensions developing in some. A big one was trying to figure out who got the most of them—the church and its organizations or the home. They wanted to be a good wife and mother, but they also wanted to serve in the church, now beginning to open its doors to them just a bit. I recall that tension in myself before Walter died and even more so after he was gone. My family needed me, and I enjoyed taking care of them, but it was also fulfilling to be together with adult women after a day wiping noses and changing diapers and talking only to people three feet and under. Yet one didn't dare admit to such a longing. A mother lived solely for her family. Mother's Day was an important celebration in church life where women were identified by motherhood.

If women's roles were changing, so was church life as churches were drawn into the exciting new methods of marketing the gospel. The life of real service and witness was posed as belonging to the sphere of the church building. The church was the building. No one said it that bluntly, but as I worked at the Publishing House, reading dozens of church bulletins weekly to glean for news, I noticed most of them had a picture of the church edifice on the front cover, reinforcing this idea.

During this period invitations to serve usually included going to that building to meetings, suppers, Sunday school, teacher training sessions, workshops, conferences, sewing circles, and much more. All else didn't seem quite as blessed of God. The call to serve in the church was a new frontier, especially on boards and committees as mobility and communication methods increased. This was the time when church boards and committees proliferated. Ad hoc committees, standing committees, boards—every congregation had zillions of them and was developing more. Some people spent more time evenings in the church building than at home. Women and men needed the official sanction of a church board or committee to tell them what to do before they could say "This is the Lord's work." A few women were being elected or appointed to developing committees, sometimes amid great conflict. The path ahead was murky.

Even today some people cannot give money to a needy person as a gift to the Lord unless they get a tax receipt for it. It isn't an official work done to the Lord if it hasn't got a piece of paper and a signature attached to it. Others have difficulty using their spiritual gifts unless it is under the auspices of a church board and gets noticed in the church newsletter or annual report. It is freeing to be able to give a gift to a poor person or an organization that doesn't send back a receipt, only a thank-you note.

While living in Hepburn, where Walter was the pastor, I argued with myself whether I could be satisfied to stay home polishing and cleaning what already gleamed and shone or should I move into a larger arena to add my voice to the battle against sin and evil. Although I invested much creative energy in my children and their well-being, another hunger remained. And the church said it shouldn't be there. That troubled me for I seemed to be going against God if I was thinking of self-development. A woman's role was established by her biology. Could God even use an ordinary woman like me from a very lowly immigrant background in anything else besides homemaking?

Should I be a traditional Mennonite woman like Martha, cooking and serving, or find my way as a Mary? I can't count the many sermons preached during the early years of the burgeoning women's movement with the male preacher always coming down heaviest on the side of Martha. Some women, uncomfortable with the invitation to add a little of Mary to their lives, endorsed his statements and defended Martha by saying they could still pray as they cooked, sewed, and vacuumed. If the church didn't have Martha's, who would feed the congregation at weddings, funerals, relief sales, and church suppers? One or two Mary's was okay, but what if most women decided to become like her and sit at the feet of Jesus? The church needed more Martha's than Mary's.

Writer Gail Ransome argues that she saw women preferring to stay in the kitchen like Martha rather "than face each other as merely human, fully present, ready to be touched, changed, moved by the presence of another, by the presence of the incarnate God." The difficulty during the height of the women's movement was that the church lacked models showing how men and women could function together in the church, serving one another with love, mutual submission, and understanding. Martha's were clearly visible, Mary's were few. Their memory bank lacked images of women serving in non-traditional ways.

J. B. Toews, then executive secretary for the Mennonite Brethren Board of Foreign Missions, traveled all over the MB constituency in the 1960s, often speaking to women's groups, urging their support for missions while steering them away from Martha-type projects, like sending barrels of finished clothes overseas, and toward donating money. Missionaries overseas were finding they could buy materials more cheaply close at hand than have missionary societies make clothing and ship it to them. But faithful church women, especially the older ones, needed something to do with their hands—their greatest gift heretofore. They were accustomed to being Martha's. Their conditioning had told them that hands could do more than minds and spirits. Hands brought about quick visible results.

Well then, if the women's circles couldn't help the poor overseas in traditional ways, what about the poor in the community? I heard of one group in a neighboring community who rallied to the call to help a poor family at Christmas. They brought together eleven dolls and dozens of cookies. Another circle rose to the need by donating fifty-three nighties for one new needy baby. Women's groups were looking for direction. They had zeal. They had money. They had energy but lacked direction. Fortunately, that has changed in most women's organizations, but at the time something seemed wrong to me that, having lost a project, these women's organizations also lost their purpose. No new projects appeared on the horizon that fully involved the gifts and talents of the majority of women.

For a time the emphasis in women's organizations shifted to having what even today is termed a "program" to attract younger women to come. Sometimes I was pressured to be that program when someone had reneged. "We have to have a speaker," pled the caller. Anyone would do to fill the slot on the program. "You can speak on any subject you want." My suggestion to spend time talking to one another was met with dismay.

Sometimes I accepted a Mother's Day tea engagement or similar event to find it had become a major production with frills, doilies, place cards, and flowers and the food as fancy as the human mind could concoct. Women were looking for avenues for their creativity. When asked to speak to such groups, I floundered. How could I speak about Jesus' ministry to the poor and downtrodden when one long wall in the home where the meeting was being held proudly displayed an immense collection of silverware and gold plate and another wall a sparkling array of crystal and china? And the hostess, with hawk eyes, watched over us women for spills as we carefully ate our salad luncheon from bone china plates on our laps. My timid words fell onto the deep rug without indentation.

With growing affluence after the war, consumerism, like the traditional camel in the tent, put one foot in the door and never left. Consumer goods were filling the store shelves again in the years after the war after years of doing without. Garage sales followed soon after to become a symptom of the times. When houses became stuffed too full, the owners shoveled it out the garage door by means of a sale.

Over the years I have struggled to see the Christian life as a temporary pilgrimage on this earth. I saw too many women, including myself, getting a high shopping when they found a huge bargain for something they didn't need because they were not challenged to use their gifts.

For a while in the 1960s and beyond, Mennonite publications pushed the concept of simplicity. The late Doris Longacre set a great example by editing that popular cookbook *More with Less*. At Mennonite Central Committee meetings I saw her bring her own mug to avoid using a disposable one. I admired her conviction and worked at a simpler lifestyle the next decades with varying degrees of success. My early topics when I spoke to groups included the home, personal spiritual life, prayer, women of the Bible, but also establishing priorities as a woman. I used the title "Sugar and Spice or Salt and Light."

In November 2005, I felt freer than I had in years when I moved from my large duplex to a small apartment and gave at least a third to a half of my belongings, including an antique bedroom set, to thrift shops rather than having a yard sale. My mother had always been a great example in this. When she no longer had room for something, she gave it to whoever happened to come by at the time, whether it was a grandchild, cleaning lady, or neighbor. It was a way of life for her. I encourage people to give rather than nickel-and-dime their time through several days of garage sales.

Keeping organizations going during a time of change frequently became a burden to leaders when volunteers didn't step up as freely as hoped. The result was a careful watching of others to make sure each one bore her share of the burden by making lists of who would do what. This was the Martha approach, the sister who came to Jesus asking him to set matters straight. "Lord, look what I'm doing for you. Make Mary help me. Why doesn't she take her turn in making a meal for a sick person?"

All women were expected to make chicken casseroles and sew layettes with little regard for the individual gifts of the Spirit—of heart, money, prayer, mind, and hands. The result of years of thinking through these concerns was my book *Bless Me Too, My Father: Living by Choice, Not Default*. It deals with issues I faced in my sixties in finding my own gifts rather than falling in line to acquire the gifts expected of all women.

Jesus freed women to discover that women can set aside chores and discover the wonders of mind and spirit. They have the right to dream spiritual dreams. The right and the privilege of being a homemaker should not be in conflict with these dreams. It is not a matter of doing or not doing housework or of good parenting, but of valuing the spiritual over the material, relationships over things—always deliberately choosing.

This truth became a great breakthrough for me: It is important to choose. For years I had struggled with how to know the will of God, experimenting with fleeces and all sorts of other formulas to force God to a showdown. Now it became clear. After bringing the matter to God in prayer and researching the options, the important thing was to choose, not wait for God's big hand to push me his appointed way.

From there it was a short step to recognize that each one, male and female, had been given a gift, a grace gift, our due portion of Christ's bounty. And it was possible to name this gift, just like we can name a tool. A carpenter knows he is using a saw, not a level. A violinist knows she is playing a violin, not a drum. A cook knows he is using a mixing bowl, not a skillet. Many Christians had great zeal to build the kingdom of God but had nothing to build it with except good feelings and intentions. They didn't know their gift.

For years I encouraged women to recognize God had given them a gift—giving, encouragement, hospitality, evangelism, helps, caring, listening, knowledge, teaching, leadership, celibacy. Their task was to discover that gift and risk using it. The world was opening up to women. Why were we holding back? Some men were more ready to open doors to service than women were willing to enter. Today I rejoice to see women using individual gifts instead of falling into identical patterns.

Even as I did more speaking, I recognized I had lived too much of my life with fear—fear of what people would think of me. I was sure they were expecting someone important like Elizabeth Elliott or Becky Pippert. If I spoke, what if a real expert sat before me in the audience? Sometimes one did. To be effective I would have to let people see me as I was—at times discouraged, irritable; other times joyful and full of faith, not always brimming with wisdom. One wonderful day I realized I didn't have to worry about the flops, the criticism, as long as I had been faithful.

Some women countered my new boldness with statements like "That's okay for you, Katie. You are naturally outgoing. For me to admit to having received a gift from the Holy Spirit collides with my Mennonite upbringing, which urges modesty and self-effacement." I understood that.

Women at the time fought a history of being considered as less than whole persons. Under English common law women were civilly dead with no right to property, wages, or inheritance. In Europe, women were burned at the stake for seeking relief from the pain of childbirth. In early American history women were forbidden to learn to write out of fear that they might forge their husband's name to a legal document. If they studied geography, they would leave the family. In America married women couldn't own their own property. The right to vote did not come until 1920. In many Mennonite Brethren congregations women did not vote until well into the 1970s.

Over time the roles and organizational structures of women in church and society changed as well as recognition of their gifts. As they became more aware of the possibilities, they accepted more responsibility in community and church. Women working outside the home was no longer the big issue I faced when I started working in the 1960s, but an individual decision. The focus of women's organizations shifted to poverty and hunger, family problems, and social injustices in addition to missions and evangelism. With these changes my speaking emphasis shifted from women and their organizations to writers workshops, study conferences, church history, and later to older adult issues. I felt more comfortable with the years as I found my voice in areas other than women's concerns. I reflected this shift with a change in the title of my *Christian Leader* column to "Viewpoint" and gained a new reading audience.

CHAPTER 17

My long day's journey into the women's movement

If a man does not keep pace with his companions, perhaps it is be-cause he hears a different drummer. Let him step to the music he hears, however measured or far away.
—Henry David Thoreau

As a child I knew that women who felt called by God to a spiritual ministry had to go overseas. The church in America had no place for them. The MB church ordained women for service overseas since its beginnings in the late 1800s but not for service in the homeland, something I found strange. But even that ordination was rescinded in 1957 for some reason I never understood. A single woman who felt called to serve the church in America could achieve her goal only by marrying a minister.

In the General Conference Mennonite Church in the early 1900s, David Goerz, a man with insight and vision, recogniz-ing the plight of women with a spiritual calling but no opportu-nity to fulfill it, established a deaconess school for single women who wanted to serve the church at home and abroad. The school was patterned after the Lutheran deaconess movement in Germany with a mother-house and sisterhood. The first leader of this school was the dauntless Sister Frieda Kauffman. (See my book, *Our Lamps Were Lit: An Informal History of the Bethel Deaconess School of Nursing.*)

Some women saw the women's movement challenging motherhood and threatening their long established place in the private sphere. How could any woman break the long line of women who remained true to traditional ways to serve God? How dare she? To kneel alongside Mary at the feet of Jesus, to stand beside Priscilla and the daughters of Philip to prophesy, or to stride alongside the women hurrying away from the tomb commanded by the angel to "go tell" was not intended for this generation's women. Staying out of the public fray shielded them from being troubled, or tempted, by non-traditional ways about serving God.

As I continued writing about women's concerns, I sensed women were reluctant to expand their ministry into new aspects of church life, especially leadership roles, even as the church rapidly changed in the latter third of the twentieth century. They had accepted that a woman's role was to be subordinate, submissive, silent, working alongside the men or from behind the scenes. Furthermore, they were inexperienced, fearful, and uncertain about stepping outside long-held views of women's roles even though they knew they had a contribution to make.

Because women seldom participated in real church decisions, they couldn't see the big picture of what was taking place in church and conference and where they might fit in. Such negotiating skills are not achieved overnight, and women, who at forty and fifty, even sixty, were beginning church committee work in the 1960s and 1970s, were kindergartners compared to men the same age with twenty to thirty years of experience behind them. Even a young man elected to some position as a representative of young adults had the edge over most women. He knew that as a male he was entitled to a position of leadership. His identity as a man was connected to being at the head.

Over my decades of observing church life, I find Mennonite Brethren have usually dealt with the issue of women's roles reluctantly, often with great pain and discomfort on the part of all concerned, because it is enmeshed in firmly entrenched cultural mores. We are not a church that has learned to deal gracefully with conflict. Over the years I heard slowly increasing comments from women about the neglect of their spiritual gifts in the church. In private, I heard a few men speak up supporting women's greater involvement but unable to do so publicly, which made the issue seem to me more like a political than a theological one. The issue was power, not theology.

Yet theology had to be dealt with. Mennonite Brethren have seen themselves as a people of the Book ever since seceding from the mother church in the Ukraine in 1860. Therefore, any discussion about women's roles has always started with Bible passages like the Genesis record of creation or Paul's admonition in 1 Timothy 2 for women to keep silent in the churches. The interpretations of such texts have always been literal. Even after examining other passages, these two passages have been the arbiters in the matter. For example, in 1973 the Faith and Life Commission chairman of the Southern District MB Conference wrote to the district leaders sharing conference concerns that it might violate Scripture to nominate women to the Faith and Life Commission as well as the Church Extension and Evangelism Commission. But was that really the root problem? Which Scripture would it violate?

My own stance was that this theological discussion should take place at the grassroots level where fear of women's greater participation resided in both men and women. Lodging the dialogue in the highest echelons of church hierarchy meant that only men made decisions about women's well-being. At a Hillsboro MB Church council meeting in the late 1980s, of which I was then the only woman member, I heard that widows were concerned the appointment of a woman to the diaconate would restrict them even more to the company of only women. They preferred the husband/wife team concept. Women enjoyed the ministry of men and the company of men. However valid their response ("because I am more comfortable this way") it was not a theological but a personal and social response.

Church statements produced in the 1970s and 1980s included grand phrases such as "all believers have spiritual gifts which they should use"—only to be refuted by another coming soon thereafter that women should not be appointed as lead pastors. I argued that to have integrity the earlier statement should say that all believers have gifts and that if a woman believes God has called her to the pastorate, she has misinterpreted the call. She should be counseled to suppress it, even deny it, because God does not give this gift to a woman. That never happened.

In her autobiography *God's Hand Over My Nineteen Years in China*, which I shortened into a small booklet early in my writing career, Paulina Foote, her heart set on missions in China, asked church leaders in Oklahoma for freedom to preach in China. Her MB conscience told her that women don't preach. She had been accepted by the mission board. At her ordination in 1922, the ordaining minister gave her freedom to preach. "Go tell," he admonished her, using as his text Gospel passages in which Jesus told the women at the tomb to tell others what they had seen. In China she preached and wrote home about her ministry. If only all women had such gumption.By the 1970s few ministers had this freedom to charge women to "preach it, sister."

My own personal journey as a woman in ministry in the Mennonite community has been a never-ending roller-coaster ride, yet here I am, not where I began but on a much surer level. It took a while before I realized I was part of something much bigger than my little thoughts, an idea whose time had come, even as it had been coming, off and on, for centuries. I think of it as wispy spider webs floating in the atmosphere, pulled together first by one person, then another, until a strong fabric results.

At first my journey was lonely because I thought I was walking it alone—therefore there must be something wrong with me. I was a misfit. I felt God's call to a spiritual ministry, but the doors swung shut just when I reached what looked like an opportunity. I have mentioned several of these doors in earlier chapters. At nineteen I was elected leader of our young adult group only to be told two weeks later by the church council that was unscriptural. In Kitchener I offered to teach a mothers' class only to be told women were not to teach. Let these examples suffice.

Why was I misinterpreting God's voice consistently? Why were women encouraged to live vicariously through husband and children even after the children were grown or their husbands might have died? How often I heard that wives were to ask husbands about church decisions. Church polity was not their realm. But what about all of the husbandless women, widowed, single, and divorced?

As the women's movement gained momentum, so did the backlash. Its proponents argued that women wanted to be the same as men, thereby destroying gender differences. I have yet to meet a woman who wanted to be a man.

As I read Betty Friedan's *The Feminine Mystique* in the 1960s, I couldn't believe other women thought the way I did, hundreds of them, maybe even thousands. I wasn't alone in my feelings about being set aside when it came to use of gifts. Other women identified with Friedan's words also, although some Christians saw her words as heresy when she advocated women not be forced to accept a role determined solely by their reproductive organs. Women had minds and creative gifts to offer society besides baby making. I had often pondered why I hid my intellectual achievements after I finished high school. I had won the Governor General's Medal for all Saskatchewan the year I finished Grade 12, but I didn't want anyone to know, especially young men because they didn't want a smart girl friend. Now I understood.

Friedan's observations were fighting words. The postwar years were conservative as men returned from the military or alternative service and women left factories and offices to take up full-time home-making. Though freed of the drudgery of home cleaning by new appliances, standard in every home, some women were desperately unhappy and couldn't understand why. "Career woman" was an oxymoron. Magazines showed the prevailing image of a housewife at that time to be that of a childlike, fluffy sex kitten, content in the world of bedroom and kitchen. No man helped with childcare or housework. When he babysat his children, he was substituting for his wife. That was her job. Motherhood was strongly endorsed as the full-time and only occupation of women after World War II.

I had promised myself as long as my children were small that they would always find me at home when they returned from school. No stranger would ever babysit my children. They would get my full attention. It took years to accept I made a better mother when my own intellectual and creative needs were met. The involuntary enclosure of modern women in the home is not a biblical precept. I studied the ideal woman in Proverbs 30, often held up at the time as a model to mothers, to find a Hebrew woman of many skills and occupations who moved in numerous spheres. She was no stay-at-home mom. Nor were the women who followed Jesus during his years of ministry.

A friend wrote me "Friedan's book has done more for me than I care to broadcast—and only after one reading. I really don't tell anyone about my inward aspirations, doubts, etc.— too many probably think I'm a little nuts already. I'm so glad you're saying something challenging and worth thinking about in all your writing. . . . I sure get sick of continuous small talk."

My first venture into an organized effort to bring clarity to women's roles came in 1973, when I attended the Evangelical Perspectives on Woman's Role and Status Conference sponsored by the Conservative Baptist Theological Seminary in Denver. It brought together an impressive array of theologians, anthropologists, sociologists, psychologists, and numerous opportunities for interaction. As the sessions moved to a close, I sensed the presenters and all audience members were no longer comrades in exploration. The presenters were moving steadily in the direction of greater freedom for women in the church. The sponsors had predetermined a more conservative resolution. Edgy about the outcome, they canceled one last presentation on Jesus and women of the New Testament by Dr. Paul Jewett of Fuller Theological Seminary because his theological position was not in harmony with theirs. They closed the podium to avoid the outcome they didn't want.

I recall that attendees quoted a name new to me then, Bill Gothard. He was a powerful spokesman for the traditional interpretation of Scripture comparing the relationship of men and women to the centuries-old chain of command theory. In brief, God, on top, holds the father who is depicted as a hammer, who comes down on the mother (a chisel), who in turn chips away at the teenager, a diamond in the rough. Individuals in the chain of command are not responsible for those above them—only for those below. Women have no leadership function in this chain. The husband is the head, the one with final word. Always. People flocked by the hundreds to Gothard's seminars.

Another book that had wide reception among conservative evangelicals at the time was *The Total Woman* by Marabel Morgan, whose answer to all marriage conflict was total submission. This included meeting her husband nude, wrapped in plastic film, when he came home from work.

In 1975, I was ready to attend the Evangelical Women's Caucus, held in Washington, D.C., but as a closet feminist. I knew that for many people the word *feminist* was pejorative. Adding "evangelical" or "biblical" didn't make it easier to accept. "Women's libber" was quickly attached to any woman or man with feminist leanings. The gathering, a first for the evangelical Christian community, was basically a time of finding one another as sisters in Christ because of our common concerns.

I came apprehensively, wondering whether I would find a group of raging women libbers, with swinging breasts, hostility toward men etched on their faces. Instead I found gentle but bruised women (and a few men), many of whom wept to be among people who did not judge them. I had entered a huge women's red tent of Old Testament times, a place of rest and spiritual mentoring for women. These women from all denominations had come together to study the biblical basis for Christian feminism, the historical record regarding women's roles, and to reaffirm and explore gifts and lifestyles for all women, including singles.

Of the three hundred women present, about thirty were from Mennonite denominations. The late Herta Funk, a vigorous Mennonite women's leader, called us together for a breakfast meeting. We looked each other in the eyes and knew we shared an undisclosed hurt—often unarticulated even to ourselves. I found myself bonding with women who did not see me as someone out of her mind.

What we had been hearing were half-truths and capsule answers such as "being a wife and mother is the greatest calling of women in the world," or "It's a woman's fault if she feels trapped. If she'd accept her role in life which God intended for her, she'd be happy." Some ministers, such as the late popular Canadian MB preacher and university professor, F. C. Peters, made ex cathedra statements in a letter to the *Mennonite Brethren Herald*, "I also hope that we will not have to discuss the matter again for the next few years." This was in 1975, when the discussion was just beginning. He dismissed the matter as if women were children who could be sent out to play with a giant-sized bottle of detergent and a washing machine.

My friend wrote again: "We generally just see the men's viewpoint in our Christian journals which seems strictly to say, 'Mothers say home.' Just last Sunday on Mother's Day one young man behind the pulpit in eulogizing mothers said that a really Christian mother will not want or need outside interests. Her whole being will be so devoted and fulfilled in meeting the need of her family, she will be completely happy. His young wife had just had her third baby in as many years, and I only hope this male philosophy will sustain her throughout the coming years. It left me wanting to bang my head hopelessly against a wall.

"Personally, I have never had a better winter. Studying and writing papers [for a Ph.D. program] are such a tremendous challenge and so exciting that housework doesn't compare. It has to be done, and I do it uncomplainingly and love to look after my family, but it doesn't absorb me completely. Fortunately I have the kind of family that understands."

I was appointed member of the Mennonite Central Committee Women's Task Force as the Mennonite Brethren representative, but I had no one to report to. No MB board or committee asked for a briefing or accepted responsibility for the issue. The task force's goal was to identify the issues regarding the place of women in Mennonite churches and work toward solutions. I also helped with the *Women's Task Force Report*, a publication discontinued a few years ago, occasionally writing articles. The main benefit of my participation in this task force was learning to know women leaders from all branches of the Mennonite church.

I admit I worried how I would be perceived by my church constituency, the Mennonite Brethren, who as a body had not yet found the need or desire to travel the journey toward gender equality. The deeply engrained Russlaender mentality that men were always in charge was not easily sloughed off, even after several generations.

I couldn't silence the voice that told me that to describe women's roles only in terms of limitations, rather than opportunities, was wrong. If something is evil and sinful, it should be spoken against. I couldn't understand how resolutions could affirm women with words encouraging them to use their gifts—yet leave them powerless in practice.

By then the broader women's movement was in full swing, with those speaking up openly received a full dose of ridicule and trivialization. Writing about the issue was a monologue, not a discussion.

A group of MB women attended the Elkhart, Indiana, Women in Ministry Conference sponsored by the MCC Task Force on Women for all Mennonites. Those of us who had been involved in recent years felt the time was ripe for broader conversation about the matter and particularly for education in the congregations regarding the use of the gifts of all believers.

Young women were graduating from college and university and moving into leadership positions in their chosen careers, only to find out they were ignored when they turned to the church to use these same leadership gifts.

Mennonite Brethren women needed some MB board or committee to accept the issue as part of their ongoing agenda. I wrote Dennis Becker of the Board of Christian Education, Dwight Wiebe of Contemporary Concerns Committee, and Henry Dick of the Board of Reference and Council, an all-male body, asking if they would accept responsibility for the issue in the MB church. None felt free to do so without official action by some other body. No one said, "The buck stops here." Women were encouraged to attend a study conference on the role of women but without the financial travel assistance these men would receive. What woman could take that amount out of the household budget?

I eagerly read publications like *Daughters of Sarah, Priscilla Papers,* and others. I lined my shelves with all the new books about women coming out. I watched and studied what was going on in the broader Mennonite constituency and elsewhere. I clung to these contacts like a rope flung to a drowning person and welcomed every opportunity for ministry that came from them. It took me a while to accept that power, tradition, and lack of understanding, not just biblical interpretation, shaped understandings of women's ministry. Support of women had its risks. One minister who had spoken up publicly on behalf of women told his wife when he came home, "I will probably never get another call to a church after what I said today."

Some of us MB women saw the need to make women of the churches more aware of the legacy of service and church involvement earlier women had passed on to them. I received a grant of $2,000 from the Board of Christian Literature to edit a book of women's biographies, a longtime dream. I wanted to provide young women with role models of service in premodern times. I plunged ahead before the light changed to red.

The ad hoc committee planning the book's contents agreed to stay away from feminist issues in the book and let the women's lives of committed service explain themselves without attempting to establish a bulkhead in MB feminist literature. It was difficult to locate material on women long dead and writers willing to do the difficult research, but we accomplished our task. The book was mildly criticized by stauncher feminist readers for not making a stronger statement about these early women as feminists, but we had brought to visibility fifteen women and their accomplishments in many fields. We had lifted the fog slightly.

People chuckled when they sensed the double meaning in the title: *Women Among the Brethren: Stories of 15 Mennonite Brethren and Krimmer Mennonite Brethren Women* (one missionary and fourteen others) from all stages of life in Russia, Canada, and the United States. In researching women's lives for this book, I became aware I was looking at the underside of Mennonite Brethren history, rich with women's contributions.

I had to rearrange my own assumptions about these early women. I had believed that they were passive, uncreative, submissive, accepting their lot with equanimity; that they had been absent when the MB church was emerging; that they had made few contributions to the church outside the home and sewing circles in those early years. I discovered women were present in the early history of the church, only they were unrecorded in official historical documents. Women were much involved in church and missions support, only invisible. They popularized missions support. They prayed, sewed, cooked, quilted, auctioned, raffled, and donated money to missions and Mennonite Central Committee. Women's circles were the undergirding beams that made the church strong.

In 1978 I was asked to present a paper on the "Church's Response to the Changing Roles of Women" at an MCC study conference in Abbotsford, British Columbia. Delighted to have this opportunity, I recognized I was moving into dangerous territory by speaking publicly. The topic was volatile. I received many suggestions and warnings before I left Hillsboro about how to say what I had to say. But I said what I believed.

In 1981 I wrote an article for *Mennonite Life* on the role and contribution of women in the early Mennonite Brethren church in Russia, which I later presented at a Center for Mennonite Brethren Studies Study Conference in Fresno. It was eventually published in *Your Daughters Shall Prophesy*. For decades the statement was often made that eighteen men signed the original document of secession from the mother church in Russia; therefore eighteen men began the MB Church. I documented that women may not have signed their names but that the men signed as heads of household; therefore the signatories could be counted as thirty-six if all the men were married. The women were much involved but in different ways.

In those early years in Russia, the women's individual contributions were vast but unrecorded officially. They served to the limit of what was allowed them and some stretched the limits. They were advisers and secretaries to church-leader husbands. They offered hospitality for house churches and itinerant ministers and others, not a small matter in those days without household conveniences. They served as missionaries or supported missions and sewing circles; cared for the sick and hungry, especially during the revolutionary years; and looked after their own families but also other people's children orphaned when parents were exiled or died of typhus and starvation.

Perhaps these early MB women's greatest role was suffering alone and together with men harassed and/or imprisoned during the founding of the church in 1860 and while starting new settlements beyond the original Ukraine colonies. They took over economic and spiritual headship of the home when fathers and husbands were killed, exiled to concentration camps or forced labor in Siberia during the 1930s, and conscripted into the German army before and during World War II. When men were absent, they prayed over and buried the dead.

My research took me into footnotes, often overlooked. I had descended from a long procession of women who made tremendous contributions to their world which had never entered the memories of present church members. Historians had shoved them to the edge of the story of the founding of the MB church, making them invisible to future generations. Mennonite Brethren historians and historians generally, at the time, looked to exceptional and powerful people and for the record of their influence in official minutes of public meetings, public debates, speeches, letters, and journals. The life stories of ordinary men and women who went about their daily tasks quietly and who did not see themselves as makers of history did not usually provide the material for history books. I documented that MB women played a much larger role in the founding of the Mennonite Brethren church than historians assume. They were not just spectators.

The struggle continued. In 1982, after a disappointing MB General Conference discussion of the issue, I wrote the editors of our two publications, *The Christian Leader* and *Mennonite Brethren Herald*: "I never planned my life this way [as a woman in ministry]. All I had promised the Lord was to enter doors he opened and not break my head and spirit pounding against those closed to me. Yet I'll admit to yearning for the moral and spiritual support of my conference in my service."

Some doors were firmly locked and bolted. I continued to write and travel, mostly outside MB circles. It seemed to some that if women spoke up for women, we were men-haters. My article "Color me a person," which appeared in several periodicals, came back to me annotated with little negative comments penciled in all over.

I accepted every opportunity to speak or write papers for study conferences. At a Center for MB Studies study conference in Winnipeg in 1986 I included data about the representation of women as delegates to the Canadian MB conference over the years. After a session, a registrant from southern Saskatchewan told me that my figures were wrong with regard to the number of women delegates present at one of the 1960s Canadian MB Conferences. I had the number as zero. He told me a woman from his congregation came as a delegate that year but was not seated at the request of the conference executive committee. My count should have been one woman for that year. The matter had troubled him all these years.

I gave a response to Diane Zimmerman Umble's "A Feminist Reading of the Mennonite Experience in America Series" at the Mennonite Experience in America Conference at Bethel College, North Newton, Kansas in 1997. Umble showed that the early history accounts omitted women, but they were there—active, alive, serving.

During the 1980s, for an entire school year, as already mentioned, the Faculty Advisory Committee at Tabor College, comprised of both men and women and of which I was a member, researched the issue of sexism on campus and finally discussed it with the administration. Once we could get past the feelings level, the discussion went better. That women should be involved in all aspects of work at Tabor College, including leadership roles in administration, teaching, support staff, committee work, is a given now that the air doesn't turn thick with emotion as it did when first introduced.

In spring 1987, before the MB General Conference in Abbotsford, B.C., the Board of Reference and Council called together an ad hoc task force on women in ministry including three women to compile a resolution to present to the upcoming conference. Always men had decided what to do about the women. For the first time in MB history, women had been asked to share in decision-making regarding their role in the church. I wept openly. For about thirty years I had been asking, sometimes gently, sometimes more stridently, that women's gifts be acknowledged. Now, I and other women present at that meeting could talk about our concerns. It was overwhelming.

Our meeting in Winnipeg began with each person present laying all cards on the table so that we knew where each stood. One spoke for equality between sexes in every context as the direction the church should be moving. A pastor's wife was content with her role supporting her husband. A seminary professor had moved from a previous mild restriction on gifts to full freedom for women, persuaded in part because of his own daughter's pain as she tried to move into church ministry. A college professor admitted he was his father's son, having accepted authoritarian male dominance for decades. Now he had had a theological conversion but was still troubled by some restrictive passages. "If Katie has borne the pain for thirty years, I can bear it for a few." Another college professor came with anger, stating openly, "If it is right for women to serve, it is wrong to hinder them." The resolution we chiseled together and later presented to the conference sessions didn't make it.

In 1987, a group in St. Paul formed Christians for Biblical Equality (CBE) after the Evangelical Women's Caucus folded because of a conflict over internal issues at an earlier Fresno conference. This new organization spread the word that there was a place for both the Bible and equality. By now I had retired from Tabor College and was living in Wichita, Kansas. I was willing to take one last shot at the issue.

In 1993 I joined two women from the Free Evangelical Church in Wichita to form a local citywide branch of CBE. We sponsored meetings and seminars, one with Dr. Ruth Tucker of Trinity Evangelical Divinity School, but could not get a significant response from the women in Kansas. An MCC Women in Ministry conference in which I was somewhat involved was also only mildly successful. The issue of women in the church was losing the interest of modern women, many of whom were working outside the home and focused on furthering their careers. In the end we decided to put our energies elsewhere.

The MCC Women's Task Force had sponsored several successful Women in Ministry conferences in Elkhart, Indiana, and elsewhere, followed several years later by the first Women Doing Theology Conference in Kitchener, Ontario, in 1992. These conferences held over the next decade were overtly political acts as they encouraged women of the Anabaptist community to come together. They were necessary to give the women a stronger theological understanding as well as moral support and to make future conferences possible. I no longer felt alone in the struggle.

At the Kitchener conference I gave the opening address on "What? Me a Theologian?" I noticed several things: The women present were younger. A new group was stepping in place, an encouraging sign. Some were still angry, with open threats to leave the church. But already some did not understand the pain some of us older women had gone through.

I told the story (mentioned in an earlier chapter) of how at the end of a daylong celebration of my husband's ordination in 1953, I had returned home and taken off my new black velvet hat. Clearly evident on it were the sweaty fingerprints of the visiting minister. He had laid his hands on my head in prayer, leaving a permanent indentation. Thereafter I wore the mark of ordination on my head, although I had made no public promises and received no formal instructions or blessing for my role as a minister's wife. The young women of the audience laughed. I was shocked at first but then realized it was time to laugh at these earlier hurts. This was a new generation of women before me.

In 1993, when a seminary professor accused me of not being supportive enough of younger women struggling with their roles as women in the MB church, I was taken aback. Was this true? I examined my activities of the last years. The prior week a nationally known writer had told me my encouragement had gotten her started. Another writer came specially to a retreat to thank me for getting her started in writing. She now had one hundred articles to her credit. A young woman at the retreat told me that even then she was carrying in her purse a letter of encouragement I had sent her more than two years before, when her ministry as a woman was in question.

At the time I was carrying on an extensive correspondence with several women who had asked me to mentor them. My files are full of letters from women asking for information, advice, and encouragement. One would-be writer followed me for six to eight months to every workshop where I was speaking before she had the courage to approach me. In the introduction to her first book she traced our relationship from watching from afar to inviting me to her home. She has since won awards for her work. Some women wrote me endorsing my stance but hesitated to identify openly with me for fear of being labeled a "women's libber like Katie Funk Wiebe."

I have a file of poetry women have sent me. Both men and women have sent me manuscripts to look over on many subjects. Not long ago a young woman, recently widowed, wrote me how she had found my book *Alone* helpful. A letter from a friend in Ohio mentioned that at the Mennonite Assembly in San Jose a few weeks earlier one of the speakers, a successful college president and church leader, had mentioned, "I want to pay tribute to a woman who influenced me tremendously. She is someone I have never met—Katie Funk Wiebe." But maybe I should and could have done more to help other young women on their journey.

At the Anabaptist Women's History Conference in Millersville, Pennsylvania, "The Quiet in the Land," I found women who once felt exiled from the Mennonite community circling back. I also found those who had never considered leaving despite hindrances to service. What a joy to hear from women who had deliberately chosen membership in the Anabaptist community because of its spiritual strengths even as I continued to remain a member of the MB church despite encouragements and pressures to leave. Another name for this conference might have been "Coming Home."

The Mennonite Brethren Church was still in turmoil about the issue. The final version of *Your Daughters Shall Prophesy* edited by John E. Toews, Valerie Rempel, and me at the request of the Board of Faith and Life, destroyed the peace of many because it wasn't supportive enough of the conservative view of women's roles in the church. That element was and is still strong in some congregations.

At the 1993 General Conference of Mennonite Brethren churches in Winnipeg, the recommendation that congregations decide the issue of women in leadership locally in the interests of unity and consensus was defeated (61-39 percent). I did not expect it to pass, given the wording. It had too many unexplained implications. In 2006 the Canadian Conference finally passed a similar resolution. A friend in Winnipeg was so elated she sent me an email the same day. In 2008 the first two Canadian Mennonite Brethren women were ordained to the ministry, an amazing movement forward. The United States MB Conference has made no movement toward resolution of the issue.

During a period of despair because of the slowness of the pace, I had the opportunity to hear Roberta Hestenes, then of Fuller Theological Seminary, later a college president, encourage women who had lost hope to recall that God is active in our lives even when outward signs of hope are gone. The suffering of injustice shrinks one's world to issues of personal survival. Hope extends horizons into the future. Hope looks for solutions for the larger body, not just for self. I was not without hope but realized full equality for women in the church would probably not happen in my lifetime. I was at peace about the matter. I had been true to God's leading, but I knew it was time to leave this issue to younger women and heed God's calling to other tasks.

CHAPTER 18

What I learned from the women's movement

An invasion of armies can be resisted,
but not an idea whose time has come.
—Victor Hugo

Thousands of words have been written and spoken about women's role in church and society over the years. The resurgence of interest in the issue during the 1960s was long overdue. It was as inevitable as the civil rights movement. When I taught English literature, we never encountered women writers until the 1800s. The first ones sometimes wrote under men's names—George Eliot—as I did when I first started writing. In the medical field, clinical studies were first done only on men—men's heart studies, men's colon cancer studies. It took many years before the focus shifted to include women's bodies.

Now, in my eighties, I can look back to what I have learned from my involvement with this movement over the decades. I was able to do so because of the freedom of the country in which I live. Women in developing countries are only slowly beginning to speak up for greater involvement, but too often if there is not enough food survival becomes more important. Women are the first to go without food if there isn't enough. The girls are denied schooling if there isn't enough money for books and uniforms. During war, women are treated barbarously because they are female.

Today younger women in many cultures aren't fitting into old patterns of thinking and behavior because they don't know what these were, or they have glimpsed new light. They don't see themselves as lesser human beings and so don't act that way. When a person comes to new awareness about any matter, it is impossible to go back to square one and start again. I couldn't.

Over the years I found out there was danger in speaking about gender relationships openly, yet I decided it was important to do so to strengthen the body of Christ. And to send the message that as women we didn't want dominance over men, as some critics thought. We wanted to contribute at the level of our gifts and abilities, as full-fledged members of the human race. To treat women as second-class citizens demeaned us.

Each man or woman stands independently before God and is responsible to God alone. Other people, like a spouse or parent, are not responsible for our spiritual standing. I, not husband or children, will give account of myself before God some day. When I was married I was tempted to hide behind my husband in spiritual matters. I would slide alongside him into glory land. The women's movement taught me that I was responsible for my own sin, salvation, and spiritual growth and service.

When I started to work this out in my life, I was hampered by society's stereotypes of a woman's place before God. Church leadership of any kind was men's work. Certain doctrines, such as nonresistance to violence and war, were male doctrines. That disturbed me. In a Mennonite church, albeit one leaning on evangelicalism for support, the ethos of nonresistance was communicated in the family with reference to sons rather than daughters. Adherence to this doctrine determined whether or not the young men were drafted, and if they were what type of military service they would do.

The church's and parents' concerns were for sons conscripted into the military without the option of following an alternative form of service. Several Mennonite migrations have occurred because of this concern for sons' welfare, for example from Prussia to Russia in the 1780s. And from there to Canada, Paraguay, and the United States. Then later to Mexico. Even from the United States to Canada during the Vietnam War.

Because Mennonites' destiny was wrapped up with the way sons were involved with this issue and not with the way women experienced the truth of Scripture related to the peace position, women's response was not viewed as significant. From childhood on up my father and other young men like him imbibed this teaching that Mennonites did not go to war. It was a cultural matter, not a decision based on personal faith convictions.

The women's movement has shown me that both men and women must submit to God and then figure out other relationships. If this does not happen, we accept the roles society has given us and make idols out of them. We can make an idol out of the peace position, the position of submission, and even who is in charge.

The answer I found to the question of roles came through the writing of Dr. Mary Stewart Van Leeuwen, a psychologist and former member of the secular feminist movement before she became a Christian. She asserted that we have all become so preoccupied with individual rights, none of us—male and female—seem to realize that the most important principle is to submit to God from which "all other acts of submission and authority must be derived if they are not to become corrupt and idolatrous."

She pointed out that men have identified with God rather than submitting to him. My neighbors for a short while in Hillsboro were an elderly couple. The husband came over one morning to tell me he had to go to the hospital and didn't know what to do about his wife. I was in my fifties at the time. I offered to spend the nights in their home while he was gone. "But there has to be a man in the house," he responded. What an elderly, infirm man could do that I couldn't do was never clear to me. But a man had to be around to protect the women. That was his God-given role.

Van Leeuwen also pointed out that some acts of submission in marriages have become sinful. Women have submitted to men before they have first accepted their responsibility before God. It is easier to submit to a husband than to God. Women avoid finding their true identity, thereby losing the possibility of knowing true submission to husbands, a possibility only between equals. A husband can never demand submission. Without mutual submission husband and wife end up bereft of both real love and real personhood. Her words made me realize I had never really found out who Katie was until I was well into my forties.

During the many decades of my journey through this issue, I came up against the matter of gifts and calling time and time again. The idea had crept into our churches that not only should men always be in control but also that they were a little more able than women, had been given a few more and better gifts. Gifts had been divided according to gender, marital status, sometimes according to race and social status. The Spirit had handed restricted gifts to single men and women.

The women's movement reclaimed the acts and words of Jesus as models for today. He was friends with Mary and Martha, both single women. He told Mary she had chosen the good part by sitting at his feet. Serving meals was necessary, but women also needed to spend time with him. Women accompanied him on his preaching and teaching trips. Jesus performed his first miracle for his mother Mary at a marriage celebration. He spoke openly to women, an action frowned upon in those days. He took upon himself the role of a woman of those days—servanthood.

The gifts God gives to both men and women fall into no one pattern. The church should not ask what women can do but what a particular woman can do with certain talents, strengths, and weaknesses. It doesn't ask what men generally can do but what John or George can do.

Yet we shrink back, men as well as women, for to acknowledge our Spirit-granted gift means to step into the battle, face criticism, know the loneliness of leadership, but also to enjoy rewards and blessings. What is the answer to this important issue of roles in a broken world? I have agonized over it. What can the church say to women satisfied with their home roles so that they feel less threatened by those who suggest another approach? How can women who ache to use gifts besides cooking and cleaning or are single be released from their anxiety and guilt? And what about the men who are also perplexed?

Here's another learning: Women in leadership roles, even only by participating in committees and boards, change the climate of the world in which they function. Having lived on the underside, they understand the feelings of those at the bottom. Their voice changes the tone of a meeting. Men and women need each other in all areas of life. We each have gifts to give to one another. Our society can't function without both genders in the home, economic world, political arena, or church. Many powerful and visible men have developed their gifts and strengths only because they stand on a pyramid of invisible women—a support system of clerks, secretaries, wives, and aides. More employers are becoming aware that to speak of this large undergirding as "the girls in the office" is no better than when black men, even grey-haired men, were called "boys."

I also learned this: Language reveals our biases and sexist attitudes. Pronouns are more important than people realize. Today most people have made the switch from the exclusive "he" to some other usage. I am amused to hear TV broadcasters say "Everyone must do their assigned task." Singular subject, plural pronoun. But they've moved from the former "his," a positive sign. They are becoming aware that language is changing. In time "everyone" will become a plural subject.

Some people feel the language question is petty. But language is far more powerful than most of us recognize in conveying and reflecting our world view, our value system. I wondered often what a difference it might have made if I, as a young woman, had heard some common Scripture passages quoted to include me specifically: Ephesians 4:13: "And so we shall all come together to that oneness in our faith and in our knowledge of the Son of God; we shall become mature *women*, reaching to very height of Christ's full stature," or if Romans 12:2 had read, "Think of God's mercy, my *sisters*, and worship."

I do not advocate changing the Scriptures, but where normal language is exclusive it should be changed to show women are included. We need to find new ways of speaking to one another in our congregations instead of uttering bald statements that say, "We know the term *brothers* includes the sisters." Sometimes it does. Sometimes it doesn't. An advertisement for a ministers' school was directed to "pastors and laymen." Few women would have had the courage to become comrades in exploration about theological issues with such an invitation. For several years I urged that all documents be studied thoroughly to determine whether the use of language determined the gender of the person to be chosen for the position.

The women's movement has also shown me that historians have kept women from being visible simply by the way their names are recorded. I have done enough research to know how difficult it is to find women's names, particularly their given and maiden names, if they lived long ago. Early records often include the names of only male heads of families and identify women as John Rittenhouse's wife or daughter or by husband's name (Mr. and Mrs. Martin Kolb). Over time this changed to John and Anna Brown until finally sometimes the wife's full name was mentioned without her husband's. Women are hard to find in early history books if their accomplishments are evaluated only by the trappings and appearance of traditional power. Not powerful, not mentioned.

Another lesson I learned: Women are held responsible to hold back modernity and be the social conservators of Mennonite culture, particularly through clothing and hairstyles. Through their dress they have been expected to reinforce women's traditional role of submission, purity, and piety. They still are in some conservative branches of the church. I'm not advocating immodesty, but sometimes I want to clothe these women with a bright-colored dress and shorter skirt to add color, God's wonderful gift to humanity, to their lives,

Another learning: Life for both men and women changed when birth control became more widely accepted. Not much is written in church papers about birth control, yet attitudes toward birth control have played a part in keeping the genders unequal. Whoever determines reproduction decides woman's role in society and church. A woman who bore a child nearly every year throughout her child-bearing years had her role cut out for her.

I have studied many family histories tracing the line through generation after generation. With marriage, women faced pregnancy after pregnancy and the threat of death at childbirth and disease. Childbearing was a given. My mother told me that women in the Ukraine had dresses sewn before marriage to accommodate an expected pregnancy and breast-feeding. A man married wife after wife as each one died, often in childbirth complications. Some men sired from eight to eighteen children. Did anyone every murmur? I can only speak for the under-the-breath mutterings I hear even now when the number of children one woman bears seems too many. But women didn't and couldn't restrict the number of births if she was submissive. It was her role.

During the most difficult years after World Wars I and II, my research shows that women in Mennonite communities kept having baby after baby even in the face of great famine, harsh migrations, exile, imprisonment, and death. Was celibacy in marriage ever a consideration out of concern for the mother during these most difficult times? They bore children in good times and bad and most loved each one. The identity of women as child-bearers was rooted in their anatomy. They migrated long distances big with child. It was their lot in life. My one aunt, exiled to Siberian forced labor camps after World War II, gave birth on the packed cattle car transporting hundreds of Russian-born Germans to their doom. The infant died. At a train stop the dead body was handed out the door to some Russians and the train chugged on.

The acceptance of family planning in the latter half of the twentieth century by Mennonites changed their world as it did the rest of society's. When birth control was taken out of the sin category and placed into an acceptable category of behavior, a number of things changed, including history and theology. How?

When women gained control of their reproductive functions, that control changed their lives, their husbands', and the church's future. For one thing, women felt freer about returning to work outside the home and lessened their contributions to voluntary church work. The church now had to be concerned about membership growth of the church other than through biological growth. As long as families were large, local church growth was not an issue. Finding enough land for each son when he married was a big concern in the Mennonite colonies in Russia and led to starting daughter colonies because of the explosion of children. The question then was not how to increase local membership in a congregation. That was taken care of by the large families. The concern was missions and evangelism in the far-flung areas of the world.

Small families would have kept membership roles at a stable or declining level in Russia and also in Canada and the United States in the early years. Strong biological growth kept the body expanding. Large families kept Mennonites on the land in the early years; small families allowed them to move to the cities and become urbanized. A father with a wife and ten or twelve children did not readily move to the city. Only the older children moved away to find work there. Evangelical outreach first became a serious concern when families remained small.

As I think through my long involvement in women's issues, I wonder also why we didn't have more fun along the way as we looked for a way through the muddle. I sense the humor now in incidents that happened a long time ago, but I didn't then. Then it was serious stuff. Heart-breaking stuff.

During the fourteen years I wrote a column of Mennonite humor for *Festival Quarterly*, I discovered that much of our humor came at the expense of the most powerful among us— the preachers and leaders. Each story attempted to find the Achilles heel, to burst the bubble of pomposity associated with authority. Little humor exists about women and their roles or even about the relationship of men and women, other than as husband and wife, because men and women didn't relate in other spheres. Their roles were already determined. They were God-given. You don't make fun of sacred things.

Coming as we Anabaptists do from a long line of protesters, (we started out being against something), the poet-prophet and the humorist are not always welcome. I can hardly imagine an early Anabaptist standing with feet far apart, head thrown back, laughing at the goodness of the world. We tend to search for theological positions and constitutional changes or work to maintain those already existing. Yes, I often wish I had laughed more.

Cleaning out my files I came upon a writing from the 1960s which I called "An Immodest Proposal." I don't think I ever tried to get it published. But it was serious angry stuff, as serious as Jonathan Swift's "A Modest Proposal" for preventing the famine in Ireland by raising infants to two years and then butchering them for food.

I wrote my satire before women were allowed to attend church conferences, that all-male domain, as delegates, or to vote, so I proposed they attend in a different capacity—official cheering section, with seats to the rear so as not to distract the male delegates. Because conventions have their discouraging moments, these women would lift spirits with an occasional cheer routine and pompom waving. They would serve coffee during the sessions in attractive uniforms; take telephone messages; pin identification badges on male delegates with a gleaming smile; hand out aspirins, ballots, and official documents; count ballots; even sing a few entertaining songs now and then.

I had a solution for men who feared bringing their wives to the conference would de-feminize them—make them less tender, less sensitive, perhaps even less human if they became aware of bureaucracies and money problems. In recognition of women's more delicate nature, all women would be asked to leave the convention hall when the deeper, more serious issues like balancing the budget or discussing the Sunday school attendance record came before the delegation.

In deference to those who felt that the presence of women at church policymaking meetings might introduce error into the church, even as Eve did in the Garden of Eden, and also in deference to those horrified at the prospect of women hearing and not fully understanding and then becoming over-enthused about what they could not grasp, the doors to all committee rooms would be provided with special padlocks. The men would be advised to speak softly and in plain terms when women were around, avoiding all theological jargon. I had a great time writing this essay, but I wasn't laughing then.

I chuckle now about an incident that happened years ago. A pastor friend from a neighboring church in Hillsboro had been invited to do a series of midweek Bible studies at the Ebenfeld Mennonite Brethren Church. In the intervening weeks, she and I were both on the planning committee for an MCC Women in Ministry conference. After the conference I wrote a short article about it for our church organ, mentioning her name. Shortly thereafter the Ebenfeld pastor disinvited her because of her association with me. Dottie told me years later what happened. I tried to laugh with her.

I ask the question today why we as churches have been so task-oriented, so concerned about keeping people, particularly women, in traditional roles, and given so little attention to the voice of the poet as prophet. Why has the language of metaphor and symbol been suspect? We have swept aside the language of the poet and celebrant and neglected the voice of the psalmist/priest—the voice of confession and restoration of God's grace and forgiveness.

People need symbols to survive. Historians are more at home with established certainties than with the uncharted regions of the soul, wrote philosopher Delbert Wiens a few decades ago. They are attracted to codified statements, not to living experience, not story, whether praiseworthy or difficult. How different it might have been if poet and prophet had been allowed to speak for God to illuminate our humanness with evidence of grace.

We have not thanked men enough when they have supported women in their struggle for greater opportunity to use their gifts in the church. I wrote a litany once in praise of male feminists. Why did so few men and women speak up in the early years? Too high a cost for some.

What was that cost? The whole gamut of women being gently ridiculed for joining a secular fad to being harshly accused of heresy for having fallen prey to the sin of interpreting the Bible to fit personal preferences and cultural demands. The cost included losing the esteem of one's peers and of jeopardizing local political and spiritual influence. The cost to a man included giving up the psychological edge a man has in any mixed groups over women simply because he is male. The cost to all meant giving up the assumption that the history of the church is only about what the men were doing. The cost was to stop seeing women merely as something useful—typists, clerks, housemaids, nurses, waitresses—and not as persons who can also be innovators, creators, leaders, and futurists.

I have learned that women have a lot of power, more than we realize. We are not aware of its full strength in many areas of our lives. I was not aware of my own power through words until someone one day admonished me, "Katie, you have a lot of power." I was still seeing myself as a mistreated underling.

I want to say to all women, "You've come a long way, baby, but"—and this is a big BUT—"you've still got a long way to go." Discrimination in the future will be more subtle than it was in the 1960s and 1970s. Women can go to church without a hat, cut their hair (once a big no-no), vote at congregational meetings, teach a mixed adult class, sometimes preach. They can even wear earrings. (When I was on *The Christian Leader* staff in the 1960s, earrings were air-brushed out of photos to avoid offending readers.) By conference resolution, women can participate in many aspects of church work, but one thing is missing—a wholehearted readiness to seek their gifts and bless them openly with words, with music, with cheerleaders and pompoms, with a full-fledged party.

I've learned that much of the change regarding women's roles has happened by default, not by decision. Though our history books are filled with decisions made by large and small bodies, many more changes occurred by default. A process of slow theological evolution has taken place rather than action based on group consensus. And this is probably the way it will continue. It is possible for an individual or church body to assent to a resolution with words yet not feel its truth. Therefore, I'd like to see cheerleaders and coaches/ombudsmen and women to keep the weary from giving up, to prod, present, pray, and keep the issue open in a loving positive way. Though church people tend to think of every group decision as a movement of the Spirit, conventions are occasions when very human men and women gather, and by God's grace, something of what happens is Spirit-controlled and some of it led by selfish human motives. But God can use it all.

Regrettably many congregations have lost a generation of young women and men who, when doors to ministry were closed to them, found warm welcomes elsewhere. We have lost their gifts in our congregations because we were not ready. I and many others would probably have to strain to count the number of times we have heard a woman preach. A whole generation of children will not see a Priscilla, Deborah, or a daughter of Philip minister and prophesy to the congregation.

This generation of women will have other obstacles to overcome to move ahead in ministry, but some will be the same as those of my generation faced. Not too long ago a letter appeared in an inter-Mennonite publication asking, "How can women have a call from God when God doesn't call women?" My hope for younger women is that they will study women's history generally and specifically so that they will be aware of the road others traveled for them.

It is important for all, men and women, to hang onto a central core of identity as someone God loves and has called to serve at all times in life, even in the last decades. Discipleship doesn't end when the Social Security check arrives for the first time. We need to ask ourselves what our response is to the calling of Christ to servanthood and discipleship. The responsibility of both men and women in an age of suffering, hunger, loneliness, oppression, and much corruption is to choose according to strength, gifts, and grace given us by God—not according to gender.

I feel like Caleb, who after the conquest of Canaan at the age of eighty, said to Joshua when the land was distributed, "Give me this mountain." Although I am eighty-three, it is not yet time to pull back. I tell myself it is important to keep reaching ahead for goals I personally will not win. I want the next generation of women, including my daughters, to enjoy greater freedom in exploring their gifts and finding opportunities for partnership in ministry in home, society, and congregation. I want to die climbing.

Climbing a steep hill is easier if you have someone beside you, undergirding, clearing the underbrush. Let's climb together steadily, patiently, "for the Spirit helps us in our weakness" (Rom. 8:26). Therefore it is important to network, with the goal of finding out who we are by name and what we are doing, individually and together. That is part of the reason I wrote this book.

It is a joy and privilege to be a woman in the twenty-first century. I feel blessed. It is important to feel blessed in order to bless others. It is a wonderful privilege to have given birth and nurtured children. It is a wonderful privilege to have been given the gift of words and ideas and the opportunity to send them out to find a resting spot in someone's life. I await the *Kairos* time, a breakthrough for both men and women as we let the Spirit work. I pray it may come in my lifetime.

Photo Album

Above: *Mother gave birth to me in this little shack. In her heart she named me Katarina after her mother.. Below: I should have believed her, for decades*

later an aunt in Russia gave me this picture sent to her, probably by my parents. Written on the back (bottom right) *"Good day, Grandpa. Elfrieda, Anna, Katarina, Jakob." Why then did everyone call me Katie?*

I liked being Katie Funk, high school student.

Above left: *During the last years of high school I became Kay because it sounded more sophisticated.* Above right: *I was always just one of the Blaine Lake Funk girls. Here we are: Frieda, Annie, Katie. Sue, four years younger than I am, is missing from the picture.*

Right: *Kay Funk, stenographer-bookkeeper in Saskatoon, Saskatchewan.* Above: *Miss Funk, office secretary and student at Mennonite Brethren Bible College.*

Left: *I could now proudly call my-self Mrs. Walter Wiebe.* Above: *My children called me Mom. I knew people called me a widow.*

Left: *Etiquette said I should still call myself Mrs. Walter Wiebe, but I changed my name to Mrs. Katie Wiebe, editorial assistant.* Right: *Tabor College students called me Mrs. Wiebe at first, later just Katie.*

Above: *Still Mom thirty years later*
Below: *Mrs. Katie Wiebe, writer*

Left: *Katie Funk Wiebe, writer, teacher, and speaker.*
Below: *Grandma Katie with Matthew Harms*

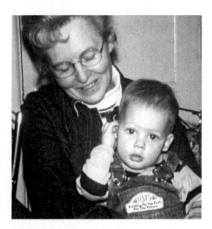

Above: *Great-Grandma Katie with Joanna Wiebe-Baer, her son Bill Smith and wife Dana and-daughter Zola*
Left: *And still Mom in 2008 with James, Susan, and Joanna*

Katie, not Katarina, and liking the name.

PART IV

CHAPTER 19

Words from an amateur at growing old

No wise man ever wished to be younger.
—Jonathan Swift

I write about aging as an insider. No longer does the waitress ask if I qualify for a senior discount. She just looks at my white hair and wrinkles. I have crossed the border, but I don't know exactly when. I wrote about growing older when I was looking ahead to this stage decades ago, pondering what it would like. Now I know firsthand.

Aging in a particular culture shapes the way a person ages and its meaning. While some cultures see elders as men and women to be honored and cherished, our society is burdened with dread and loathing of aging. This attitude rubs off on those approaching this Third Age. I've watched countless men and women do a soft shoe dance for several years after retirement, sometimes for decades, hesitant to cross over and identify themselves with older adults. "Am I old yet or aren't I old?" "When am I old?" These are questions new retirees ponder.

Maybe they can keep old age at bay if they work at looking youthful and don't associate closely with their age group. People who see *old* as a four-letter word fight the cycle of life. They avoid identification with their years the way I avoid tofu hamburgers. Successful aging is to pretend birthdays after forty never happened, that life tasks at the end are the same as at thirty. One woman said she didn't want anyone to know her age even at death. She wanted to be buried in her best dress with all her makeup and jewelry to assure her mourners she died young.

But then somehow it happens whether you wanted it to or not: You are old. Your step is slower, your eyesight dimmer. You lack the energy you had even ten years ago. It is troubling to plan ahead when you don't know how many years you will be given. You identify with the man described in Ecclesiastes 12 who is afraid of heights and dangers in the streets.

At age eighty-three, my greatest concern is not whether I can slow time by hanging onto a youthful face and figure but whether I can keep my inner being alive and well. I have been studying the mystique of aging for more than the seventeen years I have been retired. Advertisers urge me to apply creams to my skin to erase the wrinkles that have taken up a permanent home there. I am more concerned about what to apply to my soul to prevent it from becoming a shriveled sack of bitterness, regrets, criticism, and irritability.

I want to affirm daily that moving from one developmental stage to another is normal. That death is not an abnormality. It is part of God's plan. I am one of a growing group of amateurs in aging figuring out what the last years are all about in a more positive way than our culture informs us.

After I finished teaching at Tabor College in 1990, I moved to Wichita, about fifty miles away, to live closer to son James and his wife Kathy and daughters, Susan and husband Roger and son and daughter. Christine moved there in 1992 from Chicago. At my sixty-fifth birthday celebration the year before, the family launched me into this new stage with much hoopla, cake, and pictures. But how would I manage without the crutch of a daily job? I now had more than two thousand discretionary hours at my disposal each year. Moving into this unknown, unstructured life was scary, especially when I visited a small nursing home and saw the rows of silent, impassive masks pasted on those residents slouched in wheel chairs in the entryway.

I studied retired friends to learn what lay ahead. It didn't take long to see the waste of older adults' resources just as I had seen it earlier in women's lives. Now the constraint was lifespan. One day these almost-retirees were rushing about, responsible for significant specific tasks. The next day they're sitting on the sidelines, sentenced to keeping busy so they can say, "I don't know how I got everything done when I was working." People assume the warranty for meaningful life expires at sixty-five.

They are encouraged to volunteer their time and energy. An earlier view of volunteerism was that retirees became the extensions of the hands and feet of directors and administrators of organizations and institutions. A newly retired business administrator told me, "I have a thousand horsepower engine inside me and I am being given hundred horsepower jobs to do." Stuffing envelopes and shelving books was not for him. I felt the same. An identity as a volunteer lacked the dignity and meaningful work he craved. Fortunately, that attitude toward volunteerism is changing. Today organizations are tapping the creativity and managerial skills of retirees and asking them to take on leadership and advisory tasks.

When I retired in 1990 I saw an emphasis on health, exercise, and keeping finances in order. I saw the denial of aging, as if growing older was shameful instead of a joy. Some over-eager organizers pushed mindless activity on people over sixty, like bingo and casual crafts. Some in this age group devoted themselves to resting in an easy chair watching soap operas and taking naps, important as these are. I'm at the daily nap stage myself. I saw people without portfolio, without identity. There had to be another side to the whole matter of aging. Elbert Cole, Methodist minister and founder of the Shepherd's Centers of America, handed me the key at a conference on aging I attended at Messiah College in Pennsylvania in 1993.

The Mennonite Health Association had asked me to write/edit a book on aging. Something felt right about this assignment. I had a long shelf of books on the subject. I had occasionally spoken on the topic. I was interested in my own aging. I didn't want Old Age to drive over me with a steam roller, leaving me flattened out. Aging is a one-time experience unlike childbirth. For my first daughter's birth, I had been drugged. I might have given birth to any kind of creature. The second time

I was better prepared. I opted for natural childbirth. When it comes to aging, we are all amateurs with our only resources our skills in having mastered earlier development tasks, like moving from adolescence into young adulthood, and so forth. But the resources are available to learn about aging.

At the conference, Cole said simply, "The faith community has the missing piece of the puzzle regarding the aging society." Cole's point was that society keeps asking the wrong questions, even though necessary questions. People with oversight responsibilities for this age group keep asking maintenance-type questions: "Are our elders warm, eating well, getting their exercise, taking their pills?" Envisioning the older population immediately directs our thinking to the frail over-eighty-five age group living in care facilities, yet only five percent of the elderly live in nursing homes. Few retire to a care facility. The rest are fairly healthy, active, very much alive. The church should be asking other questions, Cole said. God has a theological task for older adults. It is to find meaning in old age by discovering the unique contribution each can make.

His point was to put content into aging, which means going beyond caring for physical and financial needs to attend to needs of spirit, mind, and emotions. Members of this age group need to see themselves as growing people, always pursuing the wonder of the day, ready to wear red with purple. But it means identifying with and accepting the role of an elder. And that was the issue. What was my identity at this stage of life?

For the first years after retirement I hated to be introduced as a "retired English professor." It sounded as if I was looking for a rocking chair, when I wasn't. I needed a new identity. To identify myself by what I used to be wasn't the solution.

Identity problems crop up at various times in life. In Bible times teenagers as a specific development group didn't exist. A young boy or girl became a man or a woman at about age thirteen or fourteen. Today we keep teenagers children until they are in their late twenties and sometimes early thirties. "When am I an adult?" is a question this group wonders about.

Another time of identity questioning is marriage. Most women used to change their surname and place in an alphabetical listing upon marriage. When I changed my name from Funk to Wiebe, I remember how strange this felt. At the time, women's identity was established by the men in their lives. Unmarried women were identified as the daughter of . . . , married women as the wife of . . . , but seldom were men identified as the husband of . . . unless the wife was an important person.

At a committee meeting years ago, a woman was nominated for an open position. Her strengths were listed. One insecure pastor asked loudly, "But who is her husband?" His frame of reference for a woman was always the husband. When I was teaching at Tabor, a frequently asked question was which of several men named Wiebe on the faculty and staff was my husband. As a woman surely I belonged to someone.

Widowhood and divorce are also thresholds into a new identity. You no longer come in two's. Often this change means you move to the bottom of the social ladder. I had been Mrs. Walter Wiebe for about fifteen years and Emily Post decreed I should continue to call myself that. With no husband, who was Mrs. Walter Wiebe? I had lost my identity. I felt as if the solid ground under my feet had turned to shifting sand.

A change in job or profession can also bring on an identity crisis, especially when the shift is from a white collar profession to a blue collar job or unemployment. Some people go through a midlife crisis, suddenly aware of being mortals who will not live forever. In contrast, in countries with a low life expectancy such awareness emerges at a much earlier age.

A spiritual turnaround also means a change in identity. The ancient patriarch Jacob became Israel. The zealot Saul became the apostle Paul, missionary to the Gentiles. The disciple Simon Peter, outspoken, tempestuous, became Peter the Rock. Jesus said to him, "You are Cephas, a rock and upon this rock I will build my church."

The big question for many at retirement is "Am I a worthwhile person even if I don't make money?" Society wastes people who don't add to the GNP. In the case of men, retirement means the provider and protector role is reduced, a key factor in their lives for forty or fifty years. Position, power, and significance in the eyes of others are lessened. For women who have never worked outside the home, growing older means the caregiver role in the family is reduced as children leave home. Their source of meaning is gone.

Travel often fills this lack of meaning for some time until money or health run out for some retirees. A whole generation of older adults is on the move. To verify this, take a trip to Branson, the entertainment capital of the world, and survey the acres of tour buses parked there in front of the theaters. A relative who operates a travel agency told me that ninety-five percent of his business comes from this age group.

Cole had said that the church should be asking in a play/leisure society, "Is that all there is to life when one is older?" The church needs a new agenda for the older adult. They are the young people's link to faith. Only an old person can assure the younger ones that faith in Christ is sufficient when life closes in. Cole's suggested the church should spend as much of its budget on this age group as it does on young people, a shocking statement to some.

Retirement becomes the threshold to a new identity in this era because retirees are handed the unexpected gift of twenty to thirty years their parents never had. People are living longer because of better nutrition and sanitation, advanced medical technologies, and better care in the latter years. Older adults may spend more years in this new life than they did working at their previous profession or job. Therefore it is important to find their identity as an elder.

I had difficulty responding to the question, "Who are you?" I heard retirees referring to themselves as "retired teacher," "retired business man," and so forth, clutching to descriptions of themselves connected to the "other" life. I was no longer a college English teacher. So I started searching for an identity and meaning in these last decades of my life. Rabbi Abraham Heschel writes that one ought to enter old age the way one enters senior year in college with anticipation. I plunged in to find this new identity for Katie Funk Wiebe, former college professor.

I was tempted to reach back and imitate the way my mother aged. But I couldn't. Our lives were too different. She never worked outside the home but moved through the life stages always engaged in the one task: homemaking. Her identity never changed. She was always a homemaker. Her relationships remained fairly stable. Yet I sense she worked at her aging. Somehow through the years my mother picked up the identity of "elder" in her small congregation, not in the organizational structure, but in the spiritual sense. Everyone in her small congregation knew and respected Grandma Funk, one of few old women in their midst. She enjoyed that identity. She remained alive and alert until her death at nearly age ninety-nine despite increasing disengagement from life because of health issues.

On one occasion, as we said good-bye after a visit, she made her usual comment: "This may be the last time we will see one another, Katie." I lived in Kansas, she in Alberta, Canada. Her next words are memorable: "But life is still so sweet." However, some aspects of aging troubled her. Her friends were dying, she told me. She lacked the psychic energy to reach out. But I remember her positive attitude toward life as an elder.

Elderhood, according to Zalman Schachter-Shalomi and Roland S. Miller in *From Age-ing to Sage-ing,* is a state of consciousness that calls us "to engage in life completion, a process that involves specific tasks—coming to terms with our mortality, healing our relationships, enjoying our achievements, and leaving a legacy for the future." Taking on the identity of an elder is "an ongoing transformative process" enabling us to "harvest our lives, to bless all that we have lived through and to convert this rich experience into wisdom." Quite an assignment!

I wanted to be an elder. I didn't want to be a golden-ager, a senior citizen, or even a retired college professor. People don't know what to call our age group because the essence of what it means to be old is changing. To slap just any used-up label on this group no longer works. "Old person" has lost its currency of dignity. Old no longer means old, according to one dictionary but "deteriorated through age or disuse." If someone dies at age seventy-five we say, "Too young to die." At sixty you can still jump over a fence, at seventy climb under. Only at eighty or more do you head for the gate. Seventy-five is young.

"Senior" is usually reserved for people with power, mostly men, as in senior officer, senior pastor, terms that can carry awesome meaning. "Senior" as used to describe someone on Social Security ordering a "senior coffee" at a reduced rate at a fast-food place tries to sidestep negative connotations associated with being old. "Senior" in this sense is not associated with power.

I wanted to craft a new identity. I began researching and writing about aging. The first book was *Life After Fifty: A Positive Look at Aging.* I followed with *Border Crossing: A Spiritual Journey*, in which I traced my own journey across the border into old age. Next came *Prayers of an Omega: Facing the Transitions of Aging* and then *The Storekeeper's Daughter: A Memoir.*

Before long I was asked to speak at older adult retreats. I don't know when I've had as much fun as at these gatherings. I found that if I enjoyed my topic and audience, they did also. This was the most relaxed group to speak to. I traveled to many parts of Canada and the United States to share my insights.

At the church I attend I, with the help of others, started an organization called PrimeTimers. Our program at first was probably too zealous. We had to trim it down. I edited a newssheet *The PrimeTimes* to keep this older adult group informed about upcoming activities and themselves. I taught Bible classes for a number of years. In 2000 I resigned from these positions because of my daughter Christine's frequent emergencies. She needed me more.

In 1993 I began attending the East Wichita Shepherd's Center, which sponsored an Adventures in Learning program for older adults. It offered classes in a wide variety of courses each Tuesday for eight weeks in fall, winter, and spring. Over time I taught a number of writing courses including poetry writing, memoir writing, journaling, storytelling, and others. I became a member of the board and program planning committee. I was forging a new identity as writer and speaker.

This organization was the lifesaver I was looking for. At the Shepherd's Center, I find it stimulating to see a woman over ninety teaching piano to students over sixty-five. Or to teach a class of people myself, some in their eighties, to write poetry or memoirs, and marvel at the nuances of meaning they have discovered. I've watched hundreds in this age group attend lectures, learn to draw and paint, and read new books. I tell myself again: *You don't grow old, you become old when you quit growing.*

How could I keep growing?

I moved along in life with great fervor for a number of years, traveling, teaching, speaking, living. Then slam-bang, my health faltered. Adjusting to physical changes didn't sit well with me. Walking any distance became impossible. Travel was curtailed. I didn't like to drive long distances by myself. Weakening eyesight made it hard to read for any length of time. Clothes didn't fit as well. Loss of health felt like a major assault. How could God let this happen to me? Yet why should I be spared? I had talked to groups about turning losses into gains during this life stage. Now I could test my theories.

I worked at health concerns by walking, first in the golf course across the street after the golfers had picked up balls and clubs for the day. Next came a few years of arthritis water exercises followed by several years at a local health club. In 2005 because of increasing hip problems followed by surgery, I knew it was time to move from my large duplex to an apartment. How would I dispose of all my precious stuff? This meant, in essence, saying, "Enough is enough. Enough doo-dads and knick-knacks. Enough buying new. Enough shopping. Enough."

Following my mother's model, I got rid of as much as possible. Instead of bemoaning fewer household effects, I felt freed from a heavy burden. Why have ten sets of sheets filling my shelves? Why twenty towels when six or seven do as well? This does not mean a Spartan existence. My one-bedroom apartment is still full, especially my bedroom office. Books and papers are not as easily disposed of.

Family changes came one after another in the years after I moved to Wichita, sudden yet not totally unexpected. My precious daughter Christine died in 2000 after twenty-seven years of struggling with lupus. She lived with me six of the last eight years when independence became problematic. She was a poet, musician, writer, lover of beauty and friendship. She enjoyed preparing and delivering homilies.

Another daughter went through a difficult divorce, another remarried. One fall day a wonderful new grandson I had never met stood on my doorstep searching for his roots. He had been born to a daughter thirty years ago when she was in college and it was taboo to admit to such births. Grandchildren moved through school and on to college, work, and marriage. Friends died. Before I knew it I had a great-grandchild. What I was experiencing is normal for someone my age. This is the stuff of life. Deal with it. This is where meaning enters life. This is where God's grace becomes apparent.

I acknowledged that mortality is not God's goof. It is not so much to be feared as to be accepted. My mother in the last weeks of life when asked by a nurse where she wanted to go when she was released from the hospital stated openly, "I want to be with the Lord." The puzzled nurse had her pen poised to write a street address to which mail could be forwarded. Mother was ready to leave this life for a better one. I hope I can also say that boldly when my time comes.

As the years flew past after retirement, I asked myself, what did I want out of life when the years ahead were fewer than the years I had lived? My revised goal was to praise God for this life stage, not just fill the hours with empty activity. I wanted to live with courage when walls enclosed smaller rooms. I wanted to experience the gospel as good news to the end of my days even when bones ached and the doctor's diagnosis wasn't favorable.

Elbert Cole's earlier words encouraged me. He said that the greatest thing we can do for the younger generation is to reveal to them that life never loses meaning. Then it will mean more to them. We need to keep telling them that life is precious at all stages. The greatest tragedy is not death but never to have lived.

To live means to keep developing the inner life and stay in relationship with people and God. How is my inner life different now than it was thirty years ago when I was in my prime? Then I didn't have to pit culture's views of my age against my own feelings about myself. Then I was still forging ahead as far as career and reputation were concerned. Then I was in daily contact with people. Then something was expected of me daily. Cole had said we must see ourselves not just as people being maintained but as God's people with a vision of God's life for us and in turn become contributors to life with whatever gifts God has given us. It helps to like living with yourself.

The inner life staggers when burdened with old grudges. I often spoke publicly about the need to release others through forgiveness to get out from under the load of unfair pain. The Spirit told me it was time to forgive the Saskatoon Mennonite Brethren church council who in 1944, after I had been elected youth group leader, asked me to resign. Something about the shape of my body made that task impossible. But I was still carrying that load of criticism.

"Forgive," urged the Spirit.

"But this story is a great way to poke fun at the paternalistic church system," I responded.

"Forgive," said the Spirit. "What is on their conscience is their problem. Your task is to forgive." I forgave.

But that wasn't enough.

"Forgive the Canadian MB Youth Committee who refused to allow you to become editor of *The Youth Worker* because you were a woman even though you had been doing the work under your husband's name." I swallowed hard and forgave.

Even that didn't satisfy the Spirit. "What about the Sunday school superintendent who denied your request to teach a women's Sunday school class in Kitchener because women were not to teach in the church?" Would this list never end?

The spiritual task of those who carried the first heavy-handed brunt of opposition and often trivialization of women's ministry is to forgive and not carry those burdens into the evening of life. Grudges and hurts may have stockpiled in memory banks. Aging is a time to forgive and let go in all areas, including family conflicts. I forgave and felt lighter than if I had given away several households of stuff. Without forgiveness I would have been spiritually crippled to my last breath.

I look forward to my time after breakfast when I write in my journal and spend time with God, meditating, praying. Yet if I can't make time for this, I am no longer perturbed as I was in my college days when missing that fifteen minutes in devotional exercises brought great feelings of guilt

In 1988 I wrote *Bless Me Too, My Father.* I was asking for a blessing from my church upon my life as a woman in her early sixties. I knew what I wanted and needed. I was probably asking for something conservative church leaders could not freely give. I needed to turn to God for a blessing. At age eighty-three I keep asking God to bless my life: I want to see my added years as God's gift to me. I want to age as a single woman without stigma. I want to be able to stand tall inwardly because I am a child of God, made in God's image, worthy of respect from myself and others. I want the courage to re-format my thinking about aging so that this stage becomes a time of vibrant elderhood in a culture that speaks about it in empty euphemisms. I want my companions on this untraveled road to feel blessed with me. I want to be able to bless others.

The theological issues that almost consumed me at an earlier period now have less strength. I still ponder issues related to pain and suffering. I still wonder about pluralism and the validity of other world religions. Is there power in prayer? I keep on praying even though I have no formula for answered prayer. I believe classes directed toward older adults should aim at interpreting God's ways to humanity in changing times rather than focusing on more Bible knowledge. We in our age group need help thinking through the big questions so we can refuse to rubber-stamp all popular thinking because we grew up with it.

Harvesting one's life, according to Schachter-Shalomi and Miller, is necessary for good living in old age. I am trying to do that in this book. A civilization can be killed in a few generations if no one passes on the accumulated wisdom, only the facts about the elders. Real elders gravitate toward this task. Basically it means seeding the future with wisdom by sharing the stories of life's transforming moments. Storytelling has inherent power to inspire. Stories are shared with people you trust. Stories acknowledge that you have gathered wisdom and this is your way of sharing it. Meaning comes by giving yourself away in your stories, being present to them.

The all encompassing task of elders, as I see it, is to craft one's life, not just learn new crafts. Simply put, it means to learn to be real. That is the most desired identity. The Velveteen Rabbit, a new toy in the playroom, and the Skin Horse, a much-played with toy, discuss "What is real?" in Margery Williams's *The Velveteen Rabbit*. Rabbit asks, "Does it happen all at once?" The Skin Horse replies that becoming real takes a long time and involves becoming quite shabby—but that's not a problem "because once you are Real, you can't be ugly, except to people who don't understand." When an older person becomes real, the person and not what he or she can still do is valued.

With time I no longer identified myself as professor emeritus of Tabor College. I left the old identity behind and am filling the new one with experiences on my journey toward becoming real. I am an elder. I am a mother, a grandparent, a sister, a friend, a storyteller, a futurist. What name does God use when he calls me? Faith gives me the name "child of God." "Old" can mean finished and done for, or still traveling. I want to keep traveling in the spirit. On that path an artificial hip and a few other physical ailments don't count.

CHAPTER 20

Harvesting my life

Take from the altar of the past the fire, not the ashes.
—Jean Juares

At a luncheon, the guest soloist sang romantic songs of the 1930s and 1940s. Suddenly I was catapulted into the on-again, off-again, intense infatuations of my youth. Nothing could top having handsome young men, a few in uniform, at the door to pick me up for a movie or concert. Despite a vicious war overseas, we young people lived in Peter Pan's Never-Never Land. Nothing was impossible in that age of innocence and invulnerability. Better stated, nothing was impossible to me as I lived in innocence and with a sense of invulnerability.

Then suddenly, the music stopped; I was jolted back to the present. I looked around to see a large group of older men and women. Many were widows and widowers, some wives with ailing husbands or vice versa. Most had gone through pain and heartache. My own life had not always been easy. At nineteen I never expected problems ahead. I had grabbed the world by the tail ready to sling it around with vigor and abandon. I never expected to live with a purse so close to empty that my husband and I couldn't even plan a budget. I never expected my husband to be sick for four years followed by death. Or that a daughter would struggle with lupus for twenty-seven years and also die. That I would face health issues. That two daughters would go through a divorce. I could go on and on.

What I was doing in those few minutes at the luncheon was a mild form of harvesting my life. I was acknowledging early experiences that had influenced me for a time and then been discarded. Harvesting our lives as older adults basically means a conscious return to the past and then doing something with it. It's like harvesting wheat or other grain. You plant, you water, you wait for the harvest. Then you determine what to do with your findings.

Life review, or reminiscing, is an important feature of this last stage of life. Kathleen Norris writes, "Remembering is a way of finding the pattern or design of our lives, the shape which makes each life experience unique and gives it meaning." It entails sorting through life experiences as if through possessions before a garage sale. You keep some stuff, you throw some away. You look for the pattern or theme of your life.

This autobiography is my life review. I have worked on it for years, off and on, retrieving one experience and then another and then shoving both aside for something more significant. My story is not important because it is mine, but, as Frederick Buechner points out, because if it is told right, the chances are the readers will recognize that it is also theirs. He adds that it is through our stories about people we have met along the way that God makes himself known to each of us personally and powerfully. To lose track of our stories is to become impoverished both spiritually and humanly.

Life is like soil on a walkway, writes Ira Proghoff, journaling promoter. It gets hard-packed. As new experiences are added, they get stomped down until it is hard to know what lies deeply embedded back there. In this writing, my goal is to soften the soil and retrieve parts of my life I thought I had lost. I want to take ownership of my life, both the good and the bad. I want to find out what had made me who I am today. My journey is unique to me, although many people have gone through similar transitions and made similar choices. Writing this life review has enriched my days as I have looked back, gathered, discarded, and searched for even small signs of truth and integrity.

The Old Testament writers keep retelling the story of the Israelites, first from one aspect, then another, to keep reminding the Israelites how God has dealt with them. To keep them aware they are God's people. I do the same with my past. I want my children to know the strengths and weaknesses of the fabric out of which our family story was woven.

The story of my family started for me when, during the 1920s and 1930s, letters from Russia where Mother's parents and many siblings still lived arrived at my childhood home in Blaine Lake, Saskatchewan. These letters spoke of intense hardship, cold, and hunger. One family had been exiled to Siberia because the father was a minister. The letters made Mother's eyes redden and her breath come in gulps. Mothers didn't cry, so why did my mother cry? To see a parent weeping comfortless is unforgettable. She never saw her parents again after leaving for Canada at age twenty-five. As a child I wondered why I never had a grandfather on either side of the family. Later I learned one had died of typhus caused by poor sanitation and lack of medical assistance after the Russian Revolution, the other of starvation and undiagnosed illness during Stalin's rule. Why didn't God just pick them up and drop them in a better place?

As the stories seeped into my mind, I left them there, separated from the rest of my life, until I could grasp their place in the total story. Somewhere in that unreachable land across the ocean lived uncles, aunts, and cousins whose names I could never clearly sort out because they had no faces and voices. These letters and other information passed on to me over the decades taught me about lineage but even more about family values, even those broken by war, migration, and human weaknesses. But especially, that, like the children of Israel, a thread of faith, sometimes strong, sometimes weak, was woven throughout their stories.

In high school I located an old steno notebook with a genealogy of my father's family dating back to the migration trek from Prussia to the Ukraine during the time of Katherine the Great in the late 1780s. I copied it, page by page, to keep in my own drawer of treasures. I don't know why, but I knew I wanted that material. I was intrigued by a footnote for the name of Susana Jacob Funk Rempel stating she was alleged to have the power of witchcraft. Mother found it hard to explain although she had known the woman as a child. In the 1980s I finally found out more about this "witch" in my background, but I kept her in my subconscious for decades.

Genealogy provides the skeleton to be shaped with stories depicting the human condition. Storytelling, a form of harvesting one's life, in my parental home was a given. I thought all families told stories. In winter, as the frigid air, sometimes forty degrees or more below zero, shrouded our little wood frame house, we gathered as a family around the oilcloth-covered table. Dad might be working at his store accounts, Mother at her mending or knitting, and we children with our homework when the stories began. Never anything formal. Just a few statements, "Mama, that Rempel we used to know in Rosental was in the store today. Remember when he. . . . " The magic words were "Remember when." And the storytelling would begin.

Years later when we were living in Kitchener, Ontario, my husband bought *Tiefenwege: Erfahrungen und Erlebnisse von Russland-Mennoniten in zwei Jahrzehnten bis 1949* (Difficult Journeys: Events and Experiences of Russian Mennonites in the two decades before 1949) by Jacob A. Neufeld, a biography of one family's experiences during World War II, especially the tortuous journey from the Ukraine to Poland in 1943. Mother's six sisters and their families had made that horrendous trek with small horse-driven wagons following the German army repatriating all Russian-born Germans living in the Ukraine to its own lands. These included Lutherans, Catholics, and Mennonites.

All winter, I struggled through this book, page by page, while waiting for Walter to come home for lunch from his teaching duties a few blocks away. My German was limited, but I kept plodding ahead, hardly believing what I was reading. This trek included my family of origin, but I didn't know it at the time.

In May 1978 I met one of those obscure aunts from across the ocean face to face when *Tante* Truda flew from Germany to

Edmonton to visit Mother. She hadn't seen my mother, her oldest sister, since she was a girl of twelve, fifty-seven years ago. I flew to Edmonton to meet her. An *Umsiedler* from Russia to Germany, she was visiting relatives in Canada. Tante Truda was now sixty-nine. Six decades are not enough to destroy family bonds. I found it almost uncanny to meet a younger version of my mother. My "new" Tante Truda was short, plumpish. A strong family resemblance showed up in her red hair and facial features. Mother had red hair. She talked, laughed, and gestured like my mother did. She told me about war, illness, death, famine, exile, hard work, and separation from loved ones as well as stories of good times. I wrote it all down.

"What helped you the most?" I asked her in my bastardized German. She answered quickly but surely, "*Nur der Halt am Herr*" (Only by clinging to the Lord). Though life had been incredibly hard, she chose not to be governed by bitterness and resentment. I have forgotten dates and place names, but not that story, that thread of faith.

As Mother aged, she asked me to record how my father had found her family lost in the revolution of 1917-19 in Russia. I had heard bits and pieces over the years but now I started serious research. Each time I flew to Edmonton I asked both Mother and Dad to tell me the story again. I had asked Tante Truda to also tell me her version of the story, for she was one of the seven children lost during the Bolshevist uprising. I read books about the period and researched the university library for corroboration of names and places. It was tedious work but well rewarded when one day I found the name of the small Russian village where Dad found the lost family: Proghnow. If I had discovered the North Pole, it wouldn't have been more rewarding.

I made a chronological listing of all events Dad had told me about that lengthy journey on foot in 1921, in wooden Schlorre (he still had no shoes), to look for his new red-haired wife's parents and seven siblings. The remarkable story of this finding is recorded in *The Storekeeper's Daughter* and also in the *Journal of Mennonite Studies*.

But even successfully putting together what seemed like disparate stories didn't satisfy my hunger to know more about my family left behind in the steppes of the Ukraine. In 1989 I joined a tour group of Tabor College alumni headed for the Ukraine and Siberia whose families had once lived in Molotschna and Chortitza in the Ukraine. To walk the streets of Rosental where my parents had once walked and to see the building where my sister Anne was born, the spot on the hill where the Funk windmill once stood, and the edge of the ravine where possibly my Grandfather Funk had eluded his political captors brought me into even closer touch with my past.

In Moscow I met another of Mother's sisters, Aganetha Janzen Block, living with her daughter and husband and children. I had occasionally mused that my remaining relatives in Russia were probably simple peasants. I was wonderfully surprised to see the front hall of their tiny apartment lined with books. Tante Neta, even in her eighties, was a reader and a storyteller. She loved watching the Russian parliament in session on television. In our two days together, her stories spilled over. Obviously, she had told them over and over again: childhood, young adulthood, marriage, forced march to Poland after World War II, death of her husband on the Belgium front after being conscripted into the German army, exile into forced labor in Siberia for eleven years. Her Jewish son-in-law admitted he didn't believe in Christianity but "she sure lives what she speaks about." The thread of faith kept showing up.

I encouraged her to write her life story. "I am too old," she said. "Then write me one story in each letter you send me or my sister." The result was about fifty letters, each with part of her story in it in neatly scripted German. I translated the letters and compiled them into a manuscript, including the story of how my father had found her parents and siblings after world war.

Another big find in a cousin's home in Edmonton was several large notebooks filled with letters copied from the originals my grandparents in the Ukraine had sent to my parents and an uncle and aunt in Canada beginning with 1924 to the early

1930s. Then followed a gap in the letters during the terrible Stalinist 1930s, when brutality controlled the nation and brought on starvation and political oppression. The letters began again in 1943 for a brief time when the Germans "liberated" the German colonies in the Ukraine. Their letters were full of doubts about God amid underlying simple statements of faith. Where is God when I suffer had been my question also.

But then all correspondence stopped again for the next years until the death of Lenin in 1953. The people were now declared free to move from Siberia to wherever they wanted except their old home place in the Ukraine. These letters were like those Rip Van Winkle might have been written after his long nap. "Where are you?" the writers asked. "Who is still alive?" They had but one mission: to find relatives in Russia, Siberia, and Canada. I translated these and added them to my store of family records.

Now I was on a roll. I kept gathering and filing data. I wrote biographies of my aunts in Russia, my mother, Uncle Abe Funk, my husband, and others. I told my Aunt Neta's story, "From the Sunny Steppes of the Ukraine to the Cold Hell of Siberia," often to various groups. I wanted others to know about this gross inhumanity. I called it "The Other Holocaust." I was finally ready to write *The Storekeeper's Daughter*, a memoir of growing up in an immigrant home. I had come to terms with this past I once wanted to discard. I now saw in it the source of my greatest riches as a writer. Whereas as a high school student I had wanted to discard anything that tied me to my immigrant background, now I couldn't get enough.

Why was I doing this? Because researching and retrieving, or harvesting, one's past is a creative process. It nurtures the imagination. The bigger reason was that I wanted to leave my family with a written account of their background. I wanted them to know where they came from. A family does not begin with a marriage certificate, range, refrigerator, and a mattress on a bed or the floor. Family begins with parents and grandparents and great-grandparents, and with the preceding generations and what happened to them and what they did to life. Each leaves a legacy of some kind.

Joseph's brothers in the Old Testament discarded their sense of family and sold their brother into slavery. "We don't want him," their actions said. They disliked his obnoxious attitude. But in the end they were reunited with him. In my own harvesting of the past, I am drawing the family together, pointing out places it might have broken or became strong. A family is a living, breathing entity, stumbling and stalling, but also forgiving, its members picking themselves up and moving on.

I tell my children and grandchildren we are part of a deeply flowing river with one generation moving on the scene to be replaced by another. Grandfather and Grandmother Johann Funk and their seven children lived on the hill at the edge of the village of Rosental near the windmill. Before that there was another windmill in Osterwick. Before that a family on a horse-drawn wagon with many other wagons rumbled down the rutty road from Prussia to the Ukraine And before that? Always movement and wandering in search of a better livelihood, greater freedom of religion, and opportunity to better the family.

I value the story my Aunt Neta told me about another sister, Aunt Tina (Katharina) Klassen and her minister husband exiled to the northern Urals in the late 1920s by the Bolshevists because he was a religious leader. Was this the aunt, Mother's older sister, I was named after? Mother had always said my name really was Katarina even though my birth certificate didn't reflect that. I look at the only picture I have of her and her family standing outside of their house in the Ukraine. Am I her namesake like my mother told me?

Aunt Neta and her family had been forced to work at hard labor in the lumbering or other heavy industry in another part of Siberia after World War II for 11 years. At the Treaty of Yalta and the division of Germany, all Russian-born German people caught in the Russian-controlled zone were forcibly returned to the USSR. Thousands of these hapless people caught in the Russian net were loaded onto cattle cars and shipped off to live out their days in the harsh winters of Kazakhstan. My aunt and her four children survived the ordeal. Many didn't.

These two sisters, Aunt Neta and Aunt Tina, the diminutive of Katarina, had not seen each other in decades. When Stalin died and people like Aunt Neta working at hard labor in the far north were freed to move, Aunt Neta determined to find her sister, reportedly living in Omsk. She received a travel permit and left by train for her unfamiliar destination.

In a huge city, how do you find a person, possibly greatly changed, you haven't seen for more than twenty-two years? Walking down the street somewhat aimlessly, Aunt Neta noticed a tall, erect woman walking on the other side of the street. She vaguely resembled her sister. She determined to call out her name. If it wasn't her sister, nothing was lost.

"Tina," she called. The other woman walked resolutely ahead, not hearing.

"Tina," called Aunt Neta again, a little louder. The other woman stopped, turned slowly and looked around.

"I'm the one calling you," said Aunt Neta and hurried across the road. It was her sister. They fell upon one another to cry and embrace. At once local Russian people gathered around them to ask what the commotion was about.

"When you called me 'Tina,'" said the older woman, "I didn't recognize my name. My husband has been dead and the children call me Mama. I didn't know my own name."

When I tell this story, listeners marvel at God's leading in bringing the long-separated sisters together. It is a mercy to be praised. Yet as I mull over this story, I consider the tragedy of living a life in which circumstances allow you to forget your own name because no one is intimate enough to use it. The sound of her name being spoken to Aunt Tina awakened in her an awareness of who she was.

My problem has never been forgetting my name. Rather I remembered it too well. I didn't like it. But as I think through Aunt Tina's life of at least thirty years in exile, away from family, friends, church, her strength to hang onto life makes me hang my own head in shame. I am glad to bear her name. I want to be worthy of her example of faith to the end. I want to remember that every time I hear my name it evokes a sense of who I am.

I am writing family histories knowing that though some offspring may have no use for them, some grandchild or even great-grandchild will find as much interest in a little footnote by a name stating the woman was a witch as I did as a child and begin a search for family roots.

To know my family's story does not mean I endorse it all. But I am learning from it. In the words of Corita Kent, "If we deny the continuing power of yesterday, we will be left with a heap of rubble tomorrow." Thus I give my children our past in this autobiography. In working through this material I see better how the pieces fit together. Especially, it has helped me better see the life cycle and accept the glories as well as dark side of each life stage. In doing so I honor my forbears with all their strengths and weaknesses and accept them. We belong together.

Rabbi Abraham Heschel writes that the real bonding between two generations is not a blood relationship but the "insights they share, the moment of inner experience in which they meet." They have discovered some spiritual truth together. I have pondered this. What insights did I share with my own mother and father? What did my parents pass on to me?

I think often of my mother at the breakfast table, reading a Bible story to us children and praying. Dad had gone to work long before. Her prayers always ended with thanks for a warm place, food, and clothing. She knew about times when the cupboard had been empty. I sensed she was talking to someone she knew, not just mouthing words like we did when we rushed through our table grace.

My father was never glib about his faith. His subliminal message was life isn't fair, but you try to make it fair for others. He gave what he had to others in need. I understood only much later why he had a strong reaction to literalism and legalism, even though at times he was literal in Bible interpretation. Once in Edmonton he preached to just me, as we sat together on the sofa, a sermon about the wind from John 3 that expressed his theology about God and the Spirit. He was back in Russia on the hill, keeper of the windmill. The wind blows wherever it wants to. He had seen that. Likewise you can't control the Spirit. That truth gave him freedom to accept a theology of conversion and to change churches.

Dad had spent time in a Bolshevist prison for political reasons because his brother Peter had enlisted in the White Army. He was convinced he would be shot at daylight as many were. Hidden in his felt boots was a small hymnal which he read and reread during that time of waiting, marking words that spoke comfort. Unexpectedly he was released in the morning.

As a young man he had wanted to become an evangelist. He loved to preach. I inherited his Bible, the leading edge deeply gouged because he always wet his thumb before turning a page. It is filled with notes to himself, or rather stories he intended to use as illustrations when he preached.

In Canada, faced with supporting a family of five children, he became a store manager to ensure his family would be provided for. He had seen too much starvation in the revolutionary years and he was opposed to serving the Lord for pay. I see in my father someone who struggled through issues yet found it hard to articulate them in English, his third language. His life experiences are his gift to me, his legacy, the bond between us. I do not see my parents as near-gods but as human, with freedom to be themselves and to make choices. I sense how both Mother and Dad tried to figure out what life is all about, each in their own way. I hope my children see this in me.

As I wrote this book I renewed acquaintance with myself. I have lived long and well and can now hold up the fragments of my life to the light of experience and savor them anew. I have known passion, waved banners, stumbled. I have known the dark night of the soul. I have unraveled some of the muddle of life for myself, hopefully also for others. I am at peace.

CHAPTER 21

Sticking with what you're stuck with

We are a conduit through which passes all of the
traditional rituals, precepts, and practices of the older
generation. . . . for the purpose of making the [newer] generation a
better generation than the ones that have gone before.
—Quoted by Robert Wuthnow

A few years ago, after an intense local church conflict, many years in the making, I found myself debating whether to remain with a Mennonite Brethren congregation or even whether to remain MB, a heavily loaded acronym which in the minds of some outsiders includes shades of fundamentalism: rigidity, narrowness, and exclusiveness. In the minds of insiders, it connotes a warm, close-knit church family with strong goals of evangelism and outreach. I grew up in an MB home and later, as a young adult, chose to become one, possibly because I saw few other options at the time.

I believe in the church. I and my late husband worked for or were closely associated with the Mennonite Brethren church and its institutions a combined total of nearly fifty years. I have written a history of the Mennonite Brethren Church as well as many researched articles. I have this love-hate relationship to the MB church. I can think of my faith without the MB church, but not without the body of Christ.

As I traveled in Canada and the United States, I sensed that MBs are an enigma to other Mennonites, maybe to other denominations also. To the purist Anabaptist, that alternative to both Catholics and Protestants, they seem to be an adulterated

form of everything staunch Anabaptist believers hold dear because MBs hesitate to wave the banner of peace and justice
boldly. MBs wave banners high for evangelism and missions.
Some evangelical Anabaptists, including some MBs, wave
both.

To gung-ho MBs, however, close association with strong
peace activists gives them a bad aftertaste. "Okay," they say,
"we'll accept you as fellow pilgrims, and, if you don't holler
'peace, peace' too shrilly, we won't ask questions about your
spirituality." MBs are not activists. They focus on spirituality,
especially a relationship to Christ.

Mennonite Brethren are also an enigma to me and have
been since I was a child in northern Saskatchewan. I was born of
MB parents, new immigrants to Canada in 1923, shortly after
the Russian Revolution and its aftermath of pestilence, famine,
and political unrest. The practice in pre-World War I traditional Mennonite churches in southern Ukraine was to rou-
tinely baptize young people at about age eighteen, when they
were entered in the church rolls as adults and could marry. Dad
had fulfilled that requirement, but then he was "born again"
and baptized by immersion in the *Bruedergemeinde* (Mennonite Brethren) in Russia, Mother in the Allianz Church. A
"born-again" experience was alien to the Kirchliche (churchly)
Mennonites in south Russia. A Russian Baptist *Stundist* had directed Dad to faith after a Mennonite elder gave him no help in
finding peace of soul when he nearly died of typhus while a
medic in the Russian army.

In their adopted country of Canada, Dad, an ordained
evangelist/deacon, with a vibrant faith only a few years old,
preached *mit Gewalt* (with great energy), said Mother. As I have
mentioned, he preached his favorite sermon to me in detail
shortly before his death. Its essence was that the Holy Spirit is
not stuck in one pattern. I think he also meant stuck in one denomination. One denomination is not the whole. He was often
perplexed with people driving half way across town to a church
when there were half a dozen closer. He had figured it out that

denominations and their varying theologies were human inventions, not God's, but didn't have the words to explain this.

All my early life I sensed my father's ambivalence with regard to Mennonites. I could never quite figure it out. Mother and Dad were members of the MB church but always looking on from the sidelines, partly because of where we lived—twenty miles from any Mennonite Brethren congregation.

Dad never felt MB, possibly because that church had excommunicated him in Russia when he married Mother, a non-MB, yet an immersed believer. MBs kept their boundaries firm then and for years thereafter in America. Because they were evangelical in their beliefs, they cautiously resisted the "other Mennonite" church because it seemed to substitute "culture" for spiritual life. *Kultur* was a bad word when associated with religious life. You said it looking down your nose. But nothing was ever mentioned openly because most of my father's relatives were members of that fold.

In or out, an emphasis on MB exclusiveness was passed on to us children, as were other emphases, a legacy I found hard to escape. At the time of this writing my siblings and my children have all moved on to other congregations as have the children of many friends. Were the MB fences too confining in a world of increasing diversity? Why have I stayed?

It took years for me to realize how several theological voices had set up a dialogue within me from childhood on up. I experienced an undefined discomfort. Our MB church across the Saskatchewan River, which froze over in winter, remained isolated from us all the cold months, October to April or later. With the roads closed, we stayed in our little village from fall until the spring thaw. The United Church of Canada Sunday school became our church home as children. Church attendance was a hit or miss affair. We learned that Jesus wanted us to be "G-double-O-D GOOD."

In winter we did wonderful un-MB things like skating in the ice rink, enjoying Santa Claus at the Sunday school Christmas concert, getting our hair cut and curled, playing hard-and-mean Monopoly late into the night, wearing shorts and slacks, and attending school movies. But no drinking, dancing, or smoking. The United Church taught a subtle tolerance of other faiths, which Dad never spotted. It was, after all, an amalgam of several faiths. He rarely attended their services but enjoyed the friendship of a British Israelite, many Catholics, and attendees at the other churches, Baptist, Doukhobor, Anglican, whatever. He liked them and they liked him.

Those few glorious months of summer meant attendance at the across-the-river church. Only in summer did we have to worry about being saved and listening to hellfire sermons. Only in summer did we sing "Are you washed in the blood?" and "Send the light." Only in summer did we have to be concerned that the trumpet of the Lord might sound and some people would be snatched away to heaven leaving dirty underwear, outer clothes, watch, and pocketbook behind.

Yet those few months were long enough to convince me I should consider myself, a young child, a rank sinner on par with the village drunk. I needed to be converted. An inner argument about my gentle commitment to Christ as a child as opposed to steady growth in the Spirit stayed with me for years. Was I saved or wasn't I if little changed after going forward at an altar call? I hadn't agonized for days about my sinfulness like the preachers shouted I should. If I was saved, why didn't my former temptations leave? Why did people keep going forward at revivals? Wasn't once enough? Something didn't jibe. In winter I could leave these questions behind and coast again. I realize now that the march up the aisle rather than one's walk was for many evangelical bodies crucial evidence that the person was saved.

Such ambivalence in my earlier life acted as a strong undertow when I began to question more serious issues. As a young person I got caught in various theological crosscurrents: fundamentalism with its strong emphasis on right and wrong (and that the greatest sins were sexual); biblical literalism and legalism with little room for grace. I chuckle now as I remember how in Bible college, a friend told us though he came home after

midnight from hours of hard physical work, he felt compelled
to spend a full fifteen minutes in prayer though he didn't know
what his head was saying because his body pulled him toward
bed.

But the little church across the river had strengths. Today I
still long for the rich bonding our family experienced with the
people in the small white building with two entries, one for
men and one for women. God forbid that a woman might ever
enter through the hallowed men's entryway. Today I think that
bonding was based as much, if not more, on the fact that my
parents' closest friends here had also experienced the harshness
of war, revolution, hunger, and immigration. They understood
one another from another land, another time. They had endured suffering together and bowed before God's sovereignty in
allowing it. Memories of a spirituality of submission to God's
will in suffering remain deeply engrained in my psyche.

At this juncture in life, I am clear about several things. I
don't want to return to the MB isolationism and platitudes of
my childhood, though sincerely spoken. Or the consistently
imposed obligation to nail people I meet asking if they have accepted Jesus into their heart, as we had to do on the streets of
Winnipeg for personal evangelism classes in Bible college. It
took me too long to realize that the Christian life cannot be reduced to only words, even words of Scripture, prayer, and witnessing. Or that an over-emphasis on evangelism without an
equal emphasis on discipleship can lead to trip after trip to the
altar and stagnation in spiritual development. A strong emphasis on individualism is hard to put next to a strong emphasis on
the church as a body. Individualism emphasizes going it
alone—solo performance—rather than working as a body.

Growing up in a home such as ours meant learning to identify only one kind of sin—individual sin, such as smoking,
drinking, dancing, murder, adultery, and so forth. Before I
could consider structural sin, sin in systems, institutions, and
organizations, I had to know what it was. It took a conversion
of another kind to come to that conviction.

It took me a long time to realize that slavery and racial discrimination were forms of structural sin, as are gender discrimination and ageism. Jesus opposed structural sin in the religious
system of his day when he spoke harsh words against the religious leaders. He did not often speak to them individually. A
person remains in bonds to structural sin until an awareness
dawns that sin is not only personal and individual. Entire cultures or even a church bodies may condone certain types of systemic discrimination and call it "good" as long as they believe
they have scriptural proof to back up their position. Slavery is
one such form of systemic discrimination that for years had
backers quoting Scripture to support it.

I am also clearer today about my thinking about eschatology. A strain of fundamentalism in the form of dispensational
premillennialism had traveled across the ocean with the thousands of MBs who came to Canada from Russia during that
open door between 1923 and 1929. It was reinforced by MB
preachers who drank deeply of its waters while studying in
American conservative seminaries. Like other fundamentalists
caught up in this teaching, some MBs delighted in figuring out
the puzzle of God's plan for humanity to the day and hour. One
missionary friend told me she carried a huge bed sheet with the
full chart of the dispensations and end-times events drawn on it
to teach nationals in the villages of India.

As a young adult, I found myself entranced by a Sunday
school study of prophecy. I like puzzles. I bought a Scofield Reference Bible and studied the underpinnings of dispensational-
ism in the footnotes. I learned to draw all the complicated
charts about the end-times. I ordered a *Prophecy* magazine. I
could explain every line and arrow in those charts as easily as I
could recite the alphabet

It took years of study before I could challenge the teaching
that the essence of the Christian life is to figure out a mammoth
cosmic puzzle according to the Darbyists, although the thrill of
making one Bible fact after another pop into place is probably
as great as finishing a double-size *New York Times* Sunday cross-

word puzzle. To change one's theology imbibed as a child is one of life's most difficult hurdles. It took me too long to understand that scouring the daily news for clues to beat God at figuring out his plan means you have to put all your energy into preconceived human conclusions and not into what is important about the Christian life.

It took too long to say to myself, *I do not, cannot, believe this. There is truth somewhere in the teachings about eschatology, but not when the result is an intricate drawing of lines and arrows.* To finally grasp that I had the power to let go of certain theologies was a major turning point in life. My father experienced a "second birth" as a young man. His church of origin wasn't into pious experiences, but he moved with his new understanding of Scripture and left behind the old church traditions and opted for the new. I didn't need to believe every humanly devised structure imposed on the Scriptures. But it also took me too long to recognize that institutions change very slowly and that leaders are very human. I have often been too impatient, too judgmental, too anxious for change.

Trying to escape early influences is like trying to get rid of your DNA. With time I could acknowledge that denominational lines are permeable and that all denominations and even individual congregations have gifts to offer the kingdom of God. I should have learned that as a child with our mixture of churches: Mennonite Brethren in summer, Russian Baptist church in our home in winter for my parents while we children attended the United Church Sunday school. I had an easy camaraderie with school friends who were Catholic, Doukhobor, Baptist, and Anglican. Religion was never an issue.

My adult life, especially since I retired, has been a second kind of growing up—sorting, learning to respond differently to old stimuli—to come up with an understanding of God that is mine—not one thrust on me by old experiences. A friend asked why I stayed in the MB church when it still restricts women's use of their gifts of service. Why stay in a church that has hindered my development? I answered her that only as a member can I continue to speak to the church. For thirty years and more *The Christian Leader* editors gave me the rare privilege of speaking to the entire constituency as a columnist about my relationship with it. And I wrote many articles for this periodical in my retirement years. It gave me a platform that reached other constituencies.

For thirty years and more I could think in public. Readers who encouraged me showed me that others were struggling with the same issues. Those who objected to my opinions wrote too seldom. When I am no longer a member, my voice is silent. I believe strongly that the church will change, maybe not in my lifetime, but it will change and open doors to women. In the Canadian MB Conference, in 2008, two women were ordained to the ministry, a big step forward, something that seemed impossible fifty years ago.

So I ask myself again, as an octogenarian: Why am I Mennonite Brethren when some MB congregations lean strongly toward fundamentalism? Fundamentalism and its variations is not something you get entirely over as you mature spiritually. Traces always linger. It's as if the master narrative you learned as a child hides in ever new crannies of your mind, decade after decade. The theology learned as a child is hard to identify and discard. But as I look back I sense even my parents with their limited education were constantly questioning what was going on in themselves and the church. What made my father hesitate to plunge fully into the MB church, or into any Mennonite church for that matter, and look for his true spiritual home among the Russian Baptists? Only because he had questions unanswered in the church where he grew up.

Members of other denominations often place me with the Mennonite church because of the opportunities for service I have found there. When I moved to Wichita at retirement I told myself I did not want to die without having experienced worship with other Christians. My new association with people from other denominations has enlarged my view of the mission of the church and stretched my understanding that God works in many ways, not just the MB way. Instead of my faith being diluted by mingling with other Christians, I am enriched. I am privileged to see the wider world, its diversity, and the common values all Christians hold dear. My faith is strengthened as I learn to know God's people outside the MB fold.

For some people, when the fundamentalism of their childhood doesn't make sense, their world falls apart. Some leave the faith. Some join another church. So far I haven't. At this stage in my life I have a clearer understanding of the messages I received in childhood. I have been able to move beyond some but to keep those I value. Even today when I feel downcast, I turn to the *Kernlieder* and *Heimatlieder* of my youth as well as familiar hymns. They still speak to my soul, bringing God's presence into my heart as modern praise choruses never will.

Robert Withrow in *Growing Up Religious* writes that it is special to grow up with a religious tradition that believes there is value in prayer and learning to serve others. Mother believed in prayer. She prayed with us children every day. She prayed with me even in her last decade at nearly ninety-nine. My father believed in helping the people in our little town without enough to eat. Just recently I heard of another story of how he had helped an impoverished mixed-race family in the community in the Depression. He had seen too much hunger in Russia to reject anyone. I am MB because of this spiritual inheritance, even though MBs are more known for a strong mission emphasis in other countries than for justice concerns. But things are changing. The change to include a greater emphasis on peace and justice will come even as women's roles are changing, if slowly.

I am still an MB because I value MB biblicism and open spirituality. Through the centuries MBs have nurtured Bible study and a personal relationship with God in Christ Jesus. I miss it when only the minister, not the members, can speak about a personal faith and pray openly.

But I sit on the fence, sometimes closer to the outside than the inside, for these reasons: As evidenced from my pew, the fortress mentality of the MB church is still strong. A group insecure about its identity is concerned about who's in, who's out. We like people to join our congregations, but we find it hard to fellowship with anyone who doesn't speak our version of God-talk. Part of the fence we have built around ourselves has to do with language. We are always screening people for recognizable God-language before we include them among the faithful. Yet I believe allowing a certain type of God-language to become our shibboleth handicaps our own personal growth. And the growth of the church.

At the local level, MB congregations find it hard to join other denominations in programs they haven't initiated. Or which aren't labeled clearly as evangelical. "Partnering," that strange modern church word, takes place at Mennonite World Conference, missions overseas, and MCC levels (also once a taboo organization), but not usually where it affects ordinary MBs. As MBs we are more likely to get taken up by the big evangelical church growth programs of national leaders like Rick Warren than by local programs urging people to serve the poor and needy, even though God measures his followers by the way they treat people at the bottom. But this too is changing.

I miss a sense of the mystery of God, of transcendence, in an MB church. Like many evangelical churches, worship is aimed at people as a performance. One Sunday when I was handed a little gadget and a bottle of bubble-blowing liquid to show my joy in the Lord, I balked. Yet maybe becoming more childlike would help rid me of some of my inhibitions. So I blew a few weak bubbles into the center aisle. But I could rally no strong emotion to see this as worship.

F. Thomas Trotter writes about the "flattening of wonder" in the church through banality that leads away from the spirit of awe, wonder, and transcendence into the presence of God. Many evangelicals seem to want things clear and understandable at first glance, emphasizing absolutes, which can lead to thinking they alone have truth. They can be so anxious to get doctrine precise and achieve growth and relevancy little room is left for wonder and mystery in services. My "metaphorical soul" yearns to be nurtured. Festivals of the faith are becoming fewer and fewer as they are replaced by national social emphases like Valentine's Day, Mother's Day, Graduation Day, Memorial Day, and a multitude of others. That troubles me.

Yes, I sense an attempt at casual relevancy, but not enough evidence of a communal search for authentic ways to confront and be confronted by the enormous complexity and terror of life in this world, as Trotter writes. We are concerned about explaining away discrepancies and problems in the Scriptures without acknowledging ambiguity. Like a cat, everything has to be so housebroken that the challenge of costly grace gets lost. Church has become a natural, comfortable place to come to, not a place where we are warned that the fully committed life in Christ is risky and dangerous. But I acknowledge that the fundamentalism of my youth gave me a moral universe. I am grateful for that.

For the remaining years of my life, I would like to be a member of a congregation where women's roles are not an issue. That may not happen in the United States MB congregations, slower to progress than the Canadian ones. Our present pastor, like the one before him, has strong opinions about the role of women. Despite conference resolutions, I see no overwhelming evidence to offset the deeply entrenched belief that adult men with authority must always have the true and final word. I have not heard a woman preach more than once in my home church in the last decade. Mostly laymen with wives are deacons and moderators and hold key positions in church life.

What has my faith survived in the last eighty years? Changes in theology, changes in social mores, changes in life goals, changes in attitudes. If I hadn't grown up in such a diverse community as a child, would I have turned out differently? I don't know. I am still a seeker.

CHAPTER 22

What I learned on my way to becoming eligible for a senior discount

When the heart speaks, take careful notes.
—Quoted by Greg Mortenson in *Three Cups of Tea*

A journey by car or on foot can be retraced by road signs or landmarks passed along the way. Life's journey can also be retraced, not by street signs but by experiences that marked a turn in the journey. The markings on this journey, to use Dag Hammerskold's term, may not be as defined as a well-lighted street sign. As the traveler looks back, however, they reveal the development of convictions and beliefs that have turned into actions, and hopefully, the wonderful breakthroughs of God. They also show the times when the slide backwards became the impetus for forward movement again.

At this stage of my life, I feel as if I am standing on a high mountaintop looking back over the path my life took and searching for those markings. I recall walking into the small entry of the Russian Baptist Church as a child on a bright Easter morning. Sometimes we attended here when we couldn't drive to our own church across the frozen North Saskatchewan river. The small room was filled with people, one after another announcing jubilantly to a fellow worshiper in Russian: "Christ is risen!" to which the other replied, "Christ is risen indeed!" That joyful witness to faith is a small marking in my journey. I wanted that kind of sustaining faith.

In the Soviet Union in 1989 our tour group attended a huge church service with about a thousand believers in Kazakhstan. Although I couldn't understand a word, my spirit worshiped with these believers as they poured out their hearts in audible prayer, dozens at once, for a lengthy time. Many of them had gone through tremendous suffering in labor camps after World War II. Their desperate, yet staunch, clinging to the faith is also part of my journey. I can think of incident after incident where I witnessed expressions of faith that encouraged mine.

What has changed since I made a simple commitment to let Jesus into my heart as a young child, clinging to my mother's nightgown hanging in the closet? What have I learned over the years? An incredible amount of self-knowledge comes with age, not automatically, but with self-awareness. I know myself better now than I did when I left home at age seventeen, a naïve high school graduate, for the big city.

I have learned foremost, after eight decades, that faith is a journey with God, not just an initial turning toward him and then a long slow slide into home base. Faith is not a quick plunge into the sea of God's grace followed by basking lazily on the shore thereafter. Faith is a process of continual growth from the first simple reaching out to God, as I did as a child, to becoming more Christ-like with advancement in years. Growth in faith does not come automatically, nor does it always follow in lock step with life stages. I can't retire from this journey like I did from teaching at Tabor College. If I do, I slip downhill We older faith pilgrims can't infer that because we are more gray and wrinkled we are more mature in the faith. There are beginners as well as seasoned pilgrims in the faith life at all ages.

I wish I had known this sooner, but we live with what we encounter over the years. I like the way theologian Paul Ricoeur describes the faith journey. We start off with simple faith, a kind of naiveté. Little internalization of truth. Few questions. Just a childlike trust in Christ. As a child I gave my heart to Jesus and meant it. I said I was in.

However, crisis conversion theology, with which I grew up, doesn't mesh with faith as a lifelong journey. When I was young, preachers aimed mostly at getting sinners inside the door. Growth in Christ was expected to come naturally thereafter. For some it turned into a placid treading water in place. As a child I accepted that at the moment of giving my heart to Jesus "all things became new." Old lusts and desires disappeared. What the preacher most often mentioned was freedom from the urge to drink, smoke, and carouse–and there were many burdened with such behaviors at the time in those home-steading communities.

But those weren't my problems. My struggles were with fighting with a sister for more drawer space or share of the blankets, whose turn it was to do the dishes, or with jealousy because my hair was long and lank and my friend's was Shirley Temple curly. Drinking and smoking didn't translate into such child-like sins. It took life experiences to learn that "instant change" thinking without discipleship teaching does not allow God to keep breaking into life with new light. It doesn't encourage growth as a Christ-follower. The new birth should be the deciding point, but only the starting point.

Ricoeur speaks of a second stage in the faith life as confusion and disillusionment. This may be triggered by grief, loss, life crises, rebellious children, death, empty nest, divorce, retirement, illness, financial failure, and more. Doubts arise regarding God's promises when what you accepted as truth about God's ways doesn't match daily experience. However, faith at this stage can be as real as the doubts that torment it.

Until my husband's death, faith was present in strong measure. If ever I was a David confronting Goliath, it was then. Walter and I believed God was leading us into a literature ministry within the church. When the doors opened to enter the United States to begin work at the Mennonite Brethren Publishing House, I was ready, if hesitantly, for an earth-shattering miracle regarding Walter's health. There were too many coincidences to think otherwise.

His death just seven weeks after we entered the Promised Land of Hillsboro, Kansas, brought me up against one of my biggest challenges. My security was shattered. Was our earlier strong belief in God's leading a mirage? I was now solely responsible for myself and my four children in a strange land without assured income. I could no longer hide behind my husband to lead in making decisions and guiding the family. I faced the major question of how can a good God allow children to grow up without a father—and I had no friend to discuss it with in this land where I was an alien resident with a green card to prove it.

At this stage I grew dissatisfied with shallow preaching and teaching, especially platitudes tossed at a congregation like so much confetti. Should I reject my faith as unworkable in the face of real problems or continue? I have written more about this in *Alone: A Widow's Search for Joy*. Some people reject their faith in God when the way ahead becomes murky and they feel confused.

Years later, while visiting Central America in 1992 with a Mennonite Central Committee Learning Team, I understood better what I had gone through at the time. A Catholic priest on his way to hide a man from political persecution briefly described his own spiritual journey to us in a library hallway. His word was "confusion is grace." Confusion allows a person to regroup and start again. "Who passing through the valley of Baca [bitterness] make it a well," writes the psalmist. This priest was explaining how when I passed through my valley of bitterness in a new land, my confusion allowed opportunities for God's grace to move in.

After my husband's death I consciously sorted, affirmed, threw aside, reducing my faith to the essentials, to what was non-negotiable. I jettisoned what no longer served me. I had gleaned from various sources as a young Christian that God was my personal ATM machine, ready to supply my every need. I inserted a prayer credit card, God answered—a simple, mechanical transaction. Drop a prayer into the slot and answers pour out. I had also accepted that as a Christian I lived in a pre-determined path, labeled God's Plan A, like a wound-up toy, not a free moral being. My task was to discover that plan and then wait for God to shove me into it. I was a puppet in God's hands. Prayer was part of the windup.

I found a signpost the size of a giant Sequoia on my life's journey that stated: Believe in God because God is God and not a blessing machine. Faith means trusting in both favorable and unfavorable circumstances. God is with us at all times, not just when my car narrowly misses being smashed in an accident or death takes a loved one. Or when there isn't enough money for all the hairspray and hose the girls want. God reveals himself by words, deeds, prayer, and his still small voice. I chose to move in the direction of this marking and set aside the whole health, wealth, prosperity theology that would have taken me elsewhere.

During this lengthy period of probing, I began nailing my own Ninety-Five Theses to my Wittenberg door. Slowly. Surely. I had thought I could explain my faith by going to the little green *Confession of Faith* booklet, and one by one, affirming each doctrinal statement. But faith doesn't work like that. My journal entries for these years show questioning, doubts, discouragements, near despair. Yet out of this period of searching came the firm conviction that the Christian life is a meaningful relationship between me and God based on trust. It is an intelligent relationship. Exercising faith does not mean eliminating the mind.

Each step forward in the faith journey must be claimed separately. Despite many stumbles backward, each small faith-inspired action into the unknown cleared the mist a little. My answers to suffering and related issues came in small bits and pieces, which I have explained more fully in my books.

I found another signpost that directed my way. One day I had an awakening experience. This sign said clearly that God does not expect me to be an invertebrate slouching along in the hidden cracks of life. What glory does that give him? I stumbled upon Christ's familiar words "Thou shalt love thy neighbor as thyself" as if for the first time. By now I was a grown woman, supporting four children while pursuing higher education, yet in search of an identity like a teenager. The light burst through. If God loves me, I can love myself.

Love myself? At age forty plus? Yes. I learned to love myself the way God had made me with my own talents and gifts, hopes and dreams, weaknesses and faults, despite what church and society cautioned me was out of bounds as a woman. That experience was like having another conversion. Like the bent woman Jesus healed in the temple, I could stand erect. I could follow God's call to serve with my gifts. I could respect myself. God's invasion of my life did not wipe out my personality but enhanced it. His indwelling love meant I could reach out to others with joy and freedom. Though people called me a writer at the time, I now claimed that calling for myself. Writing was no longer a hobby. And the person with a calling is more powerful than the person with a spreadsheet and wall charts.

Then I took another step in my faith journey, a big one. I became a theologian, if only a lay one. Theology is as important as Bible study. Theologies, which are human systems of thought to figure out God's relationship to his children, have fads or trends. They are subject to human error. Yet we live according to our thinking about God. How we relate to today's world, the strength of our relationship with Christ, and our understanding of sin and evil and its moral implications depends on our theology. The task of theology is to root believers firmly in Christian truth and to help them better show God's love to others. To allow preachers to spoon-feed us our theology is backtracking to the Middle Ages when only the priest had access to the Bible and interpreted it.

Two outstanding early women theologians are the Hebrew midwives Shiprah and Puah (Exod. 1). They had no seminary training, no walls of books to guide them, no august body of theologians to support their thinking. With their simple faith in God they faced the difficult assignment of the Egyptian ruler: Kill all male Hebrew babies. Pharaoh's command didn't square with what the midwives thought God expected of them. They theologized (this is wrong), then acted (they let the babies live). I wanted to be that kind of theologian who could discern God's will together with other believers and act upon my findings. My thoughts about lay theology were published in *Bless Me Too, My Father*, a book that won the Silver Angel Award.

I maintain to this day that conflict over interpretation would be lessened if it was hammered out within the faith community in prayer and humility. I regret now that church members are not able to freely discuss what is close to their hearts when a conflict arises. Years of persistently "making nice" has shut that door to them. Yet didn't we, as a church, struggle through this whole issue of wearing masks in the late 1960s and '70s? I think of the numerous books I bought on the subject and workshops I attended at the time. Is the church condemned to repeat its battles? I openly promote adult classes that allow for student interaction and have a conscious goal of straightening out theological concerns as well as increasing biblical knowledge.

At the time my theology was being battered by the conflicting views on the role of women. I studied the Scriptures and writing from all sides of the argument. I feel remorse today about having demanded other people change more rapidly than I could myself. Attitudes change slowly. Why did I expect men and women deeply entrenched in their views about men's and women's roles to do a quick turnabout when it had taken me years to accept a different view myself? Their thinking was as normal to them as breathing. But I was sinking in deep water, searching for an identity that matched my being, flailing arms and legs in a struggle to stay afloat.

The moment I became aware of the way some women anguished about being barred from opportunities for services that matched their gifts, I became more like the person I am now. Over the years I saw a gradual returning to the person I had once been, almost a metamorphosis, changing yet becoming a different Katie, more in love with life. I was finding that old self, the fearless self I'd been so proud of in high school, who spoke out on issues.

Ricoeur calls the third stage in the faith journey the second naiveté, in which a wave of grace pours over the believer. We're back to a child-like faith in God, unburdened by all the questions and doubts of the second stage. Ambiguity is not the big issue it once was. Our relationship to God is restored, with or without evidence of God's sudden outpouring of money, health or miracles on our behalf. We can affirm God's unconditional love and place in life. We are able to deal with unpleasant realities like sickness and loss knowing God is with us in the tough stages of the journey, not just if all goes well. I think I am approaching that stage.

Stages one (first naiveté) and three (second naiveté) are similar in quality of trust, but faith in old age has been tested by the muddle of living. I find as an octogenarian I can accept life's uncertainties better and am less critical of flaws and inconsistencies in human behavior. Life is not always as I would like it to be, but that's okay. I can't quick-freeze the best times or alter events I don't even want to remember. I have to keep living in the present.

Present popular societal views on aging conflict with an encouragement to be. Older adults are encouraged to keep doing. Don't withdraw. Don't look for a rocking chair. Keep active. I see doing as important but not always possible, especially for the frail elderly. What if you can't do? I find this acceptance of a gradual transition from an emphasis on doing to being, when the inner being gains dominance, difficult to explain to myself or others. How can one serve by being? Blind poet John Milton attempted an explanation, "They also serve who only stand and wait."

Human infants are the purest example of being, writes William H. Thomas in *AARP Bulletin*. They do almost nothing except eat, sleep, and fill a diaper. Adolescents, on the other hand, are moving toward a clear preference for doing. When two adults meet, before long one will ask, "What are you doing these days?" Some race through the day from the first alarm clock buzz until their heads hit the pillow at night determined to leave no minute undisturbed.

Thomas suggests the shift to being occurs when relationships have more value than possessions. Getting jars filled with cookies by baking with a grandchild isn't as important as being with the child. I value my writing class of older adults for the relationships we have developed, not how many words get written. Being does not mean stagnation but a reaching out to something significant in the spirit. This group of older adults has taught me the importance of shared laughter as well as shared triumphs, mistakes, and failures.

I am searching for a better understanding of what it means to be, knowing the time may come when being may be my daily agenda. I have read that as people age there is a change in consciousness about self, shifting from doing to being. There is no specific physical trigger, but the change comes as result of personal experience as well as the shared public understanding of the elderly. As I have often said, it has to do with hanging onto a central core of identity as someone God loves and has called to be his child despite circumstances.

We need older adults in our midst as a visible presence, as a reminder to the young how the gospel works itself out in people's lives throughout the life cycle when doing is impossible and one can only be. I think of ninety-five-year-old Ed in our congregation with his rheumy eyes and swollen hands. Each time I say hello he reminds me of the power he once brought to the church music ministry with his strong baritone voice and directing ability. He is now a be-er, not a doer, but just as valuable. The best way to love anyone, young or old, is to receive that person's gifts whether of being or doing.

But enough of that. Along life's journey I have also learned the power of a story. The story-markers were multitudinous throughout childhood, but I didn't recognize them until much later. Stories, like cream, have a way of coming to the top. We five children were raised on two kinds of cream. Mother used cream to cook and bake—about a quart every week delivered to the door by some local farmer. Food wasn't food without cream in it. We also grew up with stories, all kinds.

When Dad came home from the store, he told us stories he had heard during the day's business transactions. Mother and Dad told stories during the long winter evenings in northern Saskatchewan when we all sat around the oilcloth-covered oak table under the gas lamp. "Anna, remember when. . . . " Those were the magic words to take me back to the collective memories of our extended family as we heard about my parents' early life, their parents, and grandparents.

Storytelling took place when relatives gathered and reminisced about ocean crossings, making watermelon syrup, dodging cannonballs on a hike across no-man's land to visit a girl friend. Dad told stories when he preached. His sermons were mostly stories out of his life related to a text, not made-up anecdotes or retrieved from some book.

We children told stories, or rather, I should say my oldest sister, Frieda, gathered all five of us into one bed. Snuggled under comforters on cold winter evenings she told us continuing stories, night after night, stopping just when the story was getting interesting.

Why were stories important to me? They helped me understand the family I belonged to and where I had come from. They helped me understand who Katie was.

Stories are healing for teller and reader. Readers shared with me how my story of widowhood in *Alone* was healing to them. It assured them they were not traveling their journey of loss alone. Everyone's story matters. Our true wealth is in our stories, not in our possessions.

Another learning: I'm not as afraid as I used to be. It's a scary thing to suddenly be faced with the support of four children without adequate training or education. I can remember when every phone call was a risky venture, for everyone was a stranger. It's a scary thing to be desperately seeking an identity when you are over forty. It's a scary thing to feel the need to push against prevailing thinking, knowing you are in a minority. In some settings I knew critics were listening for daring statements contrary to their traditional beliefs or for glaring errors of biblical fact. Some people seemed determined to make sure I knew readers' animosity about a book or article. It's a scary thing to recognize the evil of raw power, even in church institutions.

At times the fear, indecision, lack of clarity regarding the future devastated me. I read through old journal entries and come up with statements like these: "In a few weeks I will be fifty-two—and that seems like the end of something instead of the beginning." "I am under strain and I am not sure what it is. At any rate I feel depressed. I'm pushing through clouds for air and can't make it through."

Today I'm less afraid of not having certitude about all aspects of the faith life. Every time Jesus said, "Fear not," he had people like me in mind. The fears lessened as I wrote about my concerns not just in my journal but openly in publications. Putting words on paper are spirit-strengthening.

I have learned to take joy in simpler living. I don't need as much stuff around me to keep me happy.

The journey is never over. The goal is never accomplished. Young women will have different obstacles to overcome than those I and my generation faced. Even now some of them think their freedom to function freely was always there. But some will be the same as those we faced. The struggle never ends.

I have learned that God has a place and name for each person. I may have thought my parents never gave me a real name but I know now I always had a name. I only needed to make it mine.

The Author

Katie Funk Wiebe, Wichita, Kansas, prolific author and still on the speaking circuit in her eighties, continues to examine her life, moving into aspects not mentioned in previous writings.

Was her name Katarina or Katie? Or a variation? *You Never Gave Me a Name* is a refreshing retrospective look at Katie's search for identity. For new generations it holds potential to bring the power of a woman's perspective to faith issues, especially related to women's roles, and to be useful for group discussion or personal resource and inspiration.

Katie begins her story with attending a conservative Bible college in Canada and early married life and motherhood. Although she had been intent on being the best full-time stay-at-home "mom" possible, early widowhood pushed her into the workforce to earn a livelihood for her family of four. This, in turn, led to a professional teaching career. With each new stage in the journey, she found her name changed. What was her real name? She concludes, "Our names, being the gift of others, aren't really ours until we make them our own."

Katie traces the influences, hurdles, and helping hands that led to her becoming a writer, speaker, biblical feminist, and, especially, lay theologian. Over the decades she expanded her ministry to the broader Mennonite community and, in her later years, to the larger community.

As she examines the threads woven into her life, the pattern changes, causing her to pause to reflect on what she learned thus far and how her world grew as a result.

Lightning Source UK Ltd.
Milton Keynes UK
13 December 2010

164335UK00001B/100/P